The Open Canoe

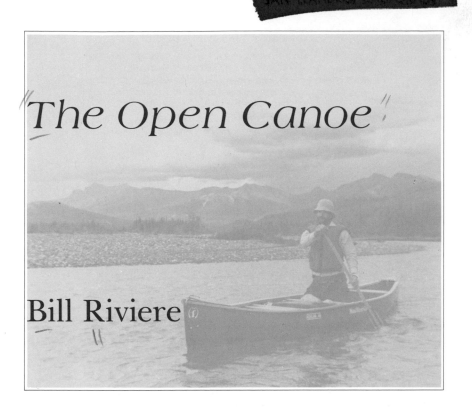

"The Open Canoe"

Bill Riviere

Drawings by L. Randal Boyd

LITTLE, BROWN AND COMPANY • BOSTON • TORONTO

[C1985]

FIRST EDITION

Figure 7-1 by Bill Riviere, Jr.
All other drawings by L. Randal Boyd.

Library of Congress Cataloging in Publication Data

Riviere, Bill.
  The open canoe.

  Bibliography: p. 286
  Includes index.
  1. Canoes and canoeing. I. Title.
GV783.R52   1985   797.1′22   85-4311
ISBN 0-316-74768-8 (pbk.)

MV

Designed by Dede Cummings

*Published simultaneously in Canada
by Little, Brown & Company (Canada) Limited*

PRINTED IN THE UNITED STATES OF AMERICA

Contents

Acknowledgments

In the Winter 1969–70 issue of the United States Canoe Association's *News Letter,* Heinz Wahl wrote: "Boiling it all down, authors of canoeing books make it most obvious that there is NO ONE person who has the all-embracing knowledge of the sport to pass himself off as an oracle. No book has been written yet that is a 'complete' book on canoeing." Taking to heart this pithy admonishment, I contacted every canoe builder known to me, more than 150 of them, and I inquired into the work of more than 275 now-defunct manufacturers. I visited several dozen shops, and I sought out experts in the field, notebook and camera in hand.

Personal contacts were especially fruitful. Combined with queries by mail, they elicited a volume of data that required four file drawers to house. The number of persons who responded was so great that I had to set up an alphabetical file so that I could later acknowledge their contributions. Assistance took many forms — photographs, catalogs (old and new), technical papers, and many lengthy letters expressing design theories and paddling tips, to say nothing of numerous invitations to go canoeing.

So it is that *The Open Canoe* represents the contributions of close to 100 paddlers and builders who shared their knowledge with me. Many of them enjoy the stature of experts in their specialties. Others, although less well known, gave unstintingly without hope of special recognition. They know who they are and so do I. I am deeply indebted to:

Harriett Barker, Marlin D. Bayes, Harold "Doc" Blanchard,

James J. Brady, John C. Breiby, Jerry Cowles, Jeff Dean, Gary DeBacher, Mark C. Dilts, Glenn A. Fallis, Glenys Gifford, Richard Gitz, Gordon Harris, Gilbert Henderson, Thomas Hill, Robert C. Hughes, Theodore L. Hullar, Verne Huses, David C. Joyce, Weston Keyes, James A. Leavitt, Michael H. Levy, Larry Edward Marnes, Roland Marston, Kevin Martin, Willard E. Millis, Jr., Ph.D., Anne and Greg Morley, Bill Ness, Herschel Payne, Bernie Roth, Gary Schell, Joseph T. Seliga, Dan Sheehan, Phil Siggelkow, Walter J. Simmons, Larry Strout, Jame Thompson, Martin Torodash, Jeff Trapp, and Ralph J. Vincent.

And I am further indebted to:

Howard Amidon, formerly with Grumman Boats and now with Alumacraft, who stops by often just to talk canoes.

John Berry, president of Millbrook Boats, a national champion who has racked up some 130 wins in slalom and white-water racing, all but a few in canoes of his own design. He shared his thoughts, thus greatly enlightening me.

Arthur M. Bodin, Ph.D., who provided a copy of his *Bibliography of Canoeing*, at the time of its publication probably the most complete ever compiled.

R. H. "Bob" Cockburn, who operates Headwaters, a Canadian program of wilderness canoe travel. His views on packing and the use of tump lines are a vast improvement over my previous opinions.

Stewart T. Coffin, who also shared his thoughts in lengthy letters discussing paddle design and construction.

John Cross, whose long, handwritten letter revealed information about Canadian canoe builders that had long escaped me.

David Curtis, operator of Canoe Specialists, who, by way of replying to my request for information, graciously invited me to attend one of his annual canoe seminars, from which I returned far better informed.

Thomas S. Foster, director of the Outdoor Center of New England and an instructor for the American Canoe Association and the American Red Cross, whose formula for determining paddle length makes more sense than any other.

V. T. "Gil" Gilpatrick, author of *Building a Strip Canoe*, who also teaches others how to do it.

Robert D. Gramprie, president of Sawyer Canoe Company, who

described at length some vital innovations that have advanced the performance of canoes.

Bob Hartt, president of the Stowe Canoe Company and an innovative builder of paddles, who stops by occasionally, always with enlightening information.

Bart Hauthaway, who builds small canoes of his own design, and who did not mail me the information I requested. He brought it personally, his visit the equal of a week's apprenticeship in a canoe shop.

James "Jim" Henry, president of Mad River Canoe, who also happens to be a superb photographer. He provided many of the photos that appear in the following pages.

Edward "Zip" Kellogg, formerly special collections librarian at the University of Maine's Fogler Library, who researched for me above and beyond the call of duty.

Robert "Bob" Lantz, chairman of the Blue Hole Canoe Company, whose information packet was among the most complete I received, and who added details in a personal letter.

Rob Linden, of We-no-nah Canoes, who supplied me with background information on Jensen-designed canoes.

Duane MacDougall, who sent along some revealing thoughts regarding the effects of rocker in competition canoes.

Bill Miller, builder of the famed New Brunswick salmon-fishing canoes. He welcomed me to his shop and spent several hours explaining building techniques.

John D. Minehart, president of the North American Birch Bark Canoe Association, who compiled a list of present-day birchbark canoe builders, a task that had stumped me. He also provided photos.

Nick Nickels, author of *Canoe Canada,* who operates a Canadian canoe-trip planning service and who formerly published a superb canoeing newsletter, *Che mun,* always packed to the gunwales with paddling information.

Dwight Rockwell, formerly public relations director for Grumman Boats and now the moving force behind the American Canoe Manufacturers Union, who, whenever I was stuck, came up with the answers.

Jerry Stelmok, owner of the Island Falls Canoe Company, and author of *Building the Maine Guide Canoe.*

Omer Stringer, owner of the Beaver Canoe Company, which still produces fine canvas-covered canoes.

John Whitney, sales representative for Old Town Canoe Company, who not only sells but also paddles his products, and who calls at my home every now and then for some good canoe talk.

To John Viehman, editor and publisher, go special thanks for permission to quote from *Canoe Magazine,* which I did unabashedly, in each instance, of course, citing the magazine as my source. Due to the frequent appearance of *Canoe Magazine* in the text, I may be accused of crass commercialism. I am in no way connected with the magazine. I do own a complete set, though, including the original, April 1973 issue. I consider the magazine a veritable encyclopedia, no doubt the best source of information on modern canoeing. *Canoe Magazine* deserves much credit for the information I obtained from it.

And, finally, I am most indebted to my wife, Eleanor, who is my favorite bow paddler, editor, and grammarian. She patiently read and reread my copy, made numerous suggestions regarding its organization, and corrected my ubiquitous split infinitives and dangling participles.

Introduction

Reviewers, upon receiving a copy of *The Open Canoe*, will likely exclaim: "What? Another canoeing book?" When they have read it, I trust they will agree that it has a place in today's canoe literature, whether or not they like the style or organization, and even if they disagree with portions of the text.

Despite the modest success of my *Pole, Paddle and Portage*, published in 1969, certain shortcomings became apparent. Many developments in canoe design and construction that have occurred during the past five years were not even drawing-board dreams in 1969. In addition, although dozens of excellent canoe books have appeared in recent years, none has touched upon modern designs and sophisticated building techniques. No longer is it true that "a canoe is a canoe is a canoe"! I have not sought merely to update my earlier book, but rather to develop an entirely new work that, while not forsaking the cherished traditions of an earlier canoeing era, will actually be a statement for canoes and canoeing in the 1980s. This, then, is why I have written "another canoeing book."

As the title implies, I have dealt only with the open, or Canadian, canoe — no kayaks, not even covered canoes. These are a specialty field that deserves a book of its own. Nor have I discussed sailing canoes, for two reasons. First, I know next to nothing about them; second, like kayaks, they should have a detailed text specifically devoted to them. I have also omitted outboard-powered canoes, which, frankly, have changed little, if any, over the years. Thus, only open canoes, propelled by paddles, are discussed.

There is another deliberate omission: repairs. With the proliferation of new materials and construction methods, it would be ludicrous to attempt to elaborate on the repairs of all kinds of canoes within the confines of a single chapter or two. The bibliography suggests some superb repair manuals.

As a professional writer, I prefer to deal only with subjects in which I have more than a casual interest. Canoeing is indeed more than an interest of mine. It is a deeply felt love. To me, there is no lovelier watercraft than a canoe, and none moves so gracefully. Thus, *The Open Canoe* is also a personal narrative.

I submit the book in the hope that it will enhance your enjoyment of paddling and that canoeing will bring to you the same rich fulfillment it has tendered me.

BILL RIVIERE
NORTH BERWICK, MAINE
JANUARY, 1985

The Open Canoe

Chapter 1

~·~·~·~·~

Canoeing Today

THE CANOE INDUSTRY IS RELATIVELY SMALL, its retail sales, not including accessories, amounting to about $60 million in a good year. If this seems like a tidy sum to you, compare it with the sport-fishing industry's sales of well over $500 million. Prior to the 1982–83 recession, canoe production totaled only 100,000 to 125,000 units per year, with roughly 40 percent of these turned out by the two giants, Coleman Marine and Grumman Boats.

The 1985 *Canoe Magazine* Buyer's Guide listed 109 American and Canadian manufacturers, who together produce 920 different models and lengths. My files reveal an additional 58 active canoe builders—albeit many of them small "woodshed" operations—which brings the total to 167 builders, with a projected output of 978 varying models. Then there are about 275 canoe makers no longer in business, whose canoes may well still be available in the secondhand market. Obviously, there's an extensive inventory of new and used canoes from which you can choose —at least 1,000 models, each one varying slightly, or greatly, from all of the others.

Set out to buy a canoe and you'll discover that, paradoxically, there is both a seller's and a buyer's market. If you're seeking a fine old Peterborough, Old Town, or similar canoe for restoration, prices may shock you. As for adding a Rushton to your fleet, be prepared to mortgage the farm. Too, there are limited-production high-performance canoes produced in small shops. You may have to wait several weeks for delivery, perhaps months. These are in the seller's market.

Virtually all others, whether new or used, are offered in the buyer's market. The builders of most of today's canoes are in a highly competitive business. You can shop around. You can compare. You can dicker.

Let the Buyer Be Wary

In view of this, one can't blame manufacturers for enthusing about their products when seeking a share of the market. After all, for a business to prosper, salesmanship must go hand-in-hand with production. The trouble is that some of the copywriters who produce brochures and advertising tend to stray into the realm of fiction. Even when describing a single canoe, some are prone to sprinkling their literary chefs-d'oeuvre with such colorful phrases as "streaks through the water". . . . "nimble in the turns" . . . "tracks like an arrow" . . . "reassuring stability" . . . "carries a hefty load" . . . "feather-light for portaging" . . . "white-water wizard" . . . "lots of freeboard to thrust aside spray" . . . "climbs those intimidating waves" . . . "rhinoceros-tough" . . . "slips over the rocks" . . . ad nauseam. All of this in one canoe? It might well be called "The Unicorn." Such a canoe does not exist.

There is no "all-around" canoe. You'll win few racing trophies in a canoe built for wilderness trips, and if you try to fish from a sleek racing machine, wear your life jacket. Buy a canoe that winds, twists, and turns among white-water boulders with the moves of a county-fair belly dancer, and you'll discover that it perversely repeats these maneuvers when you try to hold it on a straight course on flat water.

While a few canoes do little more than float (and not well at that), most of them perform very well — even superbly — during one or two, possibly three, of the many phases of canoeing. Anything beyond this involves compromise. Reconcile yourself to some trade-offs. Beware of any claim that "this canoe will do anything you want it to." To choose the right canoe for you, determine which model will best suit as many of your needs as possible.

Not all catalog copy, of course, is seasoned with exaggerations.

4

Most are honest representations. Many, in fact, can be very helpful, especially those that include line drawings and diagrams, details of construction, and even direct advice. We-no-nah Canoe
catalogs, for example, explain that wood-and-canvas canoes
(which We-no-nah does not build) are "not as fragile as many
people think," and advise that "if you really want a wood canoe,
buy it." The catalog also characterizes aluminum as "acceptable."
Before Mad River Canoe discontinued one of its high-performance models, it warned that it was not recommended for inexperienced paddlers. The Merrimack Canoe Company clearly advises
that "the Merrimack (canoe) is not designed for white water."
Such candor in this era of hard sell is refreshing.

Most of us want a canoe that will withstand as much punishment
as possible — usually to offset our lack of skill with a paddle. Innovative advertisers have conveyed the toughness of hulls in some
spectacular ways. Everyone who has read an outdoor magazine in
recent years is familiar with the Old Town Oltonar/Royalex®
Tripper that flew through the air from the roof of the factory,
landing four stories below virtually undamaged. Old Town made
its point, yet the firm is quick to agree that no hull is indestructible.
My own Tripper's bottom, scarred from repeated ricochets off
rocks, is still sound. On the other hand, a friend tore a hole in the
bottom of an identical canoe on a jagged ledge in a Canadian river.
It can happen.

When Coleman Marine first introduced its polyethylene (Ram-
X®) canoe, it circulated a videotape and color photos that depicted
a 69-pound rock (1) bouncing off a Coleman hull, barely denting it,
(2) plummeting through a fiberglass canoe, and (3) badly denting
an aluminum hull. Yet Coleman makes no claims of absolute in-
destructibility, being satisfied to describe its canoes as "extraordi-
narily tough."

Such demonstrations are convincing sales tools, and should be
accepted as such. They prove only the relative toughness of various materials, sometimes not conclusively. Given the right circumstances, any canoe can be punctured, beaten into uselessness,
even wrapped securely around a midstream boulder.

Catalog specifications can be helpful. Sometimes, though, an
omission may be misleading. For example, some materials are so
flexible that they require a keel to stiffen the hull and thus prevent

"oil canning," also termed "wave walking" (the undulating or rippling of a too-flexible hull in rough water, which slows the canoe). The presence of a keel may not be mentioned; yet if you're headed for white water, a keel is the devil's own invention.

Early Canoe Designs

Buying a canoe today is not the simple matter it was during the heyday of wood-and-canvas. Manufacturers turned out the same models, year after year, with few modifications, and no one cried out for changes. After all, many canoes of that era, 1890–1940, were state-of-the-art examples of craftsmanship. Chestnut's famed Prospector model was the "Workhorse of the North." The venerable guide's models produced by E. M. White and Old Town were (and still are) considered the finest canoes of their type ever built, although proud owners of Peterboroughs, Templetons, and Canadians might justly disagree. The altering of these designs would likely have brought howls of protest.

On the whole, recreational canoeists of those days tended toward rather conventional crafts with a flat bottom and a fullness carried to each end. High, upswept peaks were common (no matter how much wind they caught!), especially among the "courtin' canoes" for Sunday afternoon paddling with a bit of demure femininity tucked coyly amidship under a parasol. Among such canoeists, the ukelele was a canoeing "accessory."

Then it came to pass that America fell in love with the Model T and the Model A, the Marmon, the Essex, the Packard, the Hupmobile, and myriad other magnificent exhaust-spuming beasts that made canoeing seem, as the late Red Smith once said about golf, "as exciting as watching paint dry." Canoeing went into a slump from which it did not recover until after World War II.

The Postwar Revolutions

It was then that Grumman revolutionized canoe building. Aluminum, of all things! Tough, light (so they claimed), inexpensive. Canoeing started to bounce back. Actually, the new wonder canoe was revolutionary in only one sense: it was metal. Apart from that, it was quite conventional, having a flat bottom, full ends, and a keel. It was certainly not startlingly different in design, except that it was self-righting. Increasingly, the "clunk, clunk" of metal on wet rocks was heard across the land.

GRUMMAN BOATS

Grumman proclaimed the ruggedness of their canoes dramatically in 1945.

Other materials came along: fiberglass, and an assortment of then-mystical plastics. Even with these materials, canoe builders stuck to time-honored lines. In fact, many a "Grummie" never did get wet, since they served unscrupulous builders as a "plug" from which to develop a mold that would turn out fiberglass canoes! Thus, the traditional lines prevailed for more than a decade after the war. Buying a canoe was pretty much a matter of deciding upon length and fabric — aluminum, fiberglass, or one of the newfangled plastics. However, rebellion was brewing in the wings.

The renaissance in canoeing kindled it. Traffic jams developed on popular streams. A Down East wit suggested that a traffic light be installed at Chase Carry Rapids on the Allagash River. Canoeists went farther and farther afield in search of idyllic or more challenging waters. Rapids that had been considered "impossible" became routine runs. White-water competitors sought increasingly difficult stretches. While much of the canoeing public continued to paddle "double-ended bathtubs," a segment of the paddling fraternity (and sorority!) developed levels of skill that cried out for "performance" canoes. Even those who cared little about winning trophies wanted canoes to match their abilities, canoes that were exciting to paddle. Such canoes were not available, so they began building their own.

One who was ahead of his time in this respect was Eugene Jensen. Teamed with Tom Estes, he had won the grueling 500-mile Bemidji-to-Minneapolis marathon in 1948. Not satisfied with that canoe, he built the first of his own design in 1949. In it, he and Estes then won the 1949 and 1950 marathons. Jensen is still designing canoes today, and will continue, according to the 1981 We-no-nah Canoe catalog, "until I get one that goes by itself!" Several firms now produce Jensen's designs for recreational as well as racing models. Today, virtually every major canoe builder employs one or more designers to lay out the lines of performance-oriented canoes. For centuries canoe building had relied on hand-and-eye coordination alone; the designer's drawing board was a new approach.

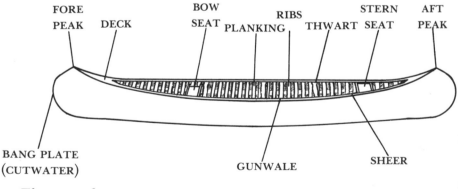

FORE PEAK   DECK   BOW SEAT   PLANKING   RIBS   THWART   STERN SEAT   AFT PEAK

BANG PLATE (CUTWATER)   GUNWALE   SHEER

The parts of a canoe

Another postwar phenomenon was the proliferation of canoe manufacturers headed by active canoeists. Ralph W. Sawyer, founder of the Sawyer Canoe Company and now the manufacturer of Sawyer paddles at Rogue River, Oregon, won the 240-mile AuSable River marathon at the age of 15! We-no-nah Canoes is owned by Mike Cichanowski, also a noted marathon paddler. Jim and Kay Henry, owners of Mad River Canoe, spend their vacations (and make their own advertising photos) on rivers in Alaska, the Northwest Territories, and northern Ontario. Joe Sedivic of Seda Products and Tom Wilson of Phoenix Products (in both cases the "products" are canoes) are former white-water champions. Bob Lantz, chairman of Blue Hole Canoes, and his canoeing partner Bill Griswold "were busy bashing their boats into southeastern Appalachian rock gardens" for several years before they built their first four canoes in Lantz's garage in 1972. Bill Masters of Perception, Inc. (more canoes) is an official of the American Whitewater Affiliation. No doubt there are many others who have paddled first, then built.

Since they are also businessmen, many use aggressive advertising while trying to sell you a better canoe than their competitor's. The result? Never before has there been such a variety of faster, easier-to-paddle, more maneuverable and rugged canoes. And never before have so many builders been so eager to sell you a canoe.

The Educated Paddler

Don't take advertising claims too literally, but by all means obtain the manufacturers' catalogs and read them carefully. They are the first step toward finding "your" canoe. Ask the advice of experienced paddlers. Visit a number of dealers who are also canoeists. Better yet, check with dealers whose shops are on, or close to, a waterway where you can try out a tentative choice.

If a dealer carries several brands and a variety of models within these, so much the better. The wider the choice, the better your chances of locating the canoe that is exactly right for you. Don't settle for one that's "almost" just right. That's like buying a pair of hiking boots that almost fit: you're in for some degree of unhappiness. You may be tempted by low-priced canoes offered in discount department stores that sell everything from panty hose to canned pistachios. But there are usually only one or two models from which to choose, and the odds are that the sales clerk doesn't know a gunwale from a side-hill gopher hole.

If you're serious about canoeing, join the American Canoe Association, which issues the bimonthly *American Canoeist* and whose members are entitled to a subscription to *Canoe Magazine;* The American Whitewater Affiliation, which publishes *American White-water,* a bimonthly journal; the United States Canoe Association, whose *Canoe News* is issued bimonthly; or, if your penchant is for wooden canoes, the Wooden Canoe Heritage Association, so that you will receive its quarterly *Wooden Canoe.*

The more canoeing publications you read and the more contact you have with experienced paddlers the greater your knowledge will be when it comes time to lay down the cash for a canoe. You won't need a degree from MIT, but if you have some knowledge of design, and at least more than a casual acquaintance with canoe lines, making the right choice will be easier.

Chapter 2

∿∿∿∿∿

The Long and Short of It

IT WAS NEVER MY PRIVILEGE to meet Howard G. "Howie" LaBrant. I envy those canoeists who did know him. He was an Olympic flat-water paddler who won his first national title in 1933, and the designer and builder of the first of the deltoid Olympic canoes, which was copied by Europeans who named it "Delta," and which went on to win innumerable national and international competitions, including the Olympics.

No one better understood, or explained more clearly, hydrodynamics as they relate to canoeing. Apropos of canoe length, Howie LaBrant once wrote: "Choose the longest canoe adaptable to your use . . . it will have more stability, more capacity, draw less water, hold its course better, and paddle faster with two or more persons than a shorter one." [1]

Even Howie would agree that some elaboration may be in order. Other matters being equal—hull configuration at and below the waterline, for example—the longer the hull at the waterline in relation to its beam, the faster the canoe will be and the more easily it can be paddled. If you're mathematically inclined, you can prove this to yourself, at least on paper. Another noted designer and canoeist, Cliff Jacobson, explained [2] that the potential speed of a canoe can be determined by multiplying the square root of the waterline length by 1.55. For instance, the square root of a 14-foot

[1] *American Whitewater Journal* (Autumn 1962).
[2] *Canoe Magazine* (1981 Buyer's Guide issue).

11

waterline is 3.8. Multiply this by 1.55 and you come up with 5.9 miles per hour. Similarly, the square root of an 18½-foot waterline is 4.3, which, when multiplied by 1.55, indicates a potential speed of 6.7 miles per hour. Granted, this is a difference only of .8 mile. However, translated into four hours of paddling, it amounts to a gain of 3.2 miles. It's no wonder, then, that the sleek racing models are capable of amazing speed. The four-man Olympic K-4 (admittedly a kayak and not a canoe), which is 36 feet long and a mere 23 inches wide, is capable of pulling a water-skier!

Cliff Jacobson explains that the formula may not hold up when applied to a shallow-water setting, because when a canoe is pushed to racing speeds, it creates water turbulence that slows it, and shallow water aggravates this problem. To overcome it, some racers choose a canoe that has its maximum width slightly aft of center, or what has come to be known as an "asymmetrical" hull.

Jacobson backs LaBrant's statement that a long canoe has a greater capacity than a short one, although their formulae differ slightly. Jacobson states that about three-quarters of a canoe's carrying capacity is borne by the middle third of the hull. LaBrant credits the center half with carrying 75 percent of the capacity. No matter whose formula you accept, it's obvious that you can stash more gear, or a greater weight, into the midsection of an 18-foot canoe than you can into the center of a 14-footer. No need for mathematical wizardry here.

In choosing a long canoe, keep in mind that LaBrant qualified his advice with the phrase "adaptable to your use." These four words are critical. Certain specialty canoes are long and lean, but probably inappropriate for your purposes. The "pro boat," for example, is 18½ feet long, but a mere 27 inches wide at the 3-inch waterline. It is built for one purpose only — to zip from point A to point B in the briefest possible time, under the urging of brawny paddlers with 3-foot shoulders and 17-inch biceps. It's a professional's craft, and is illegal in some sanctioned races for amateurs.

A more conservative "long" canoe is the 18½-foot cruising model with a waterline beam of at least 32 inches, built according to specifications of the United States Canoe Association. The USCA formula for racing canoes in the cruising class calls for the waterline beam to be at least 14.375 percent of the canoe's length. These specifications are now being built into some so-called recreational or general use models.

One long canoe whose design precludes Sunday afternoon lolly-gagging is the ICF flat-water racing model, introduced to this country in 1980, which conforms to International Canoeing Federation specifications: no longer than 21 feet 4 inches and no wider than 29½ inches.

In many cases "long" is synonymous with "big." Especially on the salmon rivers of the Canadian Maritimes, you can see canoes ranging from 20 to 24 feet, with appropriately wide beams. Then there are the "freighters" — big, high-volume canoes, some well over 20 feet long, designed for hauling heavy outfits and cargo on extended trips in the northern wilderness.

At one time, "war canoes" were popular at boys' and girls' summer camps. The 1910 Old Town catalog states that the firm's war canoe "when fully manned [18 paddlers!] passed every motor launch it has encountered in a short sprint." Until 1980, Grum-

GRUMMAN BOATS

The Peace Canoe provided group paddling for summer-camp youngsters.

man sold a "Peace" canoe, a 20-foot model minus seats but equipped with thwarts against which paddlers leaned while paddling. Currently, there seems to be only one war canoe available, a 25-foot fiberglass version built by Nona Boats.

Obviously, racing models, guides' canoes, freighters, and war canoes are among the longest. Such canoes may or may not be "adaptable to your use." Generally, among today's tandem (two-seater) models, the longest canoe will probably be in the 17- to 18½-foot range; among solo canoes, 16 feet. In the field of recreational canoes, many manufacturers offer two or more lengths within a given tandem model—16, 17, and 18 feet, for example. In such cases, the longest version is almost invariably the best handling canoe.

There are a couple of long-canoe caveats to bear in mind, however. The longer the hull, the greater the weight; and the more reluctantly the canoe will turn.

Not everyone agrees with the superiority of long hulls. Bart Hauthaway is among those who feel that "'buy the largest canoe you can ever conceive of using. . .' is terrible advice!" He insists that too much stress is placed on the so-called classic canoe trips, those once-a-year or even once-in-a-lifetime adventures for which big, seaworthy canoes are usually recommended. "Too little is said about finding one's sport close to home," he adds. "Here is where the singlehander shines; it goes wherever a muskrat swims, and, with discretion, it's equally at home on remote waters."[3]

Even if you disagree with Bart Hauthaway, his views command respect. He is a pioneer in the design and building of small canoes, ranging from 10½ feet to 14 feet. A member of the 1965 United States World Championships team, he is also an ardent, and usually successful, hunter and fisherman. On a recent visit, he brought a photo of himself in his little 10½-foot Rob Roy, from which he had landed a striped bass that weighed more than his canoe!

In a later letter, he wrote about a popular 17-foot wide-beam fishing canoe brought to him for repairs. "It has all the shape of a pregnant bathtub," he wrote. "I can't even lift it, and I can't imagine paddling it!" So much for big canoes, according to Bart Hauthaway.

There is a place for short hulls, of course, especially among the solo models that are paddled from amidship. This special breed is

[3] Bart Hauthaway, *The Mariner's Catalog*, volume 6 (Camden, Me.: International Marine Publishing Co., 1978).

Bart Hauthaway's 18-pound pack canoe is a means to an end.

treated in chapter 21. Other abbreviated specialty models are the sportsmen's canoes, usually quite short and wide-beamed for the initial stability required by hunters and fishermen. They are discussed in chapter 23.

These specialty craft should not be lumped together with run-of-the-mill 14- and 15-foot tandem canoes designed for general recreation. Quite often what the latter lack in length is offset by a disproportionately wide beam. Even those short models with conventionally proportionate beams are usually hydrodynamically inefficient since, when loaded, they draw an unconscionable amount of water, and are therefore difficult to paddle and cranky.

Small two-seaters have much appeal among newcomers to canoeing. They are lighter than bigger canoes, and thus easier to portage or to heist onto a car-top carrier. However, how a canoe handles in the water is far more important than how easily you can toss it onto your shoulders. You'll save a few dollars by buying a "shortie," but it's a penny-wise saving. Unless you have special applications in mind, go for the long one.

Chapter 3

~·~·~·~·~

Beams and Bottoms

It used to be that specifications for the midship section of a canoe described only the beam, usually at the gunwales. The specs were skimpy for the simple reason that the canoeing public was not especially concerned with a hull's true configuration. Times have changed and so have specification charts.

The 1980 *Canoe Magazine* Buyer's Guide began to enlighten canoeists with a fact to which only a handful of experts had previously given any attention: a canoe's behavior is pretty much governed by the shape of that portion which is in the water, not by the width at the gunwales. The Guide introduced a second beam specification. Along with the traditional gunwale width, it added the seemingly revolutionary 4-inch waterline beam—as the term implies, a measurement taken 4 inches up from the bottom of the canoe. Now, even without viewing the actual canoe, you can see in your mind's eye a truer image of the hull.

Occasionally you'll run across the term "molded beam," which refers to the width of some canoes at a point where the sides bulge outward to an extent greater than the gunwale width. The term is almost never used in specification charts, but it is occasionally encountered in canoe literature. Most manufacturers list only the gunwale and the 4-inch waterline beams.

Generally, if the waterline or molded beam is greater than that at the gunwales, the canoe's sides slope inward. This is "tumblehome." It is most pronounced at midship, usually tapering off toward each end. When the waterline and gunwale beams are alike, the sides are vertical, and the canoe is said to have straight sides. If the gunwale beam exceeds that at the waterline, the canoe has "flare." In canoes of advanced designs, you may encounter subtle modifications, but for all practical purposes, a canoe has either tumblehome, straight sides, or flare, and these are indicated in this manner in catalogs. But, just to keep things interesting, some flat-water marathon racing canoes incorporate both tumblehome and flare!

Tumblehome is built into virtually all flat-bottom canoes to provide longitudinal rigidity and strength. Buy a flat-bottom canoe and you'll get tumblehome. It also appears in some rather advanced racing models, since the narrowed gunwale beam makes dipping paddles easier — an advantage appreciated by racers who could probably win trophies in a log dug-out. In such models the tumblehome is often excessive. As Cliff Jacobson once wrote: "Avoid extreme tumblehome if you want a seaworthy hull. Many flat-out race designs utilize excessive tumblehome for the comfort of the paddlers, but these boats are not forgiving and should be avoided by all but highly skilled paddlers."[1] This is good advice, especially if you like a dry canoe. The greater the degree of tumblehome, the more readily waves will slop aboard. Pronounced tumblehome, particularly when combined with a flat bottom, results in a canoe that delights in flipping unwary paddlers.

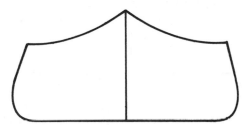

Flat bottom with tumblehome

Straight sides will turn waves more effectively than tumblehomed sides, and their longitudinal rigidity is usually more than adequate, since a canoe with straight sides will incorporate a rounded-type bottom. Unless the craft is a wide-beam tub, straight sides hamper paddling very little, if at all.

---

[1] *Canoe Magazine* (December 1981).

Canoeists who cuss tumblehome most fervently are usually the ones who proclaim flare as the ultimate virtue in a canoe, and they are probably right. When combined with a round-type bottom and even with a relatively narrow waterline beam, a canoe with flared sides is fast, maneuverable, and dry. Waves are thrust brusquely aside.

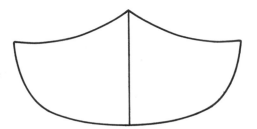

Shallow arch with flare

Over the years, it has been assumed that canoe bottoms are either flat or round. A flat bottom guaranteed stability; a round bottom signified a "fool killer." And these myths have persisted. Actually, a flat bottom is no assurance that you'll stay upright. As for the "round" bottom, few builders admit to producing a truly round-bottom canoe. It would, of course, be treacherous. "Round," it turns out, is something of a catchall for a variety of bottom shapes, including shallow arch, shallow vee, rounded vee, and deep vee.

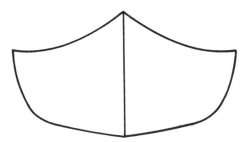

Shallow vee with flare

The most easily identified of the four when viewed by a novice is the deep vee. However, this is the one least likely to be encountered in a recreational canoe. The deep vee is found in racing models that go so fast they don't have time to tip over. On the other hand, the shallow arch, the shallow vee, and the rounded vee are

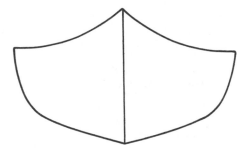

Rounded vee with flare

quite commonplace. There are no universally accepted standards. One builder's shallow arch may differ slightly from another's, and this is true also of the shallow vee and the rounded vee. The nuances are so subtle that portraying the differences in photographs would be futile: they simply do not show up. Hence, for clarity, somewhat exaggerated line drawings are used.

The flat-bottom canoe, with its inherent tumblehome and ample beam, has taken considerable written and verbal abuse in recent years; perhaps the kindest terms applied to it have been "pusher" or "bruise-water." In many instances this downplay is justified, but not always. The flat bottom is not altogether villainous. Carried well to the sides and to each end, a flat bottom increases capacity and results in a shallow draft, allowing you to poke your way along a bony creek that might ground one of the round bottoms. Also, a "pusher" will ride up and over oncoming waves, and in heavy following seas, the stern will lift readily. You may take on a bit of spray, but neither end of the canoe will knife into a wave, slopping water aboard.

The flat bottom has another redeeming feature: "initial stability." Step aboard and you'll feel relatively secure, even if you're new at the sport. Oh, there's some minor teetering, of course, but you won't feel that the canoe dislikes you and is about to pitch you out. Once you settle into paddling position, a reassuring sense of control takes over. This initial stability is important to some canoeists.

I'm one of them. For me, the ultimate sport is fly fishing for trout and salmon from a canoe. Under a bright sun these fish are easily spooked, so a long, delicate cast is needed. I can make such casts while I'm standing, but when I'm seated, my range is cut by 20 to 30 feet. So I stand, and that initial stability of the flat bottom is welcome. Others subscribe to the stand-up philosophy, too. When I worked as a Maine guide, I allowed one fisherman to stand not only on the floor of my canoe, but also on the front seat! A superb angler, he put out long casts that took salmon when other "sports" went fishless. I don't recommend acrobatics, of course, but if you have a reasonably good sense of balance, casting from a canoe while standing is not only effective, it's just plain, downright fun. But don't try it in a round-bottom canoe, even if it's tied up at the dock.

SAWYER CANOE CO.

The initial stability of this canoe is clearly evident.

Then, there are those who enjoy poling. For greater leverage and power, poling must be done in a standing position, and there's bound to be some wobble underfoot. Not only is the flat bottom's stability reassuring, but the canoe tends to "plane" as it is thrust upstream, sliding up and over the water's surface rather than plowing through it. The better it planes, the easier it is to pole.

What's more, the flat bottom readily "sets over," or ferries laterally or diagonally, to circumvent obstructions. None of the round bottoms is as steady or as maneuverable with a pole.

Fishing from a flat-bottom canoe or poling it is one thing. Paddling it is another. Lightly laden, it rides high and responds to paddle thrusts beautifully, though it's easily buffeted about by the wind. Load it to somewhere near its capacity and it does, indeed, plough through the water. I could have added "like a barge," but "pusher" and "bruise-water" are more than sufficient malignity. Howie LaBrant was a mite kinder. He called the flat bottom an "overgrown meat platter."

Capsizing a "pusher" on relatively calm waters is not easy; you have to make a concerted effort. Rough water may be another matter. Once the tilt is under way, with the hull rolling so that the gunwale is within a couple inches of the water, you are actually riding on the canoe's tumblehome surface, now transformed into a sharply rounded bottom. From here on in, flipping is easy.

The problem is aggravated in rough water because the flat bottom tends to conform to the pitch or angle of the waves, particularly if the canoe has broached (been turned broadside to the waves). The sudden tilt of the canoe can toss you out instantly, and to the amazement of many, the canoe may then quickly right itself and sail merrily out of your grasp. Two young canoeists once waded ashore to my camp on a small island in a Maine lake during a bad blow that created 3- to 4-foot seas. "We tipped over," they explained. Their canoe was no longer in sight, so I set off downwind in our motor launch. I found the canoe a few miles away, right side up, with barely a gallon of water in it. Yes, the canoe was a pusher.

Shallow-arch and the various vee bottoms are considered a mite "touchy," or "tender." Step aboard carefully. Especially if you're new to such canoes, you'll feel considerable unsteadiness. Some experts believe that these hulls are generally unstable and require considerable skill to handle. Frankly, there's more than a touch of truth in this. However, when properly loaded, with the bulk of an outfit's weight set deep in the bilge along the keel line, such hulls become remarkably stable. The early fur-trade canoemen knew this. Their great canoes were round-bottomed (probably shallow arch), yet with the tremendous weights they carried, rough seas bothered them little.

It must be admitted that the round bottoms lack initial stability. But their secondary stability can more than compensate. Especially when a round-bottom canoe incorporates a degree of flare (as opposed to tumblehome), its secondary stability is just a little short of amazing. Tilt such a canoe and you'll discover that as the gunwale approaches water level, the canoe "fetches up," stabilizing in a tilted position. It's almost as if the canoe were rigged with the sponsons that used to bedeck canoes sold to the timid. This isn't to imply that a round-bottom canoe is "untippable." A careless move will tip any canoe.

There is another advantage to the round bottom. Whereas a flat bottom conforms to a wave's surface angle, the shallow-arch and the vee bottoms tend to hold the canoe in a more nearly upright position, letting the waves slide harmlessly under. This is a concept that flat-bottom advocates have difficulty accepting.

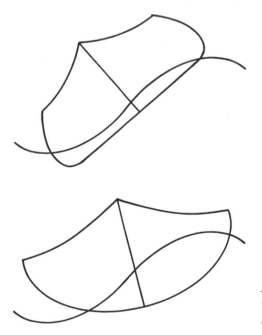

In wave action a round bottom remains more nearly upright than a flat bottom.

While they may draw a bit more water than do the flat-bottom hulls, shallow-arch and vee bottoms stay on track much better and require only minimal course correction. They paddle more easily and they are faster.

Chapter 4

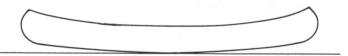

Rocker and Keels

ROCKER IS THE UPSWEEP of the keel line from amidship to each end. Its purpose is to lift the ends from the water so that the canoe can pivot readily. The degree of rocker varies considerably, from zero (a straight keel line) to as much as 8 inches in slalom canoes. Few manufacturers stipulate the exact amount of rocker they have built in. They are more likely simply to mention a "touch of rocker" or "moderate rocker."

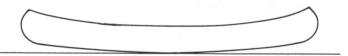

Pronounced rocker

If you want a precise measurement, you'll probably have to determine it yourself. One way is to sight along the keel line when the canoe is inverted. If rocker is present, you'll see that the ends

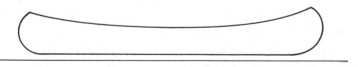

Straight keel line

appear slightly lower than the center section. But this is an inaccurate appraisal. If possible, place the canoe upright on a flat surface,

23

the showroom floor, for example. With the canoe in a level position (someone will have to hold it for you), measure the vertical distance between the floor and the point on the canoe where the keel line turns sharply upward to form the cutwater.

Note that the ends of this Millbrook rockered Model ME are out of water. At the paddle is designer John Berry, Sr.

Your canoe's primary use will determine the degree of rocker that is required. For white-water running, the more rocker, the better. In quick water, your canoe must be able to pivot so that you can dodge midstream rocks or slip into or out of eddies with some semblance of grace. Indians who lived along boulder-strewn rivers built their birchbark canoes with such a pronounced rocker that they became known as "crooked canoes."[1]

While rocker is a definite asset in white water, it will cause your canoe to waddle on flat water. Because the leading edge of the cutwater and the trailing edge of the stern are at least partially out

---

[1] For a graphic example of this, see the illustration opposite p. 31 in Robert E. Pinkerton's book *The Canoe*.

of water, it's difficult, even impossible at times, to keep the canoe on track. You'll expend as much energy correcting your course as you will driving your canoe forward. There's another negative aspect of rocker on flat water, one little realized by canoeists. As Duane MacDougall of Pembroke, Ontario, points out (and I have agreed for years), because of the upward slope in the forward half of a rockered canoe, it actually tends to climb as it moves forward, traveling vertically as well as horizontally. MacDougall would like to see a "rocker" class of canoes established, to permit separate competition from the faster, better-tracking straight-lined models. So far, racing rules continue to ignore the matter of rocker.

My own experience tends to back MacDougall's theory. I own two well-rockered canoes, and they do indeed like to stray; they do tend to bob or "porpoise" when I drive them hard on flat water. But in the rapids, they're a delight to handle.

Suppose, however, you intend to use your canoe for multiple purposes on flat *and* white water, on placid lakes and swiftly flowing rivers that may or may not be interspersed with frothy rock gardens. Compromise. Most canoes used for such purposes (known as "cruisers" or "trip canoes") incorporate a touch of rocker, perhaps an inch or so. Some rocker is almost mandatory on long cruising canoes, which otherwise would obstinately resist turning. Some cruising models may include a straight keel line with a moderate upsweep at the ends.

A flat-water canoe, whether it's a racing model or a solo cruiser, almost invariably has a straight keel line, although as in the foregoing cruiser, there might be just a bit of rise at the ends to aid in making the turns. Of course, such a canoe would be out of place in serious white water, although an occasional frothy riffle should not deter a skilled paddler.

Surprisingly, you can introduce rocker where none exists. Simply tilt the canoe until one gunwale is only an inch or two above water. This lifts the ends out so that you are now riding on the curved chine, which, in this position, doubles as a rockered bottom. Solo canoeists do this routinely when making turns.

The matter of a keel may seem closely related to rocker, but it is not. Quite the contrary. A keel would nullify the effectiveness of a rockered bottom. Nor are you likely to find a keel in a fine performance canoe with a shallow arch or a vee bottom. A keel is the enemy of maneuverability. The majority of experts scorn the keel, and they're likely to be quite explicit in expressing their contempt. Cliff Jacobson has written that a keel "will act as a cow catcher in rapids; it'll hang up on rocks and cause upsets. . . . External keels are generally the sign of an inferior canoe design."[2]

I agree with Cliff's assessment of keels in the rapids, but if you're considering a recreational or family-type canoe for use solely on a lake or pond, the keel has a place. On flat water, a keel will cut down on wind drift somewhat, though not entirely. Keels also serve as structural reinforcement on canoes built of highly flexible materials, to keep the bottom from "oil canning." As for whether the overall design of the canoe is inferior, that depends on other aspects of its construction.

GRUMMAN BOATS

Standard keel

Keels are standard equipment on aluminum canoes simply because they are required; they hold the two halves of the canoe

GRUMMAN BOATS

Shoe or river keel

together. As a concession, some aluminum canoe builders offer the choice of a standard keel or a "shoe" keel, also known as a

[2] *Canoe Magazine* (1980 Buyer's Guide issue).

"river" keel, which is little more than a bulging plate along the keel line that detracts very little from maneuverability.

The primary function of keels in canoes is reinforcement. That they also help to keep a canoe on course may or may not be desirable, depending on the water. Try to "set over" or "ferry" a canoe with a keel in running water, and you'll find that your vocabulary doesn't include the range and variety of cuss words to express your frustration. And the same goes for trying to make a sharp turn in a narrow stream, even a slow-moving one.

SAWYER CANOE CO.

The Sawyerlex 17 has an inverted or "tunnel" keel not unlike the groove in a ski.

In a 1979 letter, Bob Gramprie, head of the Sawyer Canoe Company, wrote that the then-new Sawyerlex 17' was equipped with "a tunnel or internal keel that stiffens the hull and adds directional stability without adding weight or draft, to say nothing of avoiding a protrusion to hang up on rocks, logs and become a focal point of wear." To visualize such an "inverted" keel, look at the groove on the bottom of a ski. If it works on snow, why not on water? Thus, Sawyer came up with a canoe that is manageable on flat as well as running water.

When all canoes were of wood and canvas the keel had a more prominent place. White-water running was not as popular then, and moreover it was thought that the keel offered some protection for the canvas when landings were made on a beach or pebbly shore. That protection, of course, was minimal.

Trappers, who hauled their loaded canoes over beaver dams or through marshy thoroughfares, often wanted a keel. In fact, they frequently added "bilge keels." These were wood strips, usually 4 inches wide and 6 to 8 feet long, that were attached to either side of the canoe, just within the chine line. They offered more than adequate protection, but the canoes handled clumsily.

Early canoe builders often gave the buyer an option. The 1910 Old Town catalog, describing the 15-foot "Fifty Pound Canoe," promises: "Immediate shipment can be given without keel; with keel, four days' time."

Chapter 5

·~·~·~·~·

Overview

It's been definitely established that the longer a canoe in relation to its beam, the faster it will go and the more easily it will paddle. This raises a question: Will two different models of equal length and beam handle alike? Not necessarily. The profile of a canoe as seen from overhead can be enlightening.

Note figures A and B. At a glance, one canoe may appear to be somewhat narrower than the other. Not so. Lengths and beams are identical. However, notice that in canoe A the fullness of the mid-

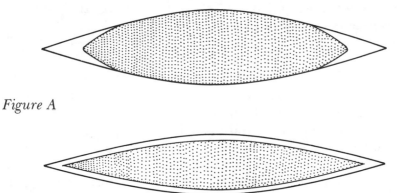

Figure A

Figure B

ship beam is carried well fore and aft, the width decreasing only gradually, characteristic of many flat-bottom models. Notice, too, that the shaded area, which represents the portion of the hull that is below the waterline, corresponds closely to the general contours of the canoe. Remember, it's the underwater portion of a canoe that largely governs its handling qualities.

Now, examine canoe B — same length, same midship beam. The gunwale beam narrows more sharply than in canoe A, resulting in more pointed ends. This is known as a "sharp-entry" hull. The shaded area — the underwater part — also corresponds to the hull's general lines.

Canoe A might be termed a "fat" boat. It is, in fact, a typical flat-bottomed, tumblehomed model, which critics insist is a "pusher." Canoe B can justly be called a "skinny" boat; it's a round-bottom design with flare. As you might expect, B is faster than A. Here's why.

As opposed to a speedboat, which may plane or skim over the water, a canoe is a displacement craft. (Some brawny race paddlers have been known to make their canoes plane during brief spurts!) The canoe displaces a volume of water equal to the volume of that part of the canoe that is below the waterline. In other words, a canoe creates a moving trough in the water. As a canoe moves ahead, its forward half pushes water aside, then the stern half allows the water to refill the trough. The faster the canoe travels, the more rapidly water is thrust aside; and, inversely, the more rapidly water closes in toward the stern. There, the similarity between canoes A and B ceases.

Howie LaBrant once compared canoes similar to A and B. In his example, each was 18 feet long with a beam of 30 inches. He pointed out that when each hull was paddled at 4 miles a hour, the "pusher" (canoe A) thrust water aside at an initial speed of 2 miles per hour — and abruptly, at that! The "fine" hull (canoe B), on the other hand, moved water aside at only .8 mile per hour — a very slow initial thrust — gradually accelerating it up to the midship section, and then gradually reducing it toward the stern. Thus, as LaBrant wrote, "both the speed and volume of displacement follow this principle of progressive acceleration and the physical law that it takes more energy to start a mass in motion abruptly than to increase its motion progressively once started."[1]

[1] *American Whitewater Journal* (Autumn 1962).

Essentially, the fine-lined canoe creates a lesser bow wave, and since the canoe will have to climb that wave, the lesser the better! The fine-lined hull also creates less friction along its wetted surface; and since it generates less turbulence, drag at the stern is minimized. Water slips smoothly by the hull, so that the wake may be little more than a pencil-thin trail of bubbles. Exaggeration, perhaps, but not much. A conclusive summation in two words: faster, easier.

Canoes A and B are symmetrical hulls; that is, each has identical shape fore and aft. Perhaps even faster and easier to paddle is a canoe with an asymmetrical hull. Its widest point — measured at both the gunwales and the waterline — is slightly back of midship, thus creating an elongated prow that parts the water even more gracefully than do fine-lined symmetrical hulls. The stern reentry of displaced water is a bit more turbulent, but this is more than offset by the efficiency of the sharp-nosed bow.

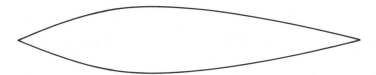

The overhead profile of an asymmetrical canoe

The asymmetrical hull is a favorite among flat-water racers, because it overcomes some of the tendency of a hard-pushed canoe to try to climb its bow wave. The added buoyancy of the stern section helps to keep the bow from climbing. This hull is at its best in shallow water, two feet or so, where bow waves are more pronounced than in deep water. Asymmetry is no longer confined to racing models. It's now being incorporated into an increasing number of cruising canoes.

An unusual application of asymmetry is found in the Blackhawk Canoe Company's Proem-85 model, designed by Pat Moore, a noted designer and paddler. The canoe is a solo sport cruiser, 11 feet 10 inches long, 26 inches wide at the gunwales, 24½ inches at the 4-inch waterline. The unusual aspect of this canoe is that the maximum beam is located about 1 foot *forward* of center, the idea being that this form improves the replacement (as opposed to

The Proem 85, a Pat Moore design built by Blackhawk Canoe Company

displacement) of water. The canoe does not have a brusque entry, however. Moore created a fine entry by building in concave lines up forward with extreme flare in the bow. This is an innovative approach, quite in keeping with Pat Moore's willingness to try something new in order to attain better performance.

When rocker is built into an asymmetrical canoe, the degree of rocker in the stern portion may be just a mite more abrupt than up forward. Both ends of the hull are never exactly alike.

Chapter 6

Depth and Sheer

DEPTH IS PROPERLY MEASURED AMIDSHIP, directly over the keel line, to obtain the vertical distance between the bilge and the height across the gunwales. Generally, the greater the depth, the greater the capacity, although capacity is also influenced by hull shape. Depth also provides the freeboard so necessary in rough water. At one time, some manufacturers specified only end depth, measured at the peaks — a misleading practice that thankfully has been largely discontinued. When both midship and end depths are stated, a truer picture of the hull is presented.

The optimal depth is governed by the uses to which you will put your canoe. If your penchant is for white-water competition, you might consider the Mad River ME model, a dry canoe even in rough water. This is a 15-foot 2-inch model with a center depth of 15 inches. Old Town's 17-foot Canadienne model, designed by Ralph Frese (who operates Chicagoland Canoe Base), is also deep (13½ inches), but for a different reason. The Canadienne is a long-distance cruising canoe, and its depth affords great carrying capacity, more than 900 pounds. Among several high-volume, load-carrying canoes is the Albany Freighter, built by Mid-Canada Fiberglass, Ltd. It's 18 feet 4 inches long and 18 inches deep — indicating clearly that, indeed, it is a freighter capable of carrying close to 1,500 pounds.

In contrast to these high-volume models with generous center depths, the Jensen C-1, designed by Eugene Jensen and produced by We-no-nah Canoes, is a one-man, flat-water competition boat,

MAD RIVER CANOE/JAMES A. HENRY

The Mad River Screamer winning the national white-water race on the Nantahala River

16 feet long but with a midship depth of only 11½ inches. The key words are "flat-water competition." Minimal freeboard and depth present no problems on flat water. The low profile offers minimal surface for the wind to grasp and it keeps weight down, both of which are important to any racing canoe.

Also with relatively shallow midship depths are a number of solo cruising models, intended to carry a limited outfit on flat water and, occasionally, through minor rapids. Depths among these run from 11 to 12 inches. Like flat-water racers, they have little need for pronounced depth. Finally, a great variety of recreational tandem canoes have midship depths of 12 to 13 inches or so. With this type of canoe, don't settle for less than 12 inches.

Naturally, since depth varies in any canoe from midship to the peaks, the gunwales generally sweep gently upward. This is known as "sheer," best seen in profile from one side. Sheer varies according to the intended function of the boat. In the white-water "banana boat," sheer just about parallels the rocker, resulting in high

MAD RIVER CANOE/JAMES A. HENRY

There is ample freeboard despite heavy load (including moose meat!) in this Mad River Voyageur on Ontario's Missinaibi River.

ends, the better to surmount boiling haystacks. In a flat-water competition model, there is usually a degree of sheer at the bow end, but in some models, there may be a "negative sheer" at the stern. In other words, depth at the stern may be markedly less than at the bow. An example of this is the We-no-nah Jensen 18½-foot cruiser built for marathon racing. Bow height is 16 inches; stern height, only 12. (Similar models are built by several other companies.)

Why sheer on a flat-water racer? Simply because flat water is not always flat. A heavy chop may be created by wind or by other racers at close quarters. Running into a chop at racing speeds calls for a slightly raised bow, to ward off spray and over-the-gunwale slop. This turbulence has little effect on the stern of a fast-moving canoe, though; hence the decreased sheer in the aft section.

Many recreational models, still patterned after the old-time Sunday-afternoon-lollygagging canoes, may have only a moderate sheer, but this culminates in suddenly ascending high peaks. These are wind catchers. Avoid them.

Why then did so many of the fur-trade birchbark canoes have such high, upswept peaks? The famed "Canot de Maitre," a 36-foot boat with a 32-inch midship depth, had 54-inch peaks! Such canoes, so beautifully portrayed by the Canadian artist Frances Ann Hopkins (1838–1918), lead one to wonder how well they handled on wind-swept lakes. Since they were nearly always heavily laden — trade goods going out, furs returning — it required massive blasts of wind to throw them off track. Howard I. Chapelle has a logical explanation for those high ends: "Some canoes were designed so that they could be used, turned bottom up, for shelter ashore." [1]

---

[1] Edwin Tappan Adney and Howard I. Chapelle, *The Bark Canoes and Skin Boats of North America* (Washington, D.C.: Smithsonian Institution, United States Government Printing Office, 1964).

Chapter 7

Gunwales and Decks

GUNWALES ARE ALSO REFERRED TO AS "RAILS," the terms used interchangeably. Whatever they are called, examine them closely before buying. There are some poor designs.

Unlike a counter-top edging, a gunwale is more than a cosmetic embellishment. It's functional, providing longitudinal rigidity. With inadequate rails, a canoe will twist torsionally or wobble in rough water. It can even eventually lose its shape, distorting the fine symmetry that was built into the canoe. Poorly designed or

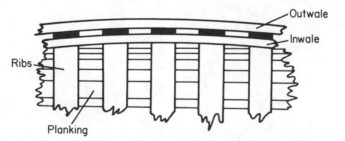

Open gunwales of a wood-and-canvas canoe drain easily.

badly installed gunwales can be knuckle-busters; and all too often, they are difficult to repair or replace. Moreover, they may make the draining of a canoe next to impossible. On the other hand, many manufacturers provide gunwales that are not only structurally rugged and functional, but also aesthetically pleasing.

No one has devised a better gunwale than that found on wood-and-canvas canoes. It is made up of two parts, an inwale and an outwale, that sandwich the ends of the ribs. This construction, rugged and durable, allows the complete draining of water. Replacing or repairing a section is easy, since the gunwale is secured to the canoe by means of brass or stainless-steel fastenings — often simple woodscrews whose heads are countersunk for a smooth finish. With the inner and outer gunwales fastened together securely every few inches, this laminated construction assures great strength. Finally, the beauty of finished wood is certainly more eye-pleasing than the starkness of aluminum or plastic. On the minus side, though, the varnished finish tends to wear off rapidly, exposing the wood to moisture and eventual rot. Annual refinishing is often necessary. Some manufacturers, rather than applying marine varnish, saturate the rails in oil before attaching them, thus deterring rot.

BILL RIVIERE · BILL RIVIERE

Robert Hartt, head of Stowe Canoe Company, demonstrates the pliability of white ash. Section did not break or split.

Woods most commonly used are spruce, mahogany, white ash, and oak. Some builders employ a spruce inwale combined with a mahogany outwale. White ash, which is easy to work, light, and resilient, is a favorite. Oak is rugged but somewhat heavy. Any of the foregoing combinations is satisfactory.

More and more builders of Royalex®, fiberglass, and Kevlar® canoes (see chapters 17 and 18) are installing wooden rails, even on white-water models that probably undergo greater structural stress than any other canoes. Unfortunately, some of these gunwales do not permit quick and easy draining. One of my favorite white-water canoes has "no-drain" aluminum-reinforced plastic gunwales, so I carry a large sponge, the type used in car washes. After flipping the canoe ashore, I can then easily and quickly sponge out the remaining water.

The draining problem has been circumvented in the gunwales specified by L. L. Bean, Inc., of Freeport, Maine, for its canoes manufactured by Mad River Canoe. Both the inwale and outwale are of wood, sandwiching a Royalex® hull. Since there are no ribs to create drainage ports, slots are indented in the inwale, next to the hull. Drainage is not quite as rapid as with a ribbed, wood-gunwale canoe, but it far surpasses most aluminum or plastic gunwales in this respect. Blue Hole canoes are fitted with similarly slotted inwales on their wood-trimmed Royalex® models.

Granted, structural integrity is more important than a dry bilge, but with today's technology, it should be possible to attain both. For instance, there is no excuse for a gunwale that is almost flush with the outside of the hull, yet overhangs it by an inch or more on

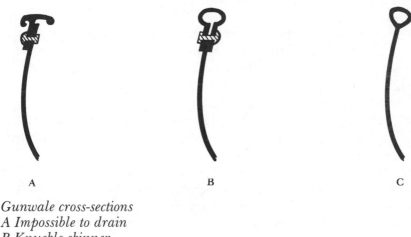

A   B   C

Gunwale cross-sections
A Impossible to drain
B Knuckle-skinner
C Drains well, no threat to knuckles

the inside. Such a gunwale holds water as effectively as a beaver dam!

Aluminum gunwales are standard on aluminum canoes, natu-
rally, and they are also used on Royalex® and fiberglass hulls.
Aluminum helps to minimize overall weight and is amply rugged.
Here again, however, the overhang is almost always on the inside.
Worse yet, gunwales may be fastened with pop rivets or bolts and
nuts that protrude along the gunwale. These are knuckle-skinners.

On some fiberglass models, the gunwales may be of wood or
aluminum, but they are encased in fiberglass, and molded as an
integral part of the hull. Suitably rounded, these are aesthetically
pleasing, drain well, and pose no threat to a paddler's knuckles.

Whatever canoe you're considering, irrespective of the gunwale
design, make sure that all fastenings are either countersunk or
smoothly rounded. You'll save on Band-Aids.

If I seem overwrought about a wet bilge, it's only because I
frequently like to stand, either to pole or simply to watch the
streambed slip by under me. A wet surface can be slippery, especially in one of the plastic hulls. I discovered this years ago, in
Wisconsin, when I tested the then-new rubber-like Royalite hull,
the forerunner of United States Rubber Company's Royalex®.
The bottom was wet. I was careless, and the tumble I took would
have done credit to a high-flying circus clown! Also, since I spend a
great deal of time kneeling, I don't relish having water sloshing
about my knees, not even in small quantities.

A canoe's decks are less critical to handling, but they do have
more than an aesthetic function: primarily they help to hold the
port and starboard halves of a hull together. In many flat-water
racing canoes, decks are minimized, even eliminated, to save on
weight. On most other canoes, decks help to keep water out, especially at the bow when a canoe plunges into a hefty wave and does
not quite make it over the top. The longer the deck, the better it
will shed such a watery invasion. Despite this, the trend is toward
minimal decks.

Decks may be of aluminum, plastic, or wood. In aluminum
canoes, the deck is part of the flotation chamber and is riveted
solidly to the hull. Plastic decks vary greatly, sometimes being no
more than a cap fitted over the peak. Wood is being used increasingly to "dress up" otherwise drab synthetic-material hulls.

Chapter 8

~.~.~.~.~

Seats and Foot Rests

Seats

THE INDIAN'S BIRCHBARK CANOE HAD NO SEATS. A paddler knelt on
the bottom, thighs resting on calves, feet turned in, the rump
lodged solidly on the instep. Conditioned to this position by generations of canoeing, Indians could squat in this manner for hours
without ill effects. For those of us without canoeing ancestors, this
position becomes torture in a matter of minutes. Builders of early
Canadian canoes added thwarts several inches below the level of
the gunwales. Canoeists still had to kneel, but they could lean
against the thwarts, or even rest on them. Today's canoes have
seats—all sorts of them.

Wood-framed caned seats are undoubtedly the most attractive,
and reasonably comfortable, although I've heard paddlers com-
plain that they are somewhat slippery. They're cool and no pool of
water will form on them. The frame will probably last the life of the
canoe, though the filling is less durable. In time, cane will crack,
then part. Using a seat cushion will lengthen the life of the caning,
and it also helps to keep it well varnished. Such seats can be re-
caned, of course.

Another wood-framed seat has rawhide lacing much like that on
snowshoes, a nice woodsy touch that will usually outlast caning.
Still another has lacings of nylon, which is virtually indestructible.

41

BLUE HOLE CANOE CO.

*Nylon-laced wood-framed seat
on the Blue Hole Model OCB*

However, both nylon and rawhide lacings create a physiological
phenomenon known as "waffle butt," unless a cushion is used.

Slat seats, a series of hardwood strips fitted crosswise, are installed in some canoes. They may seem flimsy, but those in my

BILL RIVIERE

*Slat seat in foreground on
Chestnut Prospector model;
folding canoe chair rests
against thwart*

18-year-old Chestnut Prospector are as sound as they were on the
day they left the Fredericton, New Brunswick, factory. Every year
or two, I touch them up with spar varnish. They, too, are inclined

to imbed their imprint into flesh resting thereon. Yes, I use a cushion.

There are also plastic and aluminum seats that are slightly concave. They enhance comfort and help keep your body locked into a firm paddling position; however, when spray flies, it tends to seep by to form puddles in the seat. Drilling three or four holes to drain the seat, as often suggested, actually is an ineffective remedy.

Aluminum-framed seats with woven plastic strips not unlike those used in folding beach chairs have a short lifespan. You're likely to find these in bargain canoes, almost certain to be deficient in other ways.

Probably the most efficient seats are the bucket type. They are form-fitting, as if someone had imbedded buttocks in plaster of paris. Usually they are just large enough to accommodate a paddler's derriere, so that flying spray is less likely to puddle in the

BILL RIVIERE

Stern bucket seat in a Sawyer canoe, with foot brace permanently attached

seat. Best of all, they afford a sturdy "body grip," enabling the paddler to become a part of the canoe. These seats are not built into run-of-the-mill canoes, but into high-performance tandem and solo models. Some bucket seats are rigged on a pair of runners, so that they can be adjusted fore and aft to trim the canoe.

One seat that has no redeeming value whatsoever is the flat bench, usually of aluminum or plastic, that extends from gunwale to gunwale. On this type of seat you'll slide from side to side, finding it virtually impossible to maintain a center position.

BILL RIVIERE

The Mad River "three-seater," which adapts to solo or tandem paddling

An unusual innovation is a three-seat canoe built by Mad River Canoe. It has the conventional tandem seats, wood-framed and caned, fore and aft. In addition, a third seat is located slightly back of amidship, its forward edge tilted downward. The canoe can be used for tandem paddling or for soloing. The center seat is tilted, so that a solo paddler may either sit on it or kneel with the derriere comfortably lodged against it.

On solo canoes, pedestal seats are coming into common use. These are not attached to the gunwales or to the sides of the canoe, but to the floor. We-no-nah Canoes has such a wood-framed seat with cane filling that can be adjusted fore and aft for trimming. A Wabash Valley Canoe Company solo model has a similar arrangement, except that the seat is of the bucket type, and is also adjustable.

In a more conventional recreational canoe, I'm fussy about the stern seat. I spend much time there. I want it just below gunwale

Adjustable, wood-framed caned pedestal seat

Adjustable bucket seat

height, and fitted far enough back so that I can wedge myself solidly between the gunwales. From this position I can ply my paddle vertically, for a direct thrust and better control. During a flat-water cruise some years ago, I paddled a heavily-laden 18-foot Peterborough while sitting on the rear deck — the most comfortable three days of paddling I ever enjoyed.

I have never learned why, but bow seats in most tandem canoes, and especially in the "pushers," are located too far back. I suppose this permits an easier lift of the bow over the waves, but it's a damnable position from which to reach the water, particularly with the shorter paddles now commonly used.

Some of these bow seats are "bear traps." They are hung so low that extricating yourself from a kneeling position is like trying to break a wrestling hold. If I flip, I want to be able to bail out quickly, without having to skin my calves and heels in the process.

As for the practice of placing flotation under the seats, that's just plain poor design. This construction is less expensive than fitting the foam into the peaks. But it makes it impossible to kneel while leaning against the seat with your legs extended under it. The few manufacturers who persist in doing this are simply cutting corners.

Competition cruisers and many solo models are designed to be paddled from a sitting position. Generally, the seat(s) is hung at a propitious height, somewhat lower than the gunwales. This lowers the center of gravity and, more importantly, locates the paddler closer to the water for more efficient use of today's shorter paddles.

Foot Rests

Ardent flat-water paddlers point out, quite correctly, that efficient paddling involves using the muscles of the shoulders, back, waist, and even the legs. A contoured seat at the right height helps attain this coordination, except that the leg muscles cannot be brought effectively into use. So, foot braces are added.

These can be improvised. One method calls for a heavy dowel — part of a broomstick, for example — or a flat piece of hardwood to be tied at each end by a nylon cord that runs back to the seat. Adjusted to the correct length, the cords hold the brace firmly as the feet push against it, thus transmitting leg-muscle power to the

BILL RIVIERE

Improvised foot brace

paddle stroke. The brace can easily be removed when not needed.

A more permanent arrangement employs two blocks of wood that are attached to the hull's bottom, some 14 to 16 inches apart, with a hardwood dowel or pieces of aluminum tubing bridging them. Harry Roberts, a well-known racer who believes that paddling should be done in a sitting position, has published detailed instructions on installing floor braces.[1] If you're about to buy a new canoe and like the idea of foot braces, chances are the manufacturer can add them for you at little extra cost. Some manufacturers provide braces as optional equipment.

Thigh Straps

I've no idea where or when the idea originated, but thigh straps are probably the cleverest gadgets to pop into canoeing literature and onto the rivers since Longfellow wrote: "I a light canoe will build me. . . . " Straps are attached to each gunwale, just forward of the stern seat, and run through a U-shaped bracket on the bottom directly over the keel line.

Why thigh straps? When a kneeling paddler thrusts his knees under the straps, they lodge solidly against his thighs, so that in effect the paddler is not riding in the canoe, he's wearing it! If you have ever tried paddling full out in a race, you know that your knees slide forward, away from the seat, so that you have to

[1] *Canoe Magazine* (September 1980).

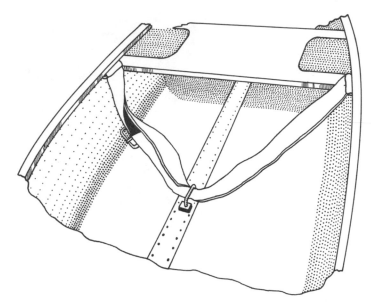

Thigh straps help lock a kneeling paddler firmly into position for better control.

"hitch" yourself back into position every few minutes. Thigh straps lock you into place; with pads under your knees, you can concentrate on driving your canoe. The straps are equipped with a buckle, of course, so that they can be adjusted.

Thwarts

Thwarts in Canadian canoes mentioned earlier were sometimes up to four inches wide, and doubled as seats for short rests from kneeling. However, thwarts now serve primarily to guarantee the hull's structural integrity. Too few thwarts result in a wobbly hull, especially if the fabric is somewhat flexible, such as ABS laminates and polyethylene. Manufacturers usually provide the right number of thwarts and locate them judiciously, but not always. My 17-foot Royalex® canoe was originally rigged with only a center thwart. I immediately added another, about 3 feet forward of the stern seat. This not only eliminated the wobble that developed in rough water, but it's also an efficient foot brace when I'm poling.

Chapter 9

Flotation

WITHOUT SOME SORT OF BUILT-IN FLOTATION, aluminum, fiberglass, and most plastic canoes would sink when swamped. This added flotation is usually closed-cell foam, inserted into each of the peaks and locked in position by some sort of bulkhead. This is adequate to keep the canoe afloat, but quite often just barely so. While you can climb into a swamped wooden canoe and hand-paddle it ashore, most other canoes except aluminum models lack sufficient buoyancy for this. On a warm summer day in water that isn't too cold, minimal buoyancy poses few problems: your life jacket will keep you afloat while you go about rescuing your canoe. In the turbulence of heavy white water, it's another matter.

Should you spill in white water, you may be able to guide your canoe into a quiet eddy—again, assuming that you're wearing your life jacket. However, a canoe that barely stays afloat is about as easy to guide through a rock garden as a pine log. With additional flotation, *beyond* the manufacturer's allotment, your canoe will ride higher and respond more readily to your efforts. If, as often happens, it gets away from you, a barely buoyant canoe is more likely to become wrapped around a boulder. A high-floater will bob downstream, perhaps bouncing off an occasional rock, but with a good chance of survival without serious damage.

Manufacturers of white-water models often recommend that extra flotation be added, especially to competition canoes that are likely to tackle the roughest of rapids. Experienced white-water runners don't need this advice; they have been adding extra buoyancy to their boats for years.

A popular approach is to wedge blocks of foam under the thwarts. This not only adds buoyancy, it also keeps a flexible or "mushy-bottom" hull from "oil canning." Often, paddlers straddle these blocks, half kneeling, half sitting, thus attaining a better grip on the canoe for the utmost control. There are variations of this method. Sometimes, a single large block of foam is trimmed to

MAD RIVER CANOE/JAMES A. HENRY

The foam-block straddle position in a Mad River TW Special on the Youghiogheny River

conform to the canoe's contours for placement amidship, the block slightly higher than the center thwart and grooved. The thwart is removed, the block put in place, the thwart then fitted into the groove and rebolted to the hull. Thus, the foam cannot escape.

There are more sophisticated forms of buoying. Some manufacturers attach foam strips, forward and aft, under each inwale. This not only adds buoyancy, it also guarantees that the canoe will float

SAWYER CANOE CO.

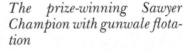

The prize-winning Sawyer Champion with gunwale flotation

in a level position should it swamp. Foam-strip flotation can be added to almost any canoe as a do-it-yourself project.[1] Another method for installing sidewall foam-plank flotation involves the installation of eyelets, tabs, and tie lines to hold the foam in place. A brochure explaining this system is available from Coastal Canoeists, P.O. Box 566, Richmond, Virginia, 23204, or from the Blue Hole Canoe Company.

A large truck-tire inner tube will also provide superb flotation. It is easy to install—wedged amidship under the thwarts—and to remove. Be sure that the tube is securely tied to the thwarts. Otherwise, in a spill, it could pop out and float merrily on its way. The inner-tube method has another possible shortcoming: inflating at streamside with a hand pump can be a long and tedious chore. The

[1] Bob Carlsen, writing in the September 1980 issue of *Canoe Magazine*, gives full instructions.

tube can be inflated at a gas station beforehand, but then you have a rather cumbersome, oversized rubber doughnut to transport.

Air bags designed specifically for canoes are available. Generally made of 20-mil vinyl, they are easier to inflate and deflate than tire

BILL RIVIERE

Fore-and-aft air bags rigged in a Blue Hole solo model

tubes and come equipped with nylon tie-downs. Several sizes and shapes are offered, for use amidship in a tandem canoe, or at the ends in solo models.

When should you add flotation to your canoe? Anytime you feel the inclination to romp in a boulder-strewn pitch of heaving water, whether in competition or simply for an afternoon's fun, add the temporary foam blocks or air bags. If your canoe is one of those that floats when swamped, but only reluctantly, the permanent sidewall foam planks are ideal, since they take up little room and add almost no weight.

Chapter 10

~~~~~~

Capacity and Seaworthiness

WHETHER CANOE CAPACITY SHOULD BE RATED seems to be a matter of contention. The 1976 Old Town catalog states: "Old Town believes that common sense, experience, type of canoe, and weather-water conditions are the best guidelines in such matters." Yet more recent Old Town catalogs specify rated capacities. Blue Hole lists "recommended working loads (not capacity)," seemingly suggesting that actual capacity may be greater but is not recommended. Sawyer lists specific ratings. We-no-nah publishes no figures, and its catalog states: "maximum capacity figures are largely irrelevant, and they are often exaggerated. . . ." Grumman specifies capacity "with six-inch freeboard." Alumacraft provides ratings based upon a formula devised by the Boating Industry Association. Mad River also stipulates load-carrying capability with 6-inch freeboard. (In fact, Mad River actually loads each new model with 50-pound sandbags until the 6-inch freeboard is reached.)

Clearly, these canoe manufacturers — certainly among the most prestigious in the United States — do not agree among themselves about the need for capacity ratings or how these might be determined.

Some years ago I ran across a formula that, at a quick glance, seemed logical: weight of canoe $\times$ 10 = capacity. Closer examination, however, revealed that this formula verges on voodoo; it's horrendously oversimplified, taking into account neither the configuration of the hull nor the material used in its building. Some 60-pound canoes *will* carry 600 pounds. On the other hand, an 18½-foot Kevlar® trip canoe, weighing only 72 pounds, should certainly be capable of more than 720 pounds.

No capacity ratings take into account 4-foot waves on a big lake, or the heaving haystacks at the foot of a wild-water pitch. Ratings give no indication of how well or badly a canoe will behave under its maximum burden, nor do they consider the skill or lack of it among likely paddlers. There is one formula that holds up well: keep your outfit's weight, including that of yourself and your partner, at under 85 percent of a canoe's rated capacity. If your canoe is not rated, maintain a minimum of 6 inches of freeboard. Keep in mind, too, that heavy cargo, even well within a rated capacity, makes any canoe behave sluggishly.

How you stow your gear affects handling, too. Place the heaviest packs on the bottom along the keel line, and distribute lighter gear fore and aft to help trim the canoe and to lighten the ends so that they will lift readily over waves. Generally, a canoe is at its best when trimmed to a level position. But there are exceptions. When running downstream in swift, though not necessarily turbulent water, the bow can be down just a bit; thus the current cannot easily grasp the stern and swing it about. For upstream travel and lake traversing, especially when working into the wind, lighten the bow slightly.

Seaworthiness is closely related to carrying capacity, of course, but it must also reflect the fact that canoes are frequently only lightly loaded — perhaps two paddlers and a picnic lunch. Seaworthiness is vital at all times, not just under maximum loads. Canoe catalogs, however, discuss it in a rather general way, usually in glowing terms. Understandably, no canoe builder is going to deny that his canoes are seaworthy!

Remember, too, that some canoes are seaworthy *only* when used for the purposes for which they were designed. For example, a sleek flat-water racer is a safe boat when used as such; but exposed to tossing waves on a wind-lashed lake, it would quickly become unsafe.

The fact is that most canoes produced today are seaworthy

within their design limitations — the exceptions being poorly designed and constructed "bargains." The truth is that while canoes are usually seaworthy, paddlers often are not. Flipping is almost invariably the result of human error or of pushing a canoe beyond its capabilities.

Claims for seaworthiness may be colored by a personal preference for one type of canoe over another. Harry Roberts has written: "A lean boat is less subject to be turned by wave action. A boat that doesn't slide off the face of a quartering wave and broach in the trough is a far more seaworthy boat than is a fat boat which skids around at the mercy of wind and wave."[1]

Perhaps rashly, I agree with Harry only partially. Inexperienced paddlers trying to ride out heavy seas in a "fat boat" are most certainly in trouble. But those same paddlers in a "lean" boat would almost certainly flip. Novices caught in a bad blow, in either a lean or a fat canoe, are in danger.

How about skilled paddlers? A canoeist capable of handling a lean canoe in rough water can also handle a pusher safely. As for the "fat boat" sliding off the face of a wave, no paddler who knows his way around canoes would stand for such nonsense. During the many years that I guided in the Maine woods, we used mostly Old Town and E. M. White guide-model canoes — "fat boats" by today's modern design standards, and flat-bottomed to boot. In these canoes I was (like most other canoe guides) often embroiled with wind and wave, but I was never at their mercy. I never doubted the seaworthiness of these canoes, although I was concerned at times about my own skill and strength.

It boils down to the seaworthiness of canoes, which is usually a certainty, as opposed to the seaworthiness of paddlers, which is often very much in doubt. If your canoe is suited to the use to which you put it, and if you're skilled enough to make that canoe bend to your will, that canoe is seaworthy.

Man has long sought to improve the seaworthiness of canoes. During the era of wood-and-canvas, "sponson canoes" were fairly common. The sponsons were air chambers attached just below the gunwales, tapering to a sharp point and blending into the hull at each end. The 1910 Old Town catalog depicts what appears to be

---

[1] *Canoe Magazine* (March 1980).

an 18-foot sponson model, with six adults sitting on one gunwale, their feet dangling in the water! According to the caption, the canoe's interior "remains dry." However, sponsons added considerable weight, they made paddling somewhat more difficult, and they were anything but aesthetically pleasing. Despite the fact that they imparted stability to a canoe, they have for the most part disappeared.

The 12-foot Sportspal equipped with foam sponsons

Some makers of aluminum canoes seek to enhance stability by building sponson-like bulges into the hull just above the waterline, so that the canoe appears to be suffering from a minor case of the mumps. Too, there are lightweight aluminum canoes, among them the Sportspal, built by Meyers Industries, the Sportsman, produced by Lincoln Canoes, and the Radisson, turned out by Norcal Fabricators, that are equipped with foam sponsons in the traditional position just below the gunwales.

Outrigger pontoons are reassuring to novices.

There also exist outrigger pontoons of foam, which may be attached amidship—reassuring to a novice or timid paddler, but doing little to enhance the art of canoemanship. I suppose that, like bicycle training wheels, they can be removed when the paddler attains confidence in himself.

Chapter 11

~·~·~·~·~

Weight

THE IMPORTANCE OF CANOE WEIGHT has sometimes been overemphasized. After all, any healthy male can heist a 75-pound model atop his car once he's learned the knack of the one-man pickup. And certainly, any physically adept young couple can carry a 70-pound canoe from a riverside parking lot to the water. If your canoe toting is restricted to such short distances, there are few canoes in today's market that can be considered excessively heavy. But hold on — there's more to canoeing than car-topping a double-ender.

Scan the catalogs attentively and you'll be struck by a consistent pattern — the racing models are substantially lighter than the general run of recreational and tripping models. Perhaps the racers are telling you something; if minimal weight is important to them, perhaps it is to you, also. Other things being equal, the lighter the canoe, the less dead weight your paddle strokes have to drive through the water. Admittedly, 5 to 10 pounds isn't going to make much difference in your pleasure level during a leisurely afternoon cruise. But when seconds count in a race, or when there are miles to go before you can rest, every ounce counts.

You may regret concluding that your canoe will spend only a brief time on your shoulders. One day, you'll hear the siren call of far-off waters. The back of beyond doesn't come easily, however. The aroma of campfire smoke rising among the pointed firs may necessitate some rather miserable portages. A 90-pound canoe will feel as if it's driving your feet 6 inches into the portage trail. On the other hand, as Bill Mason has written, "with a 60-pound canoe you start fighting with your partner for the privilege of carrying the canoe instead of the packs."[1]

While some canoeists believe that manufacturers are guilty of "white lies" ranging from 5 to 15 percent when reporting canoe weights, the discrepancy can be even greater. Once, while inspecting a canoe-building plant, I asked about the weight of a 16-footer resting upright on the floor. "About 75 pounds," the company's owner told me. I reached down to the center thwart for what should have been an easy lift. It was two weeks before my sacroiliac ceased hurting, during which time I learned that the canoe actually weighed well over 100 pounds. I suggested that the company provide a small crane as optional equipment. The owner was not amused. I later learned, too, that he had never in his life paddled a canoe!

Usually, discrepancies are not that radical. Just by way of satisfying my curiosity a while back, I weighed four canoes then residing in my barn (canoes come and go here!), using bathroom scales. Here is what I found:

CANOE AND LENGTH	MANUFACTURER'S WEIGHT	ACTUAL WEIGHT
Grumman Fiberglass, 18'	90 lbs.*	96 lbs.
Coleman, 17'	79	82
Chestnut Prospector, 16'	75	72
Old Town Tripper, 17'2"	79	75

* Grumman notes that weight is approximate.

Granted, there may have been inaccuracy in the bathroom scales, but since two of the canoes were overweight by 7 percent or less, and two were actually "underweight," it's difficult for me to label canoe manufacturers as robber barons out to con you with deceptive claims. If you're still skeptical, it's been suggested that you carry bathroom scales while shopping; but that's carrying skepticism a mite far, methinks.

[1] Bill Mason, *Path of the Paddle* (Toronto: Van Nostrand Reinhold Ltd., 1980).

If you've been working out at the gym, the weight of a 90-pound canoe shouldn't faze you. On the other hand, a 65-pounder might prove hefty if you rarely exercise. The best way to tell whether or not you can lift a specific canoe gracefully is to lift it. If you antici-pate loading and unloading alone, try the one-man lift; if your spouse or partner is shopping with you, use the tandem lift. And don't simply pull the canoe up off the floor a few inches; hoist it up over your head as if you were slipping it atop your car. The sales-man will probably chew his fingernails up to his elbows, so be careful.

When lifting a strange canoe for the first time, be a little tenta-tive. When I picked up the first "stripper" I ever saw, I nearly heaved it over my shoulders, thinking I was hoisting the usual gut-straining 75-pound 17-footer. It weighed only 55 pounds!

A good rule of thumb dictates that the lighter a canoe, the more fragile it is. Strength and durability almost inescapably add up to weight. There are exceptions—hulls of Kevlar® or certain "pro-prietary lay-ups" (more about these later)—for which the rule of thumb converts to: the lighter *and* more durable it is, the more expensive. There is another incontrovertible premise: a low-priced, flyweight canoe is likely to break up when a rolling trout splashes it.

Chapter 12

~\~\~\~\~

Birchbark

THE POET ARTHUR KETCHUM described the birch tree as:

> . . . *a Dryad thin and white*
> *Who danced too long one summer night.*

Indeed, the Dryad-turned-birch dances to this day, not only on hillsides, but also on the waters as a birchbark canoe.

How far the birchbark canoe antedates recorded history, no one knows. It was already in an advanced stage of development when Jacques Cartier, the French explorer, entered the St. Lawrence River in 1534. Captain George Weymouth, who had sailed from England in 1603, was impressed when two-man Indian canoes outpaced his longboat during friendly encounters on the Maine coast, on what is now Penobscot Bay. Weymouth later remarked about the quality of the craftsmanship he saw in the canoes.

On May 2, 1670, Charles II of England signed a charter that granted close to one-third of the North American continent to his cousin Prince Rupert and 17 of Rupert's associates. These 18 men thereafter operated as The Governor and Company of Adventurers Trading into Hudson's Bay, now known as the Hudson's Bay Company, or, in Canada, simply "The Bay." The charter granted not only a vast unexplored tract of land, but also its resources, and even the authority to administer civil and criminal justice.

The "Adventurers" themselves remained in England, but sent

employees, led by a "Governor," to establish a post on the shore of Hudson's Bay. There the English remained for more than 100 years, rarely venturing inland. To trade for English goods, Indians brought furs down the great rivers to the post. Some of these treks required an entire summer in birchbark canoes.

© 1978 BY JEFF DEAN

A Tom MacKenzie birchbark canoe. Note spruce-root lashings on stem.

Meanwhile the French, who controlled the St. Lawrence valley, began to invade "Rupert Land" (the Hudson's Bay Company's territory) by traveling across the Great Lakes and into the interior of western Canada, "The Bay's" backyard. It was a somewhat disorganized, but effective and highly profitable form of poaching. The Hudson's Bay Company did nothing about it. The French and Indian War did; in 1763 came the treaty under which France ceded Canada to England.

Enter the "Nor'westers," a group of Montreal Scots who openly defied the Hudson's Bay Company's territorial rights by organizing The North West Fur Company. They implemented an organized system of raiding "The Bay's" backcountry, and by the early 1800s they had the Hudson's Bay Company virtually on the ropes; its profits dropped to an all-time low.

No wonder, for the Nor'westers, in their great canoe fleets, brought trade goods right to the tepee doors! The Indians were delighted. No longer did they have to make the long trek to Hudson's Bay to obtain the white man's mirrors, hatchets, blankets, and trinkets.

© 1979 BY JEFF DEAN

Indian-made bark canoes at Thousand Islands Museum

Along came Lord Selkirk, who took control of the faltering Hudson's Bay Company. He confronted the Nor'westers aggressively, bringing in troops via the Great Lakes in 1812. They confiscated Nor'wester furs and supplies. Fighting broke out, and quickly escalated — ambushes, raids, and barn burnings. Blood flowed. Not until 1821, back in London, did common sense prevail. The Nor'westers and the Adventurers amalgamated their two companies, under the name of the Hudson's Bay Company. Today, the firm is one of the world's greatest retailers.

The opening of the Canadian wilderness, the widespread beaver-fur free-for-all, and the founding of a great retail firm — all came about because someone in the dim recesses of unrecorded history discovered that birchbark could be used for boat building.

Tom MacKenzie at work in his Madison, Wisconsin, workshop

Without their canoe fleet, the Nor'westers probably could not have challenged the Hudson's Bay Company, and without bark canoes, the Indians could not have made the long voyages from the interior to the shores of Hudson's Bay.

From 1700 to 1765, the French maintained a canoe "factory" at Trois Rivieres, on the north shore of the St. Lawrence below Montreal. Employing both Indians and French Canadians, the factory turned out the famous Canot de Maitre (literally, "Master's Canoe"), a 36- to 40-footer, and the equally noted Canot du Nord, or "North Canoe." About 25 feet long, the Canot du Nord was capable of hauling up to 3,000 pounds.[1] Smaller canoes were also built, including a "half canoe" — about 20 feet long — and 10- to 15-foot "light canoes."

The Canot de Maitre, also known as the "Montreal Canoe," hauled freight on the Great Lakes and on Canada's larger rivers, while the Canot du Nord was used west and north of Grand Por-

---

[1] Grace Lee Nute, *The Voyageur* (St. Paul: Minnesota Historical Society, 1955).

VOYAGEUR CANOE CO./AQUA PHOTO TECHNOLOGISTS LTD.

Glenn A. Fallis, president of Voyageur Canoes, portages a Kevlar®/fiberglass replica of the 25-foot Canot du Nord.

tage, located at the western end of Lake Superior. The smaller canoes were used for local travel and on sheltered waterways.

By today's standards, the birchbark canoe was fragile. Part of the voyageurs' nightly riverside chores consisted of applying pitch to cracked skins. Yet the birchbark was — and still is — remarkably tough. Robert E. Pinkerton reported that "for three dollars I once bought a twelve-foot birch that weighed little more than twenty pounds and never leaked a drop in an entire summer's travel."[2] On Prince Edward Island I once examined a 70-year-old bark canoe whose hull was so firm that, had I struck it with my fist, I would have injured my hand and not damaged the canoe.

A birchbark canoe is actually a wooden canoe with an outer skin of bark. To build one, the Indian drove stakes into the ground to form a canoe-shaped frame. Within this, he unrolled birchbark, soaked in hot water to make it pliable, perhaps resting stones on the bark to keep it from curling. Those who see a birchbark canoe

[2] Robert E. Pinkerton, *The Canoe* (New York: Macmillan Publishing Co., 1914, 1942).

JOHN CROFT

Jack Minehart removing bark from a birch tree. Bark is taken from trees scheduled to be cut by loggers.

for the first time are often surprised that the bark is a reddish-or-ange color, not white. That's because the inner surface of the bark becomes the outer surface of the hull, so the familiar white faces into the canoe. This provides a smoother outer finish.

The canoe usually consisted of several sheets, sewn together with finely split roots of the black spruce, and later waterproofed with pitch. Once the bark was roughly in place, the builder then lay in the planking of split cedar, against which he propped the ribs. These lodged the planking solidly against the bark. With the ribs and planking positioned, the gunwales and thwarts were then added — these, too, being lashed with spruce roots. Until about 1850 no nails — no metal of any sort — were used. After that date, builders began to use metal fastenings. Pinkerton complained early in this century that some slipshod construction resulted in the shifting of the planking, exposing the bark to easy puncturing. The later practice of nailing the planking to the ribs, as is done with today's wood-and-canvas canoes, eliminated the problem.

The foregoing is, of course, an oversimplified description of birchbark canoe construction. Adney and Chapelle, in *The Bark Canoes and Skin Boats of North America,* provide a thoroughly de-tailed history and explanation of building methods.

JOHN CROFT

Jack Minehart (left) and Bill Hafeman with a birchbark canoe approaching completion

Unfortunately, birchbark canoes are highly perishable unless kept under cover when not in use. Few of the early ones remain except in museums. Yet now and then a few turn up, discovered in their hiding places in attics. Once, when a rumor reached me that a birchbark was among the items being offered at an estate sale a few blocks from my home, I literally ran toward realizing a lifetime ambition — owning my own birchbark. I met the canoe, a lovely, mint-condition 14-footer, coming out the door in the arms of a friend. He'd paid $10 for it! In 1976, Bill and Fern Stearns, well-known Maine canoeists, obtained a 15-foot birchbark built by the St. Francis Indians in Canada. A relative wanted to dispose of it, and Bill and Fern got to the head of the line. Such finds, however, are lifetime highlights. Picking up a fine birchbark canoe at a garage sale is about as unlikely as finding an autographed first edition of Ike Walton's *The Compleat Angler*.

Birchbark canoe building nearly became a lost art at the turn of

JOHN CROFT

Bill Hafeman displays laminated stem ready to be installed.

the century, with the coming of its canvas replacement. But not quite — thanks to Bill Hafeman, of Big Fork, Minnesota. Now well into his 80s, Hafeman is semi-retired; he recalls that when he moved to Big Fork more than 60 years ago, birchbark canoes had virtually disappeared, except for a few decaying and beaten-up relics. They fascinated him. A friend, Fred McLean, described how, as a young man, he had spent time with a band of Chippewa Indians and had observed them building canoes. Luckily, although he was well advanced in years at the time, McLean remembered vividly many of the construction details. This was enough for Hafeman, who set to work building the first of his more than 100 birchbarks. After the publication of Adney and Chapelle's work, Hafeman further embellished his acquired-the-hard-way knowledge of bark building, and became the continent's master builder.

Hafeman has shared his expertise. Over the years he took into his shop a series of apprentices, including Henri Vaillancourt, of Greenville, New Hampshire, the subject of John McPhee's *The Survival of the Bark Canoe.* Others who trained under Hafeman and who are now producing a limited number of canoes are Lyn

JOHN CROFT

Bill Hafeman splits spruce roots used for lashing.

Gerdes, of Isabella, Minnesota; Tom MacKenzie, of Madison, Wisconsin; and Jack Minehart, of Cedar Falls, Iowa. Rick Nash, another builder, is curator of the Kanawa International Museum of Canoes and Kayaks, at Minden, Ontario, where more then 250 historic canoes are displayed. Ray Boessel, Bill Hafeman's grandson-in-law, carries on much of the work at the Big Fork shop. And Bill Hafeman's wife, Violet, is a knowledgeable birch canoe "craftsperson" in her own right. Birchbark canoe-building, it appears, is in good hands.

Many of the canoes turned out by these builders end up in museums, or as part of the decor for business establishments. But there are those who believe that bark canoes are meant to be paddled, and paddle them they do. Jack Minehart, president of the North American Birch Bark Canoe Association, has logged more than 5,000 miles in the bark canoe he built for himself. The canoe, he says, "looks a little beat up, but it is still in sturdy, straight-tracking operation."

Not many canoeists adopt the birchbark as their sole canoe, but if you hanker for some nostalgic paddling, the birch canoes being built today are of excellent workmanship — probably better than many a canoe turned out with primitive tools 200 years ago. In the fall of 1981, I was able to examine one of Tom MacKenzie's canoes; it was a thing of beauty, indeed, and as well built as some of the better wood-and-canvas counterparts.

Building a birchbark canoe is a labor of love. Today's builders, whether it be MacKenzie, Hafeman, Gerdes, Nash, Vaillancourt, Minehart, or Boessel, incorporate a level of craftsmanship that shows they place pride in their product above profit. Some turn out only one or two canoes a year, and most have a three- to four-year waiting list. The entire building process, from peeling the bark (large sheets are becoming increasingly difficult to find) to applying pitch to the seams, is almost entirely handwork.

If you're fortunate enough to acquire one of these prizes, be good to it. Enjoy the stealth and ease with which it glides over the water. Who knows, somewhere along a shaded riverbank you may see a lone figure in loin cloth, an approving light in his eyes, perhaps even a touch of envy.

Chapter 13

·\·\·\·\·\

Wood-and-Canvas

PETERBOROUGH, OLD TOWN, WHITE, Morris, Thompson, Templeton, Racine, Chestnut, Rushton.

If you're a pre-Grumman canoeist or a more recently converted "nothing-is-as-good-as-wood" paddler, at least one of the foregoing names will stir your soul just a mite, for they represent the finest wood-and-canvas canoes ever built. There are others, of course, including relatively unknown builders who operated "woodshed" shops, turning out only a few canoes each year for local use.

Remarkably, little is known about many of the long-gone builders. They left behind virtually nothing more than an occasional catalog, gleefully uncovered by a modern-day wood-canoe buff. The small shops in particular were not historically minded, and hence left no literature. Considerable research is now under way, especially by members of the Wooden Canoe Heritage Association.

Among the great builders, only two remain—the Old Town Canoe Company and the White Canoe Company, quite by coincidence both located in Old Town, Maine. But both have made a switch. Old Town's wooden canoes now have skins of fiberglass, rather than canvas; and White's canoes are now of all-fiberglass, Royalex®, or Kevlar® construction.

E. M. White founded his company in 1889, and the firm now claims to be the oldest in America. It may be a valid claim, since all companies of earlier origin are now defunct. Mr. White operated the business until 1947, when he sold it. The new owners added lapstrake-construction boats to the line. In the early 1960s, the business was sold again, after which the third owner eliminated wood-and-canvas construction, venturing instead into fiberglass canoes and highway signs. Today, E. M. White turns out ten different fiberglass models, plus a 17-foot 2-inch Royalex® canoe.

Until recent years, both E. M. White and Old Town produced superb guide models up to 20 feet long. Maine guides were openly split among themselves as to which was the better canoe. I have owned one of each, and I'd consider the choice a toss-up, although, if pressed, I might confess a slight preference for the White.

E. M. White guide model built by Island Falls Canoe Company

And glory be! You can still buy an E. M. White canvas-covered guide model, in either the 18½-foot or the 20-foot length — but not from E. M. White. White canvas canoes are now built by the Island Falls Canoe Company, of Dover-Foxcroft, Maine. Clint Tuttle obtained five molds from E. M. White in 1973, and turned out a number of guide models and smaller canoes for about three years. In 1976, Jerry Stelmok purchased the business and was joined by a partner, Rollin Thurlow.[1] Since Old Town continues to produce its own guide models, Maine guides can carry on the argument.

Especially in the Moosehead Lake region, there were guides who wouldn't give a pair of worn-out suspenders for either a White

---

[1] Jerry Stelmok has also authored the book *Building the Maine Guide Canoe* — in this case a White, naturally!

or an Old Town. Their choice was a Templeton — either of them. "Either" because there were two Templetons, Fred at Greenville and Arthur at Rockwood. Although related, they operated separate shops.

Fred Templeton developed a 20-foot mold in 1936, and in 1940, a 15-foot form. The larger canoe was a guide's model with a 41-inch beam, capable of great loads even in rough water. It became a regional favorite. Upon Fred's death, the molds were acquired by Merton Comstock, who continued the business. The big 20-footer became known as a Comstock canoe. Comstock's son-in-law, Fred Reckards, now has the molds in his shop near Rockwood. Like Old Town, Fred Reckards prefers fiberglass for the skin, not only for the added durability, but also because the beauty of the wooden hull is not hidden under painted canvas.

Arthur Templeton also built a 20-foot mold for a canoe with a somewhat rounded bottom, which proved to be very fast. The mold is now owned by Harold "Doc" Blanchard, of Greenville, who produced a limited number of canoes for a few years, including smaller ones on molds of his own design. He now conducts adult education classes in canoe building; the classes turn out eight to ten canoes each winter, and the students get to keep them for the price of the materials.

Among the great north-of-the-border builders were the Peterborough Canoe Company, of Peterborough, Ontario (formerly the Ontario Canoe Company), founded in 1879; and the Chestnut Canoe Company, of Fredericton, New Brunswick, established by William and Harry Chestnut in 1897. The two firms led canoe production in Canada for many years; but as demand fell off, it was only a matter of time before Peterborough closed down in 1961. Chestnut, which once built 60 different canoes, survived until 1979, when it ceased building only a few months after having moved into a new plant at Oromocto, New Brunswick.

Peterborough and Chestnut each produced one of the most famous of all canoes, the Prospector, often dubbed the "Workhorse of the North." In fact, at one time Chestnut built Prospectors for sale under the Peterborough label. This was probably during a brief period when Peterborough, Chestnut, and the Canadian Canoe Company had amalgamated under Canadian's name. Another famous canoe built by Chestnut was the Ogilvy, whose design is believed to have originated among salmon-fishing guides on New Brunswick's Tobique River.

Women were more adept than men at applying planking at the now-closed Chestnut Canoe Company plant.

While the original makers are gone, both the Prospector and the Ogilvy live on, thanks to Don Fraser, former sales manager at Chestnut. When that firm folded, he purchased some of its molds and opened his own plant (Donald Fraser Canoes), where he now produces the Prospector in the 17-foot length and the Ogilvy in lengths ranging from 16 to 22 feet. He also turns out three other Chestnut canoes — the Bob Special, the Cruiser, and the Guide Special — all canvas-covered.

Other far-sighted builders obtained some of the Chestnut molds, too, including Jame Thomson of the Wabasca Canoe Company; Glenn A. Fallis of the Voyageur Canoe Company; and Hugh Stewart and Kirk Smith, of Temagami, Ontario. All three include Prospectors among their output; thus a fine canoe lives on.

Workman clinching fastenings that hold planking to ribs at the Chestnut Canoe Company

Where, and by whom, the first canvas-covered canoe was built is not known. It probably evolved from the practice of patching leaky birchbark models with cloth and pitch. C. E. S. Franks states that the wood-and-canvas canoe was invented in Maine, but current

A Chestnut awaiting shipment at the original Fredericton plant

75

research is unable to substantiate this.[2] It is known that one E. H. Gerrish built wood-and-canvas canoes in Bangor as early as 1875. B. N. Morris, who started building wood-and-canvas canoes at Veazie, Maine, in 1882, wrote in one of his catalogs: "The Morris canoes . . . were the first canvas-covered canoes ever advertised, advertisement first appearing in the magazine *Field and Stream* in the year 1887."

As so often happened with woodworking shops, the B. N. Morris plant burned to the ground in 1920. Morris continued building canoes until about 1938, but on a very limited scale. In 1982, the Wooden Canoe Heritage Association reprinted an undated Morris catalog, believed to be of 1908 vintage, that includes well-detailed drawings of gunwale assemblies. The catalog also states that "the keel is regarded generally as a very essential feature . . . ," certainly contrary to the beliefs of many of today's canoeists. Nevertheless, Morris canoes attained a reputation for fine craftsmanship. When I examined a 60-year-old Morris in 1982, it was obvious that the reputation was well deserved.

One of the admirers of Morris is Joseph T. Seliga, of Ely, Minnesota. Seliga operates a canoe-building and repairing shop, and says that his work has been inspired by his acquaintance with B. N. Morris. A glance at a Seliga canoe indicates that Morris' devotion to craftsmanship has rubbed off. The late Sigurd Olson, a noted conservationist and a great canoeman, once stated: ". . . no canoe paddles as easily as my Morris-Veazie." Not only were Olson and Seliga fellow Minnesotans, they also agreed wholeheartedly about Morris canoes!

J. Henry Rushton, of Canton, New York, who had been building wooden canoes since 1873, believed that all-wood canoes were superior to canvas-covered types, but in 1902 he succumbed to the demand for canvas. Rushton hired Melvin F. Roundy, of Bangor, Maine, who had been building wood-and-canvas canoes for 14 years.[3] Rushton canvas canoes proved an instant hit. In the March 1902 issue of the combined *Amateur Sportsman and Sportsman's Magazine* is a half-page advertisement in which Rushton offers

---

[2] C. E. S. Franks, *The Canoe and White Water* (Toronto: University of Toronto Press, 1977).

[3] Atwood Manley, *Rushton and His Times in American Canoeing* (Syracuse, N.Y.: Adirondack Museum/Syracuse University Press, 1968).

canvas-covered canoes at $30, with a "higher grade" at $40. William Crowley, curator of the Adirondack Museum, wrote in his foreword to a recently issued replica of Rushton's 1903 catalog: "Perhaps Rushton did not achieve the perfection he continually sought to attain, but his craft, particularly his canoes, have rarely been surpassed by other wooden boats." The words probably apply well to Rushton's first canvas canoe, the Indian Girl, which was available in 15-, 16-, and 17-foot lengths.

The author (left) with Bill Miller, whose family has been building canoes in New Brunswick's Tobique valley since 1925

Thompson is another name linked with early canvas canoes, at Peshtigo, Wisconsin. The Thompson Brothers (there were six!) Boat Manufacturing Company turned out 17 canoes in Peter Thompson's barn in its first year, 1904. Records recently uncovered indicate that more than 200,000 were eventually sold before the company ceased building wooden canoes in 1959.

Early business was good. The Thompsons built a new factory at Peshtigo in 1911 and a second plant at Cortland, New York, in

1920. But about 25 years ago, a fire destroyed the Peshtigo shop. The firm recovered for a few years, so that by the mid-1960s it employed more than 180 people. In 1966 the business was sold, however, and the new owner phased out wooden watercraft in favor of fiberglass boats.

MAD RIVER CANOE/JAMES A. HENRY

An early Kennebec war canoe under way at Harpswell, Maine

Jeff Dean, president of the Wooden Canoe Heritage Association, has done considerable research on the Thompson brothers' endeavors, and published a well-detailed history of the Thompson canoes in *Wooden Canoe*, Winter 1979–1980.[4]

Another popular canvas canoe was the Racine. The June 1887 issue of *Outing Magazine* carried a small advertisement that reads: "Racine Hardware Mfg. Co., Racine, Wisconsin. Hunting Boats, Rowboats, Sailboats, Canoes from $20 to $70. Write for our brochure. Mention this paper." Instead, I contacted Jeff Dean. Rummaging through city directories, he established that the company was probably started in about 1875, and around 1892 was sold to L. S. Kellogg, who renamed it the Racine Boat Manufacturing Company. Ten years later, it ceased operation.

Many other famous brands have receded into near-oblivion:

---

[4] There is a collection of Thompson catalogs covering the period from 1907 to 1929 and from the early 1950s through 1959, at the State Historical Society of Wisconsin, in Madison. The search for missing issues of the 1930s and 1940s continues.

Gallop, Kennebec, Skowhegan, Arnold, Carleton, Dan Kidney, Kingsbury, Lac du Nord, Lakefield, Pacaco (Penobscot Canoe Company), Rhinelander, Penn Yan, and Skaneateles. Thanks to persistent searching by wood-canoe buffs, one of these models occasionally surfaces in good enough condition to warrant restoration.

The older the canoe, the greater the odds against finding one, of course. An unpublished University of Toronto student thesis reports that "a builder by the name of David Thompson may have constructed canvas canoes in northern Ontario as early as 1837." If indeed canvas canoes were built at that time, the chances of finding one now are virtually nil. This is probably true also of the canvas canoes that are believed to have taken part in the 1857 Peterborough Regatta.

Canoes of more recent vintage do turn up, however. Some, in fact, quite regularly. Unfortunately, the growing interest in wooden canoes and in their restoration has led many to believe that they are as rare as early English first editions, resulting in some price-gouging. Battered wrecks that require complete rebuilding are offered at prices that, when combined with the cost of restoration, can reach as high as $2,500 or more! Fortunately, there is now an evident downward trend in prices.

Whether it was built in 1910 or 1940, no other canoe lends itself as well to restoration as the wood-and-canvas type. Since all of them were literally handmade and assembled piece by piece, rotted or weakened sections, even a single rib or a lone bit of planking, can be removed with relative ease and replaced. I don't mean to imply that restoring an old canoe can be accomplished some sunny Saturday afternoon. It is a lengthy and tedious chore, but patience and careful use of hand tools can restore a battle-scarred hull to its original beauty.

Don Fraser once graciously permitted my wife and me free run of the then-new Chestnut Canoe Company plant at Oromocto, New Brunswick, for an afternoon of observing and photographing. The delightful aroma of cedar was pleasantly distracting, but watching a canoe being assembled, meticulously and efficiently, was fascinating. A rib-and-plank hull is built on a mold, or form, that resembles an inverted metal canoe. First, the stems and inwales are positioned. Then ribs (as many as 50!), usually of white cedar and steamed to make them flexible, are bent over the form and locked into place. When the entire canoe has been ribbed, red-cedar planking is attached to the ribs with copper nails that, upon penetrating the ribs and striking the metal form, clinch themselves, securely locking the planking to the ribs. While one or two strakes of planking still remain to be applied, the hull is removed from the mold. The remaining planking is then attached, and the hull examined for protruding nail-heads or unevenly matched sections of planking. A thorough sanding follows. Brawny male paddle pushers may be surprised to learn that women do most of the careful fitting, matching, and finishing.

The canvas comes next. It can be stretched over the inverted hull, but that is doing it the hard way, since it requires a great deal of inefficient tugging and pulling by hand. Wrinkles form and are difficult to remove. Most builders prefer to insert the hull, right side up, into a canvas pocket or envelope that is suspended from overhead. The hull is forced downward into the pocket. At each end, the canvas is overlapped to cover the stems, which will later be protected by a bang plate. The outwale is then attached. A filler is applied to the canvas to "kill the weave," thus producing a smooth surface. Set aside to dry and harden, the canvas surface is later sanded and painted, following which the interior is varnished.

If a fiberglass skin is applied instead of canvas, the process is somewhat simpler. Usually, two layers of fiberglass cloth — six-ounce seems to be a standard weight — are laid carefully over the hull. The resin is then brushed on, thoroughly saturating the cloth. When this has hardened, more resin is applied, to attain a smoothly finished surface.

Which is preferable, a canvas or a fiberglass skin? With either, you can choose the color, although most fiberglass advocates seem to prefer a clear finish, so that the beauty of the wood hull is actually enhanced by the see-through fiberglass. Some experts feel that canvas allows the hull to flex more readily in rough water; fiberglass and resin, which bond directly to the hull, are stiffer and certainly tougher. Either is easy to patch in the field. As for the claim that canvas is quieter than fiberglass, that's reaching a mite. I've paddled both types and, although I'm a stickler for stealth when sneaking up on riverside wildlife, I've done equally well with fiberglass and canvas. So much for that controversy. Except for aluminum, which is decidedly the noisiest of all canoe fabrics, stealth is a matter of skill with the paddle.

Canoe built for Alaska's rough waters by John Breiby of Eagle River

Wood-and-canvas canoes simply do not stack up with ABS Royalex®, polyethylene, fiberglass, or aluminum when it comes to impact resistance and general durability. But the "frailty" of the wood-and-canvas canoe, like Mark Twain's demise, has been greatly exaggerated. Admittedly, a dub paddler who doodles in heavy white water aboard a wood-and-canvas canoe is going to inflict damage, perhaps total, and will likely get dunked in the process. But if you have a reasonable amount of skill, you don't need to pamper a wood canoe. Want proof? See Bill Mason's graphically illustrated book, *Path of the Paddle.* That canoe you see plunging through rock-strewn rapids is a 16-foot, canvas-covered Chestnut Prospector. I wouldn't attempt the runs that Bill Mason negotiated, but my Prospector, identical to his, has been knocking around for 18 years. Total damage: one cracked plank, plus multitudinous scratches on the gallant thing's bottom.

Maintenance — that's another matter. If you use a wood-and-canvas canoe extensively, you bring upon yourself an annual chore of scraping and repainting, if you want to keep your canoe in top condition. During my guiding days, I used an 18-foot Kennebec

Three styles of fiberglass-covered wooden canoes built at Leavitt Quality Craft Canoes

guide's model for both canoe trips and fishing. Come the end of the season, the canoe was pretty well battle-scarred. I stored it "as is" under cover for the winter, so that it would dry thoroughly. When I heard the first honkings of wild geese in the spring, I went to work. First, the interior: I daubed that with varnish remover, and scraped it clean with a dull hunting knife. After a day or two of further drying, I applied steel wool until the wood shone clean and bright. The residue I wiped out with a cloth dampened in paint thinner. Another day or two of drying, then two coats of spar varnish, applied lightly and with two days' drying between them. The exterior got exactly the same treatment; despite claims that paint remover will damage canvas filler, I saw no evidence of this. More sanding, two thin coats of marine-grade paint, then a coat of spar varnish. Battle-scarred in the fall, like new in the spring.

To take such pains, however, you must love your canoe; otherwise, it's drudgery. If wild geese set your soul astir as ice-out approaches, by all means buy a wood-and-canvas canoe. If not, you'll probably be happier with something else.

Chapter 14

.·~·~·~·~·~

Strippers

THESE ARE NOT X-RATED CANOES! The term "stripper" derives from "cedar-strip canoes."

I confess to overenthusing about the beauty of birchbark canoes. As for wood-and-canvas, my Chestnut Prospector, its woodwork glistening in the grayish light of my barn's interior, gets loving glances almost daily. But for sheer, glowing loveliness, the cedar-strip canoe, with the patina of highly smoothed wood shining through its clear fiberglass skin, approaches sublimity. Afloat in the sunshine, it is an artistic *chef d'oeuvre*.

And it's practical, not as delicate as it might appear to be. Gil Gilpatrick, of Fairfield, Maine, who wrote *Building a Strip Canoe*, supplies strippers he has built to clients whom he guides on canoe trips. He admits that if you use a stripper in white water long enough, you will probably damage it; but then, that's true of almost any canoe. Apart from guiding, Gil paddles 500 to 600 miles per year, most of it in mid-summer when water is low and rocks are exposed. "During most seasons," he says, "I come through with just a lot of scratches, nothing that needs repair." Nevertheless, most canoeists who paddle strippers pamper them, restricting their travels to flat water, venturing only occasionally into minor rips.

Since it has no ribs, a stripper's weight may be considerably less than that of a wood-and-canvas canoe. Of course, if the builder uses a 10-ounce fiberglass cloth (instead of the more common 6-ounce), plus an appropriate amount of resin for a more rugged

83

Stripper built for wilderness trips by Gil Gilpatrick

craft, its weight will approximate that of a wood-and-canvas model. Bear in mind, though, that a canvas canoe that is used extensively absorbs moisture, thereby taking on weight. A stripper, tightly sealed in fiberglass, does not.

The earliest builders of strippers are unknown. In 1887, Rushton offered a "smoothskin" hull, actually a lapstrake with the strips beveled and sealed in varnish (since waterproof glues were unknown in his day). It is possible, too, that strippers, in one form or another, were produced in the Peterborough-Lakefield region of Ontario prior to 1879 (including the Stephenson, in which battens backed up the cedar strips).

It has only been in recent years that strippers have caught the imagination of canoeists, not only because of their beauty, but also because their construction limitations are few. The thin cedar strips can easily be molded into lively canoes that respond like living things. A growing number of small shops are turning them out in limited numbers; since they require labor-intensive methods, mass production is not feasible. But while strippers produced commercially are not inexpensive, they can also be built at

MORLEY CEDAR CANOES

The use of clear fiberglass skins highlights the beauty of stripper hulls.

home at modest cost — if you discount labor. Anyone reasonably adept with woodworking tools can build one. In fact, many of the commercial builders started by constructing one for themselves, and once set up, found it was easy to continue production.

85

A stripper is built on a "strongback," which resembles a heavy wooden ladder, the rungs of which are the stripper's "stations." These are usually of half-inch plywood cut to resemble a cross-section of the canoe, not unlike a bulkhead. When the stations are in place, you have the rough outline of an inverted canoe. Strips may be of pine, redwood, or white cedar, the latter most commonly

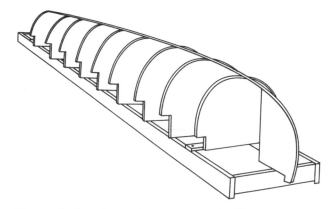

"Strongback" on which cedar-strip canoes are built

used. Planking is cut with a band saw from cedar boards, producing strips ¼-inch thick by ¾-inch wide. Thickness may vary slightly; Jensen Canoes uses ³⁄₁₆-inch strips in building their 18-foot model, which weighs a mere 47 pounds.

In most home construction processes, the strips are edge-glued and applied to the form, held in place by staples until the glue dries. The staples are later removed and the hull sanded smooth, after which a coat of resin is brushed on to seal the wood.

There are variations in technique. Instead of using woodworking glue, some builders utilize the more sophisticated WEST System®, whereby the strips are saturated with an epoxy that bonds them into one solid unit, thus greatly enhancing overall strength.

The exterior of the hull is then fiberglassed. Some builders apply minimal glass and resin, to keep weight down; but this can result in a rather fragile hull, which may fly over the water, but will "crunch" sickeningly when it meets a rock. Other builders use medium-weight fiberglass, applying a single layer above the waterline, a double layer below. Polyurethane varnish is applied by a few

Cedar strips being edge-glued and stapled during construction of a strip-per. Staples are later removed before fiberglassing.

builders; others believe that this accomplishes little more than adding weight.

Kevlar®, much lighter and stronger than fiberglass, is not used on strippers, because it is not transparent and would hide the natural beauty of the cedar strips.

After the canoe is removed from the form, interior work—sanding and fiberglassing—is completed. Trim is then attached.

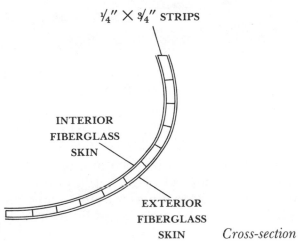

¼″ × ¾″ STRIPS

INTERIOR
FIBERGLASS
SKIN

EXTERIOR
FIBERGLASS
SKIN   *Cross-section view of stripper hull*

This is a somewhat standardized process of construction, but many a stripper builder has his own methods. Nor is the foregoing intended as a set of instructions. It merely illustrates that building a stripper does not require the skills of a cabinetmaker. Of course, you'll need plans, which are available in the form of full-size templates. There are also instruction books. You can shortcut some of the labor by buying a kit that includes precut strips, decks, and thwarts, as well as seats. Old Town Canoe Company offers such a kit. You will, however, still have to build your own strongback.

YONA PAYNE

Strippers built by Herschel Payne, Ottawa. 18½-foot model in foreground weighs 54 pounds; 15-foot canoe held by Payne, 40 pounds.

Cedar Creek Canoes produces a 16-foot laminated hull that, while it is not a stripper, resembles one somewhat in having no ribs. Using the WEST System®, two layers of ⅛-inch red-cedar veneer are cross-laminated with applications of epoxy resin, inside and out. The resin saturates the wood, stiffens the hull, and completely locks out moisture. The finished hull weighs about 60 pounds.

Nick Nickels has described an unusual stripper built by Mel Hunter and George Stenner, both of Lakefield, Ontario. The canoe, 16 feet long and 33 inches wide, weighs 70 pounds. Not surprisingly, it is called the Lakefield. Built on a regular metal-sheathed canoe form, it requires 74 half-round ribs of elm. White cedar strips, rabbetted on both edges for interlocking, are fastened to the ribs with about 3,500 copper nails. After a thorough sanding, the hull is saturated with boiled linseed oil and allowed to dry until no oil rubs off. The oil prevents cracking and waterproofs the strip planking. No fiberglass is needed; instead, three thin coats of varnish are applied. Nick, a skilled canoeman in his own right, adds: "The finished Lakefield canoe is a thing of beauty to behold and a sensitive, responsive craft afloat."[1]

The Lakefield method of construction is probably beyond the woodworking ability of most amateur builders. Fortunately, the "strongback" method is easy and inexpensive. The form can be used over and over again, which probably explains why many a stripper builder is not satisfied until he has built a second, and a third . . .

ROBERT HUGHES

"Orange-crate canoe" built by Robert Hughes, Hartland, Wisconsin. Note vee-shaped bottom.

Another do-it-yourself project produced the "orange-crate canoe." The late W. Ben Hunt, of Hales Corner, Wisconsin, de-

[1] *Ontario Hydro News* (July/August 1969).

signed a canoe that could actually be planked with the side boards of orange crates! The building plans and instructions were published in the Boy Scouts of America magazine, *Boys' Life*. The canoe was instantly popular amoung youngsters; according to Robert "Bob" Hughes, of Hartland, Wisconsin, who owns one, literally hundreds were built. Ben Hunt used the facilities of the now-defunct Schneider Boat Company in Milwaukee to build his prototype. The original version was planked with 1/4-inch plywood, but this proved too heavy. The orange-crate planking lightened it greatly. Bob Hughes built his using 1/8-inch plywood. "Due to a goof-up in building," he adds, "it has a decided hook to the left in its keel. Being a left-handed paddler, I can paddle all day without J-stroking."

Chapter 15

~~~~~~

Lapstrakes

SEVERAL WELL-KNOWN FIGURES ARE ASSOCIATED with the early development of the lapstrake canoe: John MacGregor, Warington Baden-Powell, William L. Alden, J. Henry Rushton, and George Washington Sears.

MacGregor, a wealthy Scot, visited America in 1859, venturing as far as the Bering Sea where he observed the Eskimo kayak. Back home in 1865, still deeply impressed by the kayak, he designed and built the first of four canoes, each of which was known as the Rob Roy. Aboard these, he cruised the waters of much of Europe, and even ventured into the Middle East; he subsequently wrote three books on his canoe travels, which were published between 1866 and 1870.

Each Rob Roy was a modification of the previous one. All were decked canoes, propelled by a double-blade paddle or by a sail. Rob Roy No. 3 was designed so that MacGregor could sleep aboard; it was 14 feet long, with a beam of 26 inches ". . . not on the deck but three inches below, so that her upper streak 'topples in' amidship but flanges out fore and aft."[1] To my knowledge, this is the first mention of tumblehome ("topples in") and flare ("flanges out") in canoeing literature. Including its paddle, mast (MacGregor used his fishing rod for this!), and sails, Rob Roy No. 3 weighed 72 pounds.

[1] John MacGregor, *With the Rob Roy on the Jordan* (New York: Harper & Brothers, 1870).

MacGregor's books quickly became "must" reading among sportsmen on both sides of the Atlantic, and recreational canoeing in the United States came to life. (In Canada it had been under way, in the Peterborough area, for more than 20 years!) Canoes were no longer just for hauling furs and trade goods: they would henceforth provide exciting sport.

Enter the Englishman Warington Baden-Powell—not to be confused with his brother Robert, Lord Baden-Powell, who founded the Boy Scouts. Shortly before 1872, Warington came up with his own design, known as the Nautilus, which he later sailed in several international competitions. Like MacGregor, Baden-Powell developed several versions of his canoe.

In America, shortly thereafter, William L. Alden, a staff writer for *The New York Times,* became interested in both the Rob Roy and the Nautilus. His first canoe, the Violetta, patterned after the Nautilus, was built by James W. Everson on Long Island. Alden's canoeing activities attracted other sportsmen, and in 1871, he was instrumental in founding the New York Canoe Club. Soon lapstrake canoes, with sails aflying or with double-blade paddles flashing, cruised and raced on the waters around New York City, spreading up and down the seacoast.

In reading about these early days of American canoeing, one may glean the impression that everyone took to canoeing. Not so. It was, in fact, a sport for the well-to-do, even the wealthy. The average working person could no more afford one of the handmade canoes of that era than he can a 26-foot sloop today. But this would soon change; mass production was waiting in the wings.

Whether it was this localized boom in canoeing that prompted J. Henry Rushton to build canoes is not known. It is unlikely, however, since his home in Canton, (upstate) New York, was a long way from the metropolitan areas where canoeing was most active. Although Rushton began building in 1873, he built only lightweight cedar sportsman's boats at first, mostly for local use. It was not until 1876 that he turned out his first two lapstrake canoes, each 13 feet long, with a flat bottom and a 28-inch beam.

His canoes quickly drew attention. In 1876, the newly founded magazine *Forest and Stream* described Rushton's two new craft as "portable boats," although they were actually canoes. The magazine went into considerable detail, referring to the planking as "siding which is cedar . . . stems of oak or elm . . . ribs also of oak or elm . . . put in the boat one and one-half inches apart. . . . Being lapstreak, eight to ten boards on a side, and ribbed so closely, makes them very strong for their weight, and being very flat on the bottom are very steady." The article concludes: "They are well turned at the ends . . . have considerable sheer, which gives them a trim, jaunty appearance on the water and at the same time enables them to live in rough water. . . ."

Rushton, who was no mean promoter of his products, could not have written a better "plug" himself. Other publications soon carried stories on the Rushton canoe. Interest grew. Rushton expanded, and eventually produced several models destined for fame, including his own Rob Roy, the Baden-Powell, the Canadian Ugo, the Wee Lassie, and that most famous of all, the Sairy Gamp.

This is where George Washington Sears enters the picture. You may not recognize the name, but you may well recognize "Nessmuk," Sears's pen name. Nessmuk, when he first contacted Rushton in 1880, was 59 years old and, although unaware of it, was suffering from the early stages of tuberculosis. Yet he made three extensive solo cruises on Adirondack waters, the last in 1883. He also turned out close to 100 articles for *Forest and Stream* dealing with the woods and canoeing, and wrote two books, including the classic *Woodcraft*, still in print.

Nessmuk's cruises were all made in Rushton cedar lapstrake canoes. He'd decided earlier against Peterboroughs and Racines because "neither of them talked about a 20-pound canoe" (although he later wrote: "I liked the Peterboro canoes; they were decidedly 'canoey' "). At the time, a 20-pound canoe was unheard of; Rushton's lightest model weighed 35.

Nessmuk startled Rushton with his request for a 20-pounder, but Rushton recovered quickly and built the Nessmuk No. 1. It was 10 feet long, 26 inches wide, and 8 inches deep. Rushton advised Nessmuk to stiffen the canoe with braces "if I found her too frail."[2] Nessmuk logged 550 miles in the canoe that summer and "she needed no bracing; and she was, and is, a staunch, seaworthy little model." About Rushton, Nessmuk added: "He built

[2] Nessmuk, *Woodcraft* (New York: Forest and Stream Pub. Co., 1888. Reprinted by Dover Publications, Inc., New York).

better than he knew." Rushton renamed the canoe the Wood Drake, and built about a dozen per year for other patrons.

The second canoe Rushton built for Nessmuk was the Susan Nipper, 6 inches longer and 2 inches wider than the Wood Drake. "She was a beauty," Nessmuk wrote, "finished in oil and shellac. But she weighed 16 pounds, and would not only carry me and my duffle, but I could easily carry a passenger." The 1881 cruise of the Susan Nipper was cut short when Nessmuk became ill and the weather turned bad. He covered only 206 miles of his proposed 1,000-mile trip.

His health improved in 1883, and he ordered another canoe. Rushton built the Sairy Gamp, "the lightest canoe ever built of cedar." She was 9 feet long, with a beam of 26 inches and a center depth of 6 inches. Her weight? Ten and one-half pounds! "I wanted to find out how light a canoe it took to drown her skipper," Nessmuk wrote, "and I do not yet know. I never shall." The Sairy Gamp, like the earlier Nessmuk canoes, was without seats or thwarts. Her strength lay in the craftsman-like fitting of plank to plank to rib.

Nessmuk wrote in *Forest and Stream* that during the summer of 1883, "I had cruised her, by paddle and carry, 118 miles on the outward trip, and, by a different route, 148 miles on the return. . . . It required care and caution to get in or out of such a light, limber boat. . . . Her builder thought her too small and light for a working boat. He was a trifle mistaken. . . . The Sairy Gamp has only ducked me once, and that by my own carelessness."

Nessmuk returned the Sairy Gamp to Rushton that fall, following which it was exhibited at various fairs and in the *Forest and Stream* office. Following the Chicago World's Fair of 1893, the Sairy Gamp was acquired by the Smithsonian Institution in Washington, which, in 1965, loaned it to the Adirondack Museum at Blue Mountain, New York. The Sairy Gamp is back home, where it can be seen today.

In the meantime, Rushton had gone on to still other successes, and was considered the best builder of light wooden canoes. He also had a flair for writing advertising copy touting his canoes. In an ad for one of his wood-and-canvas canoes, the text reads: "I am offered thirty dollars for this nice, canvas-covered canoe. Do I hear more offered? Why, gentlemen, this is no price at all. Make it $31.00, $31.00, $31.00, $32.00, $32.00, and sold for $32.00!"

Building the lapstrake canoe probably calls for greater wood-working skill than is required by any other type of boat. It's not surprising, then, that I have been able to locate fewer than a dozen small shops that produce them commercially. None of the large-volume canoe builders can profitably undertake the labor-intensive process. Those few who do build lapstrakes are true craftsmen who turn out a limited production, either of solo or tandem models. Modern builders do have some advantages over Rushton, though. He either painted his canoes or finished them with oil and shellac. Today's shops can use some form of cement to seal the cedar strake overlaps, and modern varnishes as interior and exterior finish.

It's doubtful that any canoeist today wants to emulate Nessmuk: his entire camping outfit, including the Sairy Gamp, weighed only about 26 pounds![3] Nor is a canoe as small as the Sairy Gamp available nowadays, unless custom-built, as the original was. However, today's lapstrakes are practical, light, and certainly more seaworthy than Nessmuk's flyweight craft.

Some modern builders turn out lapstrakes of their own designs, while others copy early models. A popular source for working drawings is William Picard Stephens's book *Canoe and Boat Building for Amateurs,* published originally in 1885. Stephens was the canoeing editor of *Forest and Stream.* My 1891 copy, identical to the first edition, includes 258 pages of highly detailed text, plus numerous line drawings. Another source is Walt Simmons's 90-page *Building Lapstrake Canoes,* available from the Wooden Canoe Heritage Association. Atwood Manley's *Rushton and His Times in American Canoeing* does not include building instructions, but does have several pages of design drawings, plus tables of elevations and offsets of Rushton canoes.

If owning a lapstrake canoe appeals to you, finding a builder should not be difficult, although you may have to order well in advance of the canoeing season.

Most of today's builders produce true lapstrakes; that is, the planking is attached "clinker" style, overlapping like clapboards on a frame house. Rushton also built "smoothskins," in which the

---

[3] There is a little-known explanation for Nessmuk's extremely lightweight camping outfit. More often than not, he spent his nights in the guides' bunkhouses at the numerous resorts that then dotted the Adirondacks!

"streaks" (as he called them) were beveled and matched, then sealed, resulting in a perfectly smooth hull exterior.[4]

BILL RIVIERE

Kevin Martin with his version of the Rushton Wee Lassie

Unable to obtain a suitable photograph of a lapstrake canoe, I recently visited Kevin Martin's shop at Epping, New Hampshire. I was in luck! He had just finished a replica of Rushton's Wee Lassie, its planking of northern white cedar, the keel of white oak, the knees of hackmatack, and the ribs of ash. Ten and one-half feet long, with a beam of 27 inches, Kevin's Wee Lassie weighs 22 pounds—certainly a more capacious and seaworthy boat than the Sairy Gamp.

Rick Heinzen and Tony Bries, who operate Freedom Boat Works in North Freedom, Wisconsin, have developed two lapstrakes. Their Mirage is patterned after Rushton's Vesper, although the length has been increased slightly, from the original 16 feet to 17. While the Vesper was a "cruising sailing canoe," the Mirage has been adapted to use with a double-blade paddle. Another Freedom lapstrake is Solitaire, a lengthened version of the

[4] P. 185 of Atwood Manley's book illustrates a cross-section of this type of construction.

Wee Lassie intended as a solo cruiser. Though both models are lengthened versions of Rushton canoes, the same proportionate lines have been maintained.

Walter Simmons, who runs Duck Trap Woodworking in Lincolnville Beach, Maine, produces three lapstrakes, in 13-, 15-, and 17-foot lengths. "Our canoes," he writes, "are essentially Rushtons but designed and built like sea boats. . . . All three are at home on Penobscot Bay . . . with a motion in a seaway more like a lobsterman's double ender than a standard canoe."

Chapter 16

❧·❧·❧·❧·❧·❧

Aluminum

THE BACKGROUND OF THE ALUMINUM CANOE is not peopled by Rush-tons or Nessmuks, nor did the voyageurs ever tote one over a fur-country portage. There are no legendary aluminum canoes; they are absent from the annals of canoeing's romantic past. Yet they revolutionized the canoe-building industry and attracted thousands who had never before wielded a paddle. The aluminum canoe was born during exciting times, the closing days of World War II.

Even as fighter planes built by the Grumman Aircraft Corporation of Bethpage, New York, flew from the decks of U.S. carriers, the concept of the aluminum canoe was being formulated. The idea came to William J. Hoffman, an executive in Grumman's engineering department, while he was at Inlet, New York, for a weekend of trout fishing in the Adirondacks. The weekend? Memorial Day 1944, barely a week before the Allies stormed ashore at Normandy.

Hoffman, in an interview, recalled: "We flew into Limekiln Lake from Fourth Lake and fished for a day or two, using a battered and water-logged thirteen-foot wood-and-canvas canoe. Then we decided to fish in Squaw Lake, several miles away. As there was no boat there, we had to carry our paint-loaded canvas canoe that must have weighed at least 100 pounds. For a fellow who was not accustomed to carrying a canoe, this was too much. I decided that someone had to do something about that problem."[1]

[1] Dwight Rockwell, *How It All Began* (Marathon, N.Y.: Grumman Archives, Grumman Boats, no date).

And do something Hoffman did. He studied the lines of the decrepit canoe and concluded that symmetrical halves of an aluminum hull could be assembled by riveting along the keel and at the ends. A 13-foot model, he guessed, would weigh under 50 pounds. He proposed the idea to LeRoy R. Grumman, president of the company, and to its vice president, Jake Swirbul. They urged him on.

GRUMMAN BOATS

LeRoy R. Grumman was among the first to test the new aluminum canoes.

Hoffman needed a modern canoe in good condition (a scarce item in wartime) for further study; one was located at Macy's, which loaned the canoe to Grumman. It was a 13-foot wood-and-canvas model advertised as weighing 50 pounds. "We put it on scales," Hoffman recalled, "and it weighed sixty-four pounds!" Immediately the borrowed canoe posed a problem. Fore and aft, it had reverse curves, easy to create in a cedar-planked craft, but impossible to stretch-form with a sheet of aluminum. By this time, Hoffman had a small crew assisting him. They modified the design and built a die of rock maple. When they stretched the first sheet of aluminum on the die, it "formed even easier than I had expected," Hoffman exulted. "The weight was also lower than I had figured." The first canoe, made with .032-inch-thick metal, weighed just over 38 pounds. Today's standard-grade 13-footer with a .052-inch skin weighs 58 pounds; the lightweight version, of .032-inch aluminum, 44 pounds. The increase is due to the need for heavier aluminum extrusions in the gunwales and keel, for greater strength.

Alcoa (Aluminum Company of America) got word of Grumman's experiment. Russell Bontecou, an Alcoa engineer, had designed and built a 17-foot model, handmade of eight sheets of aluminum riveted together, but company officials had decided it was "too unsightly and costly to be considered seriously." However, Alcoa saw the possibilities of the Grumman approach. Bontecou joined Hoffman at Bethpage, and Alcoa's experts provided technical assistance in the selection of alloys, rivets, and extrusions. Also, they supplied longer sheets of aluminum than were then being produced commercially.

Thus the aluminum canoe came into being.

It was slow at first; then business began to boom. Grumman produced only 94 canoes in 1945, the year the war ended. By late 1946, the plant was on a three-shift schedule, with more than 10,000 orders on hand. In 1951, the canoe operation was moved to Marathon, New York, and for the next 25 years or so, Grumman was the country's leading builder of canoes.

Then, in the mid-1970s, the Coleman Company of Wichita, Kansas, introduced its low-cost polyethylene (Ram-X®) canoe, selling at well below the price of aluminum models. Coupled with the firm's excellent reputation in the outdoor equipment field, an aggressive promotional campaign shot Coleman into the forefront. At one point, if you bought a Coleman camping trailer, you could add a Coleman canoe to the outfit for one cent! Tough competition, even for the equally reputable giant, Grumman.

Grumman fought back. In 1980 it joined with Uncle Ben's wild rice products—at first glance an incongruous affiliation, but not when you consider that Indians used canoes (and still do) to harvest wild rice. With five box tops, you could buy a 17-foot Grumman at a $150 discount. At that time, the canoe listed for $479. Net price: $329, a bargain. Public response was not overwhelming, but several thousand canoes were sold. However, the pendulum continued swinging toward Coleman, and Grumman was toppled from first place in the canoe market.

Historically, the aluminum canoe had been flat-bottomed, with a relatively ample beam carried well into the ends to produce a stable, high-volume craft. It changed very little over the years, because it seemed impossible to build anything but a blunt-nose canoe with aluminum. To refine the lines, thus creating a sharp-entry hull, would have meant insufficient space in the ends for work with riveting tools.

Grumman's 17-foot Eagle, the first major redesign since the original versions

Then came the Eagle, introduced by Grumman in February 1981, and the Beaver, brought forth by the Beaver Canoe Company in November 1980. Each was an innovation in canoe building. For the first time, if you wanted an aluminum canoe, you didn't have to settle for a "pusher."

The Eagle is Grumman's answer to Coleman's polyethylene

canoe. There has been no public announcement to that effect, but if you read between the lines in Grumman's Eagle literature, the evidence is there. The Eagle is 17 feet long, with a gunwale beam of 39 inches, a waterline beam of 34½ inches, a center depth of 14 inches, and flared sides. The stems are upswept and part the water eagerly. The canoe weighs 66½ pounds, which, as Grumman literature states, is: "12½ pounds lighter than the standard 17-foot plastic canoe." Add 12½ to 66½ and you come up with 79, the listed weight of the Coleman 17-foot polyethylene canoe.

Critics of Coleman canoes and the Grumman Eagle derisively insist that "they were designed by the shipping department." They are sold unassembled (only the gunwales are attached at the factories) so that they can be nested during shipment, thus effecting a freight savings. The buyer saves, too, by assembling the canoe with simple tools. Nonetheless, the Eagle is an innovative design, considering aluminum's limitations. As a flat-water canoe, it tracks well, it's dry and tough — tough enough for Grumman to warrant it.

Designer Bill Shaw, who blueprinted the Eagle, might have turned out an even better performer if he had replaced the flat bench seats with form-fitting ones, to eliminate sliding. And a shoe or river keel, in place of the knife-like type, would have enhanced the canoe's maneuverability. But then, this would probably have priced the Eagle out of the competition with the "plastic canoe."

Just as Grumman challenged the plastic canoe, Bill May, of Taneyville, Missouri, took on Grumman and the other aluminum builders by organizing the Beaver Canoe Company. Beaver would produce aluminum canoes along lines that theretofore had been restricted to wood and fiberglass: fine hulls and sharp entries. May retained the rivets along the keel, but at the ends he joined the sheets by fusing, heating the metal just enough to bond it without affecting its temper. Naturally, he didn't proclaim the details of his process to the world, although he did admit that special aluminum alloys made it possible.

A truly sharp-nosed aluminum canoe evolved. The bottom was shallow-arched, the waterline beam 1 or 2 inches less than at the gunwales. Prototypes were tested in competition and during long-distance trips. Paddlers put the Beaver through its paces "mercilessly," and one test paddler predicted, "It would blow everything else off the water, racing in the aluminum class." Six models were produced, ranging from 15 to 18½ feet and from 40 to 65 pounds, almost 30 pounds lighter than other standard-grade aluminum 18-footers. One Beaver model was a promising asymmetrical hull, another innovation in aluminum construction. At last, a high-performance aluminum canoe!

But no. It wasn't to be. Although the Beaver was reasonably priced, the anticipated rush to buy it did not materialize. There have been all sorts of explanations, but the consensus is that most American canoeists are not yet ready for high-performance canoes. So, barely a year old, the Beaver Canoe Company closed its doors in December 1981. Nonetheless, Bill May's construction breakthrough remains a notable achievement. An aluminum canoe as sleek as fine-lined fiberglass models may yet come to be accepted.

Beaver was not the only aluminum canoe casualty. *Canoe Magazine's* 1975 Buyer's Guide issue listed what were then believed to be solid, here-to-stay manufacturers such as Browning Aerocraft, Delhi, Lund, Monark, Ouachita, and Starcraft. There may still be some output from among these firms, although I've been unable to confirm this. None of them appears in the 1985 Buyer's Guide. Apparently, they have simply closed down, been absorbed into other companies, or switched from canoes to other products.

Although Grumman remains the aluminum giant, it by no means has the field to itself. The competition continues: Alumacraft, Great Canadian, Lowe, Meyers, Michi-Craft, Norcal, Osagian, Pro Boat, Smoker-Craft, and Misty River. Even if, by the time you read this, some of these have dropped out of the market, there still remains a wide selection from which to choose.

For those who are stability conscious, Michi-Craft and Smoker-Craft innovated a sort of stabilizing foil, a longitudinal projection just above the waterline and running almost the length of the canoe, tapering at each end. Michi-Craft's "Safety Foil" and Smoker-Craft's "Unispon" are, in effect, miniature sponsons that not only improve initial stability but also strengthen the hull. Sea Nymph has a similar design.

Three unusual aluminum canoe designs include the Radisson, manufactured in Canada by Norcal Fabricators; the Sportspal, by Meyers Industries; and the Sportsman, by Michi-Craft. The latter

Smoker-Craft canoe with built-in sponsons for added stability

two are built in the United States. Their strong selling points are light weight and the secondary stability they derive from foam sponsons (described in chapter 10). The hulls are of .025-inch aluminum and the interior is lined with a thin layer of foam, which

SEA NYMPH

MICHI-CRAFT COR

*Sea Nymph has similar spon-
son-like projections.*

*Michi-Craft, one of the origi-
nators of this type of built-in
sponsons*

Alumacraft has lines of conventional tandem canoe.

not only adds buoyancy but cuts down on aluminum's natural propensity toward being noisy. All are aluminum-ribbed.

The conventional aluminum canoe is built by stretch-forming two sheets of metal over a mold, and joining them with rivets along the keel and at the ends. Somewhere during the process, the metal is heat-treated to temper it. End caps, thwarts, seats, and flotation are added, the latter usually closed-cell foam encompassed behind bulkheads in the peaks. Voilà! You have an aluminum canoe.

Aluminum by itself is too soft and fragile; so it is alloyed with silicon, magnesium, zinc, manganese, or copper. There are various alloys for differing purposes. Those used in canoe building are within the so-called "6000 series"; the most common is 6061-T4. The "6061" indicates an alloy of aluminum, silicon, and magnesium. The " T-4" has to do with the metal's temper and the range of heat applied during construction. A number of canoe builders use 6061-T6 alloys; the Grumman Eagle is of 6010 alloy, claimed to be 25 percent stronger than other alloys of its weight. Quite frankly, at this point, it would seem that if you contemplate buying an aluminum canoe, you should first acquire a master's degree in metallurgy! Actually, I doubt that any paddler gives a suspender snap about such specifications, yet like the "secret ingredients," they persist in the catalogs and in advertising.

More understandable to the layman is the thickness of the aluminum. Two are commonly used: .032-inch in lightweight models, and .050- to .052-inch in standard grades. Also used occasionally is .060-inch, in canoes intended for rough use, even abuse, such as livery rentals. There's a considerable saving in weight if you opt for the .032-inch skin, but this is not a canoe in which you can bounce off rocks indiscriminately while running Skookumchuk Rapids. On the other hand, if you want to carry your canoe a mile or two to a backwoods pond for some all-to-yourself fishing, it's a logical choice.

Grumman strongly promoted the portability of its lightweight models.

When aluminum canoes first appeared, manufacturers touted their toughness, the absence of necessary maintenance, and their relatively low cost—all legitimate claims. But they went too far. They also proclaimed their canoes to be lighter than their only competition at the time, wood-and-canvas. If you compare an aluminum canoe to a waterlogged, repeatedly painted wooden canoe, the claim is valid. But when aluminum is compared to a well-maintained wooden hull, the claim does not stand up. Length for length, aluminum canoes in the standard grades, .050- to .052-inch thickness, weigh approximately the same as wood-and-canvas.

Aesthetically, the aluminum canoe certainly isn't as eye-pleasing as wood-and-canvas or a fiberglassed hull. There are even more pertinent criticisms. The metal clings tenaciously to rocks; it chills your knees when you're running white water early in the season; left in the sun on a warm day, it becomes hot to the touch. And aluminum is noisy. Strike your paddle against the side, and the hull resounds like a base drum; small waves slapping the hull give off the effect of a busy snare drum. Wildlife scatters from the riverbanks and the quiet ambience of the wild is destroyed.

Other shortcomings may appear in some aluminum canoes that reflect slovenly workmanship or indifference on the part of the builder. I've already mentioned the "bear trap" seats set too low to allow a quick, graceful, and painless exit. Often, the bottom edges of seats and thwarts are rough, or sharp enough to cause cuts and lacerations. Sometimes, too, sharp-edged rivets are not set flush with the metal.

Thanks to the location of flotation chambers at each end, most aluminum canoes are self-righting, certainly an admirable quality. But this can also be dangerous. Unless you make a quick grab for your canoe if you spill, it may get away. An empty aluminum canoe, pushed along by even a light breeze, can outrun a scared otter! In contrast, misplaced or inadequate flotation may prevent a canoe from righting itself, and even from floating in a level position. Given a choice, opt for self-righting, and attach a grab line to each end.

If you intend your aluminum canoe as a white-water playboat, look for structural enhancements. For example, a 17-foot model should have no fewer than six ribs; seven are better. An 18-foot canoe needs at least eight. Bouncing over heaving waves and bumping underwater rocks apply tremendous pressure to the bottom. If it is backed up by sufficient ribbing, chances of serious damage are diminished. A few models intended for rough-water use may rely on diagonal braces running from the keel line to the gunwales.

Despite long and persistent criticism of the aluminum canoe, there's much to commend it. Bare aluminum is ugly, of that there's little doubt. But it doesn't have to be bare. Some makers offer a choice of colors, and even camouflage patterns for duck hunters. Aluminum will not take on weight. Rot, dry or otherwise, is unknown. It is tough. Dents can be pounded back to resemble the original lines, at least roughly. Actual punctures in the skin can be repaired at riverside with duct tape, or at home with an aluminum patch and a handful of rivets. Many manufacturers offer repair kits, or you can use a piece of aluminum flashing and pop rivets available from any well-stocked hardware store.

If there is a bit of racing blood in your veins, take heart. The American Canoe Association now recognizes aluminum canoes as a separate class. You won't have to compete with those sleek Kevlar® racers.

All in all, there are happy owners paddling aluminum canoes that look as if they've been through the wars. In fact, there are still some on active duty that were built shortly after World War II. In its price range, it's difficult to find a more serviceable canoe.

Chapter 17

·~·~·~·~·~

Fiberglass, Kevlar®, and Proprietary Lay-ups

Fiberglass

FIBERGLASS FIRST APPEARED DURING THE MID-1930s, in a variety of laboratory experiments. Owens Corning Fiberglass, now based in Toledo, Ohio, came into being in 1938, its initial sales efforts directed mainly toward the building trades. There seems to be no documented record as to who built the first fiberglass canoe, but it was probably about 1952 or 1953.

Quite inadvertently, Grumman contributed to the early growth of the fiberglass-canoe "cottage industry" — small shops and individual builders who quickly caught on to the relatively simple fiberglass building techniques. By way of explanation, fiberglass canoes are "laid up" within a female mold. To build such a mold requires a male "plug," over which the mold is formed. But developing a plug is a highly complex, time-consuming, and expensive process, beyond the means of most small shops. So, why not use an existing canoe for a plug? During the early days of fiberglass, I visited a shop that turned out half a dozen canoes a day. Their lines were strikingly familiar. When I mentioned this to the foreman, he grinned. "Grumman," he said. Although the aluminum hulls were excellent plugs, the shop's canoes were crudely finished and grossly overweight. Unable to compete with more scrupulous and imaginative builders, the outfit later switched from canoes to portable outhouses.

Streamside discussions often address the legal implications of copying canoes that are still being produced commercially. The question will probably never trouble the United States Supreme Court, but the consensus among canoeists seems to be that if you build one or two direct copies for your own use or for a friend's, there will be no great outcry from manufacturers of the original. However, when you build a mold on an existing canoe and then build your canoe within that mold, you have in essence built two boats, at more than double the price of one. To make building a mold worthwhile, you would have to construct several canoes, possibly selling some of them to offset the cost of the mold. Or you might go into continuing commercial production, which is probably more than a mite unethical, if not illegal.

The question arises because of the flexibility of fiberglass cloth, which makes it possible for almost anyone with an empty garage and a few simple tools to build a canoe, providing a mold is available.

If you want to construct only one or two canoes, it makes more sense to rent a mold than to build one. Renting, however, may not be easy. Molds are not plentiful, and it's difficult to locate the exact model you need. Also, mold owners may justly be reluctant to rent, unless convinced of your expertise; molds can be damaged. Hope may lie within a canoe club. Some clubs own one or more molds that members may use.

All in all, though, do-it-yourself fiberglass construction is not the ideal medium for amateur or casual builders.

The basic fabric employed is cloth woven of glass fibers, which ranges in weight from 2 ounces per square yard upward, the most commonly used being the 10-ounce. Another material is "roving," also made of glass fibers, but coarser and heavier than cloth. Since roving absorbs considerable resin during the building process, weight is increased. However, roving is useful for imparting stiffness to a hull. Then there is fiberglass "mat," which is not woven; instead, the glass fibers have been matted, or compressed, to form a rather bulky material. It falls a bit short of the structural strength of woven cloth, but it's highly useful in the forming of compound curves. Finally, there are chopped fibers of glass, which are used in the so-called chopper-gun process.

In one sense, a fiberglass canoe might well be called a "resin"

RIVERS & GILMAN MOULDED PRODUCTS, INC.

The 18-foot Chief by Rivers and Gilman, one of the early fiberglass builders

canoe. The fiberglass, whether it is cloth, roving, or mat, serves primarily to reinforce the resin, which of itself has little strength. Only when fiberglass and resin are combined do you attain the required strength and rigidity.

Amateur builders and those doing repairs at home lean toward the use of polyester resin, while the professional shops utilize either polyester or epoxy. Polyester is relatively easy to use, although once a necessary hardening agent is added, it "sets up" or hardens rather quickly. Epoxy resins represent more complex chemistry. Concocting an epoxy resin is not difficult; creating the precisely correct one is another matter. For in-depth instructions on the use of resins with fiberglass, see *Boatbuilder's Manual* by Charles Walbridge; for more simplified explanations, read *Building and Repairing Canoes and Kayaks* by Jack Brosius and Dave LeRoy.

The combining of fiberglass with resins in a mold is known as a

111

"lay-up." First the mold is cleaned and waxed. Next comes the "gel coat." This may consist entirely of resin, or it may include the first layer of fiberglass cloth saturated with resin; in either case, it forms the exterior finish of the canoe. If color is desired, a pigment is added to the resin used in the gel coat. At this point, there are variations in the lay-up. Some manufacturers use fiberglass mat, over which they lay in cloth. The amount of cloth used may also vary; perhaps a total of three or four layers in the bottom, two or three in the sides. Some makers finish off with roving, as a final interior layer.

The number of layers, and whether mat and roving are included, depend upon the type of canoe being built. Mat and roving often appear in flat-water canoes; they may also be used in some white-water models. A thin-skinned, all-cloth hull usually is intended for flat-water racing. The possible combinations are almost numberless, so the selection is often dictated by the builder's opinions as to what makes the best fiberglass canoe. At any rate, once all layers are laid up and properly saturated with resin, the entire unit is allowed to "set up" or harden. The hull is then "popped" from the mold. Flotation and trim are added.

Despite the seeming simplicity of the process, good workmanship is vital to producing a quality canoe. If the resin application is skimpy or uneven, some areas will be "resin starved" and show up as whitish blotches that may later delaminate. On the other hand, excess resin gathers in pockets; once hardened, these become very brittle and, of course, add needless weight.

When a keel is called for to stiffen the bottom, a wood filler is inserted into a molded depression, and then covered with mat, so that the bilge remains relatively flat. If you insist on a fiberglass canoe with a keel, this is a good construction. Also available, of course, is the "tunnel keel" described by Bob Gramprie in chapter 4.

Another form of bottom reinforcement, with or without a keel, consists of ¼-inch-thick, end-grain balsa-wood sandwich construction. This approach is utilized by Old Town, White, Allagash, and possibly others. Balsa is extremely light, porous, and — in its natural state — brittle. However, once saturated with resin and sandwiched in fiberglass, it imparts remarkable structural strength and impact-resistance to the bottom.

Invented by Lem Beach, a rather eye-pleasing and effective reinforcement method originated with the Stowe Canoe Company in its Mansfield models. Basically a fiberglass hull, the canoe has mahogany ribs, which give it the appearance of a wood-planked craft. But there is no planking: the ribs are laid directly into, and are covered by, fiberglass. E. M. White produces a similar design, except that the ribs are ash. Lem Beach and his partner, Randy Pew, who now operate the Merrimack Canoe Company, are continuing the production of this design, using cherry for ribs, mahogany for decks and gunwales, and ash for seats and thwarts.

SAWYER CANOE CO.

The Sawyer Outrage, built of Kevlar®-reinforced fiberglass or in vacuum-bagged Kevlar®

Some of the problems encountered in fiberglass lay-ups include uneven distribution of resin and the presence of air bubbles. To counter these, "vacuum bagging" is employed. Various sophisticated machines are used, but a simplified version would see a sheet of heavy plastic laid over or in the mold after the various layers of fiberglass have been laid in and saturated. The plastic is then sealed around the edges, at the gunwales. A pump draws the air from under the plastic, so that it collapses in a vacuum and transmits pressure against the entire lay-up, forcing an even distribution of the resin, and bonding the fiberglass layers more tightly. Obviously, this technique is not for woodshed operations. Vacuum bagging is associated with the professional production of better-quality canoes.

WE-NO-NAH CANOES

We-no-nah employs fiberglass and Kevlar®, reinforced with PVC cores and ribs.

The "chopper gun" process, however, is not. Here, once the gel coat has been applied, a pressure gun whose nozzle mixes resin and chopped glass fibers sprays the mold's interior, thus gradually building up the hull. The trouble with this process is that the hull's thickness may be uneven, since it involves an entirely eyeball type of quality control. It also results in a relatively brittle hull. Such canoes fall in the low price range, and are suitable mostly for passive canoeing on flat water. The interior finish lacks the weave pattern that is visible in a cloth lay-up. The manufacturer's literature may claim, quite truthfully, that the canoe is built of fiberglass; but if you pin him down, he'll probably admit that it contains no fiberglass cloth.

More than 40 major builders produce fiberglass cloth canoes (not including those who apply fiberglass skins to strippers and rib-planked craft such as wood-and-canvas) — certainly a clear indication of the wide acceptance of well-built fiberglass canoes. Except for handcrafted and expensive wooden canoes, it was not until the advent of fiberglass and the perfection of techniques for working it that designs began to make rapid advances. True, fiberglass "pushers" are still very much in evidence. But the trend is toward high-performance — fast and maneuverable — canoes.

Fiberglass adapts well to almost any design that comes off the drawing boards, whether it's one that combines flare and tumblehome in the same hull; one that calls for a long knife-like entry for speed and ease of paddling; or one with a pronounced rocker for dancing in white water. Fiberglass gives a designer/builder full freedom in his search for the ultimate canoe, and at a reasonable price to boot. Fiberglass is not indestructible, but it is rugged, and except for extreme damage, it can be repaired at streamside. Even severe damage can be repaired at home. Many a fiberglass canoe sports a dozen or more patches while continuing on its jaunty way through wild water.

Fiberglass has other canoe-related applications. It is used for reinforcing and finishing paddle blades. And Gil Gilpatrick has gone a step farther: besides building canoes, he turns out "wangans" or "wanigans" — wooden boxes with packstraps, in which supplies and equipment are carried on canoe trips. Gil covers these, inside and out, with fiberglass cloth. "They're bear-proof," he claims.

Kevlar®

Kevlar® 49 was introduced commercially by E. I. DuPont de Nemours and Company, Inc., in 1972. Woven of aramid fibers, it is lighter in weight than fiberglass and much more tear- and puncture-resistant. Not surprisingly, Kevlar® is also more expensive.

Kevlar® is compatible with most epoxy and polyester resins. Some builders use it in combination with fiberglass. For example, one of the lay-ups suggested by DuPont during the early days of Kevlar® consisted of either a gel coat or a layer of 3-ounce fiberglass cloth, followed by two layers of 5-ounce Kevlar®, a layer of mat, and then another layer of 5-ounce Kevlar®. This lay-up, according to DuPont, cut 5 to 10 pounds from an otherwise 70-pound canoe. Whether such a lay-up is actually in use today isn't known, but it's an example of the compatibility of fiberglass and Kevlar®.

More and more all-Kevlar® models are being built, with amazing reductions in weight—just what competition flat-water paddlers want. I recently viewed a 17-foot competition solo cruiser, built by Wabash Valley Canoes, with a Kevlar®/epoxy lay-up. It weighs 21 pounds! True, this is a bare-bones, needle-pointed craft built for speed, but a canoe of this length and weight could be achieved only through the use of Kevlar®. Virtually every manufacturer of fiberglass canoes offers a counterpart in Kevlar®, with weight differentials of up to 30 percent.

Never having worked with Kevlar®, I can't comment on the report that it is more difficult to use than fiberglass. At a recent repair clinic, I watched as a Kevlar® skid plate (protective layer applied to the bow cutwater) was attached to a somewhat battered fiberglass white-water model. The Kevlar® was difficult to cut—tin or rug shears are recommended—but the material conformed beautifully to the canoe's contours. Incidentally, Mad River Canoe Company offers a Kevlar® skid-plate kit with resin that will bond to a Royalex® hull.

New materials keep appearing, aimed at increasing the strength-to-weight ratio. And imaginative builders are quick to take advantage of them. Among the latest is Nomex®, a product of DuPont. This is a honeycomb-structured paper, impregnated with phenolic resin to stiffen it. One technique of construction calls for sandwiching ⅛-inch Nomex® between two thin layers of Kevlar® or fiberglass, which must be preimpregnated with resin. The mold is then sealed for the vacuum-bagging process, and both heat and pressure are applied to distribute the resin and "cure" the sandwich. It's a highly sophisticated and expensive process, but the results can be astounding: a canoe weighing 10 pounds! Shades of Nessmuk.

A similar process uses Airex®, a PVC (polyvinyl chloride) foam, as a core. Although only two layers of Kevlar® or fiberglass cloth are used, the resulting rigidity and strength supposedly equal that

VOYAGEUR CANOE CO./AQUA PHOTO TECHNOLOGISTS LTD./GLENN FALLIS

Several Voyageur models are built of a composite incorporating Kevlar®, Airex®, fiberglass cloth, epoxy.

of 14 layers of cloth in a conventional fiberglass/resin lay-up. PVC is also used to mold in reinforcing ribs.

Proprietary Lay-Ups

These are "confidential" lay-ups of fabrics in varying combinations that go beyond the basic fiberglass/Kevlar® and polyester/epoxy pairings. The fabrics may include nylon, polyester, graphite, and foam cores, in addition to fiberglass and Kevlar®. Isothalic and vinylester resins are used, along with the predictable "secret-ingredient," "aircraft-grade," and "special-blend" resins. Many such lay-ups are "pressure-cured" or vacuum-bagged. While the innovators of these complex combinations don't mind listing the materials and resins they use, they are reluctant to reveal further details — all according to the old business adage, "Does Macy's tell Gimbel's?"

At first glance, confidential lay-ups may seem like so much gobbledygook, but they are legitimate applications of advanced technology. Builders who use proprietary lay-ups include some of the most reputable manufacturers. By the same token, should you order a canoe from any of them, you have every right to know exactly how your canoe will be built. Ask questions. You might find out what the secret ingredients are.

Chapter 18

·~·~·~·~·~

Royalex®, et al. . . .

PADDLERS WILL PROBABLY NEVER call it anything but "ABS." That's understandable. No one is about to announce: "I've just bought an acrylonitrile-butadiene-styrene canoe."

Peter Sonderegger, then manager of the Old Town Canoe Company, was quoted several years back on the subject: "I shudder every time I hear that word 'ABS'. I recall in the early 1970's, an ABS boat, the Budweiser canoe. It lasted about two days. Call it Royalex, or Oltonar, or Sawyerlex, just don't call it ABS."[1]

Royalex®, a registered trademark of Uniroyal, the United States Rubber Company, is a laminate. Its vinyl outer layer corresponds to the gel coat in a fiberglass lay-up. The next layer is an acrylonitrile-butadiene-styrene compound. Then comes an ABS foam core, followed by another layer of acrylonitrile-butadiene-styrene compound, and finally, another outer layer of vinyl. Thus the complete laminate consists of: vinyl/ABS/foam/ABS/vinyl. This is Royalex®, not to be confused with simple ABS, which omits the foam core. The canoe referred to by Peter Sonderegger was not made of Royalex®; it lacked the foam core.

When a sheet of Royalex® is shipped to a canoe builder, this foam core is quite thin; it looks no different from the other layers. The forming process changes this. The sheet is heated to about 350

---

[1] *Canoe Magazine* (November 1980).

| BEFORE HEAT-MOLDING | FULLY EXPANDED | *The effect of heat-molding on a sheet of Royalex®* |

degrees Fahrenheit and then vacuum-formed in a mold. Heat causes the inner foam core to expand to almost ¼-inch thick. It is this expanded foam that provides the hull with stiffness, resiliency, impact resistance, and some degree of flotation.

What, then, is Oltonar? Or Sawyerlex? Essentially, these are Royalex®. Canoe companies that form hulls on their own molds specify that the sheets incorporate different thicknesses within the laminate; the extra thicknesses are molded into stress points in the hull. In other words, custom-made sheets of Royalex® are prepared to the specifications of the canoe builder. Oltonar is the Old Town Canoe Company's version, just as Sawyerlex is the Sawyer Canoe Company's.

Some firms use custom-fabricated Royalex® *without* the embellishment of their own brand names. Bob Lantz of the Blue Hole Canoe Company states in that firm's 1983 catalog: "If we chose to play the game, we would call our custom Royalex® 'Bluholeum'; but we'd mostly only add to the already considerable consumer confusion. . . ." This bit of tart humor in Blue Hole's catalog does not detract from its explanation, in layman's terms, of the Royalex® structure — one of the best to be found in canoeing literature.

Not all builders form their own hulls. Uniroyal, therefore, provides preformed hulls to which builders have only to add the trim. Rivers and Gilman and Thompson Brothers Boat Company are believed to have been among the first to assemble canoes from these, during the late 1950s and early 1960s.[2]

Old Town is thought to have been the first to mold a hull from Royalex® in its own plant, sometime in 1972. This was the Tripper, perhaps the best known of all Royalex® canoes.

---

[2] In 1983 Rivers and Gilman was sold to Gazelle Products, Inc. of China, Maine. This firm now produces Royalex® canoes under the original Rivers and Gilman "Indian" brand.

The durability of Royalex® is now legend. Old Town threw a Tripper off its factory roof, and, when the canoe sustained little damage, graphically illustrated the act in its advertising. Another Tripper fell 800 feet from a float plane in the Allagash Wilderness Waterway, the only damage a broken gunwale. The 1981 Blue Hole catalog portrays the firm's original model, the OCA, a Royalex® hull, literally wrapped around a rock during a race on the St. Francis River in Missouri. Yet it was salvaged on the spot, straightened, and refloated. It did not place among the winners, but it did finish the race! You can't expect much more of a canoe than that.

Few of us toss our canoes off the roof, but we do nudge half-submerged boulders with varying degrees of force. Royalex® will dent, but the foam sandwich absorbs and distributes the shock. Dents, even severe ones, smooth themselves out when exposed to warm sunlight or when warmed by a "heat gun" such as a portable hair drier. Royalex® has a "memory." It remembers what it looked like before a paddler banged it up, and, with a little help, reforms itself to somewhere near its original shape.

It is not tear-proof, however. A friend ripped a 3-foot gash in his Royalex® when he tried a shortcut over a sharp ledge in a Canadian river. With copious applications of duct tape, he and his partner extricated themselves from their wilderness predicament. Back home, they made permanent repairs with fiberglass cloth, epoxy putty, and resin. The canoe lacks its former showroom glitter, but it still plies faraway waters.

Royalex®'s resiliency — its ability to "give a little" upon impact, usually without fracturing — makes it the ideal hull material for a white-water canoe, especially for beginners. Resiliency is a decided asset but, particularly in the case of Royalex®, it results in considerable flexing of the hull; hence the suggestion (in chapter 9) that foam blocks be jammed under the thwarts.

The inner core of foam supposedly provides sufficient buoyancy to make a Royalex® craft "float like a wooden canoe." Not quite. In fact, it floats only reluctantly. Some builders acknowledge this and build in flotation, usually foam in the peaks. Again, as suggested earlier, attach inner tubes, air bags, or foam blocks if you're headed for heavy white water.

Royalex® has some construction limitations. Being a "sandwich," the material can be bent only so far before it starts to

Catastrophe . . . ?

No. Quick streamside reforming . . .

Back in the race!

rupture on one side and bind on the other. Hence, the truly fine entries that are possible with fiberglass are difficult to attain in Royalex®.

The problem was overcome a few years back by the Sawyer Canoe Company. Bob Gramprie explained how: "A resilient poly-urethane bow-bumper serves two purposes; most important is to bring the blunt vacuum-molded hull to a much sharper entry line, and at the same time, provide an ablative bow guard to take the pounding instead of the hull. The bow-bumper can be replaced when necessary."

Despite its few limitations, Royalex® is quite versatile. For exam-ple, Mad River's Courier model won the Combined-Solo class competition in the 1982 White-water Championships. Another Mad River model, the Flashback, designed by John Berry, is a serious competitor in white-water slalom. Blue Hole's 17A is built to handle big waters and heavy loads, yet it has been among the winners in the National Open-Canoe White-water Championships

Mad River's Courier model in slalom competition

on the Nantahala River in North Carolina. Yet, under less spectacular circumstances, Royalex® has become almost standard among
long-distance, wilderness cruisers, including We-no-nah's Woods-
man, Sawyer's Sawyerlex 17, Easy Rider's Ousel, Mad River's
Explorer, and of course, the granddaddy of tripping canoes, Old
Town's 17-foot Tripper, now also available in 20-foot length.

The most recent innovation is that of the White Canoe Company of Old Town, Maine. Its Duralex® fabric consists of an
ABS foam core, over which is laid a skin of acrylic, reportedly 60
percent thicker than the vinyl outer layer of Royalex®. This outer
skin can be renewed.

One of the obvious disadvantages of Royalex® among competition canoes is weight. Fiberglass lay-ups can be made considerably
lighter, and Kevlar® even more so. When there's a tough haul
ahead in a long-distance marathon, or when the froth is flying in a
close finish, weight is important. But then, if you're the type of
canoeist who goes bumpity-bump through the rapids, a medium-
priced Royalex® canoe is probably a better choice than a more
costly Kevlar® flyweight.

Aluminum has long been criticized for its tendency to stick to rocks. Move over, aluminum. Although it's rarely mentioned in canoeing literature, Royalex® holds its own in this department. True, due to its resiliency, it will slide over most rocks, especially smooth ones that have been polished by eons of flow. However, in my home canoe country, streams are well littered with rough granite that needs another 10,000 years of polishing. On these, the outer layer of vinyl tends to cling, so that my Tripper "loves to linger" while I push, probe, and prod to free it.

Chapter 19

~·~·~·~·~

Polyethylene

POLYETHYLENE HAS TWO NOTABLE VIRTUES: it is tough and it is inexpensive.

To understand its makeup requires venturing into petrochemicals, a field that I'm neither qualified nor inclined to invade. However, Eric Evans does have a grasp of polyethylene as it is used in canoe building. Referring to the Coleman Company, which uses the material under its registered trademark "Ram-X®," he has written: "Coleman buys its polyethylene in pellet form and then adds ultraviolet inhibitors and heat stabilizers. This mixture is extruded into five-foot wide, .220-inch thick sheets and vacuum-molded into canoes at 350 degrees."[1]

It's not generally known, but polyethylene does lend itself to the molding of fine-lined, high-performance canoes. So why doesn't polyethylene show up in national and international competitions? Set-up costs, that's why. Evans pointed out that a mold may cost "upward of $35,000"—and that was before the skyrocketing inflation rate of the early 1980s. The demand for sophisticated competition and white-water canoes simply isn't great enough to warrant such an investment. On the other hand, the Coleman Company more than justified the cost of molds in 1977 by producing solid, run-of-the-mill canoes that appealed to the general public. The increasing acceptance of Coleman's polyethylene design is

[1] *Canoe Magazine* (November 1980).

especially visible among rental liveries, which now stack Coleman instead of Grumman canoes.

In one respect, polyethylene is not unlike Royalex®. Polyethylene also has a "memory," so that dents will reform themselves; even when folded around a boulder, a polyethylene hull can be restored to some semblance of its original shape. You'll need new aluminum fittings, of course, but chances are the hull will not split or tear.

Unless you're a hell-a-hoopin' paddler who holds dangerous white water in contempt, you're not likely to puncture a polyethylene hull. It will literally bounce off rocks; all you have to do is stay in the canoe when it does! If you want to substitute a tough fabric for skill, polyethylene is probably for you.

But there's the usual caveat: punctures are possible. Repairing a break requires the use of a polyethylene patch, a saw, epoxy resin, 100-grit sandpaper, and a propane or butane torch. The Coleman Company offers a repair kit including detailed instructions, although I have never run across a canoeist who has had a need for the kit.

Excessive flexibility is probably polyethylene's most serious drawback. For the hull to maintain its shape in rough water, interior propping is required, including a full-length keelson recessed into a molded exterior keel. There are also vertical braces from the keelson to the thwarts. Even with this bracing, considerable flexing continues. Some time ago, I noted that the polyethylene canoe inverted in my barn for about three years showed signs of sagging along its bottom.

Weight is another consideration. A 17-foot polyethylene canoe weighs 80 pounds, give or take a pound or two.

I first paddled an early 17-foot version of the Coleman canoe only a few months after it went into production. I found the minimal rocker and the presence of a keel a hindrance in white-water pitches, where I deliberately abused the canoe. Though I nudged rocks, some of them rather solidly, the hull lived up to the claims made for it. It did not hang up, sliding over rock after rock. Polyethylene's flexibility is supposed to allow it to "wriggle over rocks." It does.

On flat water, the canoe tracked far better than either my (Royalex®) Tripper or my (wood-and-canvas) Prospector, and it

The 17-footer, perhaps the most versatile of the three Coleman models

was just as stealthy as either when I eased along the shaded shore just below the pitches I'd run.

On the whole, if you're not out to win a gold medal on flat water, and you'd like to play about in some moderately frothy pitches with some impunity, polyethylene is a good choice at a relatively small cost.

Coleman's polyethylene models, available in 15- and 17-foot lengths, are sold unassembled, although some dealers will assemble one for an extra charge. Only the gunwales are attached at the factory, so that the hulls can be nested for shipping. Assembly requires three to four hours, with common household tools. Except for the end caps, all fittings are of aluminum. The seats are plastic. The foam blocks to be inserted into the peaks are preformed to fit.[2]

---

[2] At the time the foregoing was written, only Coleman produced a polyethylene canoe. Following considerable experimentation, Old Town recently introduced its 17′4″ Discovery model in polyethylene. A foam inner core lends stiffness to the hull, so that interior bracing is unnecessary. Smoker-craft also now offers a polyethylene canoe, the 16-foot Redskin.

Chapter 20

~·~·~·~·~

Tandem Canoes and How to Buy Them

Flat-water and Casual Recreation

THE RESURGENCE OF SOLO CANOES is having some effect on the production of tandem canoes, or two-seaters. The solo canoe is making serious inroads, and there are those who insist that solo is exciting, tandem is dull. To quote a well-frayed cliché, snobbery has reared its ugly head. At a 1981 seminar for designers, builders, and competition paddlers, one of the outspoken "experts" spouted: "People who paddle Colemans and Grummans are canoers; solo paddlers are canoeists!"

"That's elitism," I protested.

"You got it. Solo paddlers *are* the elite." I could only draw upon my limited Down East vocabulary: "Whale dung!"

Most of us paddle because it's fun. While we strive to attain some degree of expertise, few of us want to break any records; we seek to impress no one; even fewer of us want to compete with a solo paddler who can make his little canoe perform like Nureyev in *Swan Lake*. Even if somewhat inexpertly, we paddle for the sheer joy of it. We dawdle along the shore, not really aware of which stroke we're using; we're scared out of our wits running Pockwamock Pitch; yet somehow we manage a stealthy approach to an overhanging hemlock in which we've spotted a scarlet tanager. We attain delightful waterborne experiences with two of us in the same canoe.

So, don't be intimidated by the rash of you-gotta-paddle-solo-

or-you-ain't-canoeing outpourings in the canoeing press. Solo paddling is exciting; it has its place, and I would be the last to deny its delights. But it's not for everyone.

"High performance" is not necessary in a family canoe

A tandem canoe will cost you less than half the price of a pair of solo models. A family can load a two-seater with a child or two, a picnic lunch, bathing suits, and a few toys for a day's outing. You can't take the kids along in a pair of solo canoes. They're "tender," which means that an active youngster on board is decidedly at risk, and so is the canoe. An extended trek into the North is possible in solo canoes, but it requires that the outfit be pared almost to spartan levels. And in rough water, most soloists scurry for shelter, while the larger two-seaters go about their business.

If you're inclined toward buying a two-seater, even if you elect to buy a pusher, this doesn't make you a second-class paddler. I'm not suggesting that you rush out to your neighborhood discount department store to buy its current offering of a Doozy Special marked down from $199 to $179.99, with a pair of seat cushions thrown in — this week only. Shop for your two-seater carefully. If your aim is nothing more than casual canoeing—no proposed white-water heroics, no fantasies about running down to Hudson's Bay—your choice of high-grade canoes is virtually unlimited. There are more than 150 models.

The old adage "buy a well-known brand" holds true, but if you are new to canoeing, remember that there are now many more "well-known brands" than there used to be. Everyone, paddler or not, recognizes the names of Old Town, Grumman, and Coleman.

GRUMMAN BOATS

One of the "old reliables," the Grumman

They turn out quality products in varying price ranges. However, I'm repeatedly surprised by canoeing friends who are totally ignorant of the dozens of other manufacturers that, although less famous, are definitely in the same league with the "big three."

Shop among a number of dealers. Obtain literature from advertisers in canoe and other outdoor magazines. Get an overall picture before you plunk down your money. And it bears repeating at this point: when you do finally make your purchase, buy the longest canoe that fits your needs.

Most first-time buyers of a two-seater have in mind a general-purpose canoe. It will be car-topped, used for fishing, perhaps a weekend camp-out, and the kids will play with it at the summer cottage. For such purposes, you don't need one of the designer models built for speed and maneuverability. High fashion is costly. So, if you're on a limited budget, stick to one of the old standards. After all, idling along in a pusher under blue skies with the greenery slipping by close at hand is hardly a form of punishment. Let the high-speed artists zip by you! Chances are, you've found something they've lost.

WE-NO-NAH CANOES

A responsive designer recreational canoe

It may be, of course, that you're inclined toward a more responsive canoe than a flat-bottom, bulgy-ended model. So much the better. Even for casual recreation, there's no reason why you can't paddle a lively craft. Consider a shallow-arch or shallow-vee bottom, possibly with a touch of flare, perhaps even an asymmetrical hull, the longer the better. Particularly among the strippers, the fiberglass, and the Kevlar® models, there's a wide choice of spritely canoes. Advanced designs add a touch of excitement. Beware, though, of the hyperactive, almost-a-flying-machine type of canoe favored by racing paddlers. These are fast — and cranky!

Chart A shows representative specifications for a cross-section of flat-water, casual recreation canoes. All have straight keel lines with some upsweep at the ends. Other than that, they vary with regard to beam, hull shape, center depth, weight, and material. If you choose a model whose specifications approximate any one of the hulls listed in the chart, you should end up with a highly satisfactory canoe.

Chart A

Representative specifications for flat-water/casual recreation canoes

LENGTH	BEAM*	HULL SHAPE**	CENTER DEPTH	FABRIC***	WEIGHT
16'	34"	FB	13"	F	73 lbs.
16'6"	35	SA	14	PL	52
15'9"	35	FB	14	Rx	65
16	37	FB	12	W/C	67
16	37	FB	12½	Al	78
16'6"	34	SA	14	Strip	70
16	34	RB	14½	KV	50
17	36	FB	13	Al	73
17	36	FB	14	PO	79
17	36	SA	13	F	78
17	37	FB	14	W/C	75
17	37	SA	14½	Rx	83
17	35	FB	12	KV	40
17	33	SA	14	Strip	55
18	36	SA	13	KV	50
18	38	FB	12	W/C	80
18	36½	FB	13	Al	85
18	33	SA	13	Strip	47
18	33	RV	13	F	72

 * Gunwale beam.
 ** FB = flat bottom; RB = round bottom; RV = rounded vee; SA = shallow arch.
 *** Al = aluminum; F = fiberglass; KV = Kevlar®; PL = proprietary lay-up; PO = polyethylene; Rx = Royalex®; Strip = stripper; W/C = wood/canvas.

Tandem White-water Canoes

Making the transition from deadwater to tumultuous pitches is much like switching from the family station wagon to a Ferrari. The results, depending upon your skill level, can be either triumphant or traumatic. Triumphant is better.

MAD RIVER CANOE/JAMES A. HENRY

Mad River's TW Special in the Snake River Canyon, Wyoming

Recognize the extent of your abilities, and those of your partner. When I asked Bart Hauthaway how long it takes to develop a good white-water team, he replied: "They should start paddling together when they're about nine years old." A bit of hyperbole, perhaps, but a sound reminder that the sooner you and your partner start paddling together, the sooner you'll become a well-synchronized team. Unfortunately, we can't adjust our lifespans retroactively. The alternative is to start now. Tackle the easy stuff at first, and gradually work up until the roar of rapids no longer frightens you, it challenges you.

First, however, you'll need the right canoe. Much of the contents of chapters 2 through 11 is applicable at this point, particu-

MAD RIVER CANOE/JAMES A. HENRY

Ultimate coordination and the right canoe are necessary in slalom racing.

larly with regard to length, rocker, depth, flotation, and weight. There's little need to repeat the information here, even in condensed form, but you might want to reread those chapters before making a decision on a white-water canoe.

Essentially, you'll be looking for a canoe with rocker, ample center depth, fullness fore and aft to lift over waves, and suitable flotation. Chart B displays representative specifications for a variety of white-water tandem canoes.

High-performance white-water canoes are not as numerous as those turned out for casual canoeing, so you'll have to search more carefully for the right model. While most dealers located at waterside will let you test-paddle a flat-water model, few will allow you that privilege with a high-performance model in the rapids. Probably the best approach is to talk with friends who are experienced. One may even be persuaded to give you a hell-a-hoopin' ride through the rips, all the while tossing in some good advice.

A local canoe club may be helpful, or perhaps you can attend a white-water competition as a spectator. When the races are completed, talk to the winning paddlers. You might also attend a white-water clinic or school where, along with instructions, you'll most assuredly get some pithy comments on which canoes perform well and which don't.

Another idea: shop among dealers who handle "designer canoes." Virtually all manufacturers turn out white-water models, but how well these perform in white water may be open to question. A manufacturer who offers one or more models designed by a noted white-water champion has gone the final step to guarantee that, indeed, its canoes are truly white-water craft. (The same is true for flat-water canoes designed by flat-water champions.) So look for such names as John Berry, Don Burklund, Al Camp, Ralph Frese, Mike Galt, Robert D. Gramprie, Bart Hauthaway, Jim Henry, Eugene Jensen, Pat Moore, Roland Muhlen, Bill Stearns, Lynn "Joe" Tuttle, and David Yost. These men are not only noted designers; they are also high-caliber canoeists.

Chart B

Representative specifications for white-water tandem canoes

LENGTH	BEAM*	HULL SHAPE**	CENTER DEPTH	FABRIC***	WEIGHT
15′8″	36″	SV	15″	Rx	69 lbs.
15′8″	36″	SV	15	KV	58
15′9″	35	FB	15	Rx	70
16	37	SA	14	F	75
16	36	SV	14	F	68
16	33	SA	13	Rx	75
16	34	FB	13	Rx	70
16	36	FB	15	Rx	78
16′2″	35	FB	14	Rx	72
16′2″	33	SA	15	F	60
16′3″	33	SA	14½	KV	55
16′8″	37	SV	15	PL	59
17	36	FB	13	Al	83
17	36	SA	13	F	78
17	35	FB	13	Al	75
17	37	RV	13	Al	80
17	36½	SV	15	Rx	75
17′2″	35	FB	14	Rx	77
18	35½	SA	13	KV	50
18	36½	FB	13	Al	91
18′6″	32	SA	13½	F	65

* Gunwale beam.
** FB = flat bottom; RV = rounded vee; SA = shallow arch; SV = shallow vee.
*** Al = aluminum; F = fiberglass; KV = Kevlar®; PL = proprietary lay-up; Rx = Royalex®.

Chapter 21

~·~·~·~·~·~·~

Solo Canoes — a Buyer's Manual

AT THE TIME OF THE FOUNDING of the American Canoe Association in 1880, virtually all sport canoes were solo models. Just before the turn of the century, attention shifted to the newfangled canvas-covered tandem canoes. Then came the horseless carriage and Ole Evinrude's contraption, which together nearly drove the canoe into oblivion. Had it not been for such writers as Robert E. Pinkerton, Sigurd Olson, Calvin Rutstrum, Carle Handel, and Ben Ferrer, who helped sustain interest in paddling, the canoe might have become a museum piece. But it persisted, admittedly in diminished numbers. And then, along came Grumman. Voilà! A renaissance in canoeing. The ranks of tandem-canoe builders, enraptured with easy-to-work fiberglass, mushroomed. Canoes, almost all two-seaters, were everywhere. A friend, observing the weekend parade of car-top canoes whizzing by his door, quipped: "The Coast Guard should be directing traffic!"

As recently as 1974, if you wanted to buy a solo canoe, you had a choice of only about 16 models, 7 of them produced by Bart Hauthaway. Through the years, he never gave up on the solo canoe. He believed it would come back, and indeed it did. By the mid-1980s more than 50 builders were turning out a total of over 150 different models.

Of course, you can also enjoy solo paddling in a two-seater. For several seasons, during July and August, I guided a fisherman in Maine, but since he fished only in the morning and briefly in the late afternoon, I was free between noon and 4:00 P.M. I roamed

Solo paddler in the tandem Mad River Malecite on the North Branch of the Koyokuk River, Alaska

Mooselookmeguntic Lake, 17 miles long and 3 miles wide, sometimes leaden flat, at other times its windward shore dashed high with spray. My 18-foot Kennebec was hardly a solo canoe, but when I laid it over on its port rail as I knelt amidship wielding my maple paddle, the canoe would, as Nessmuk said of his beloved Sairy Gamp, "get over the water like a scared loon."

Those were joyous afternoons, slipping along wild shorelines, probing bays and coves, prowling among the islands. Once I overtook a bull moose half a mile from shore, coming alongside of him easily. He turned suddenly, indicating that he wanted to come aboard. I hastily explained that my guide's license did not entitle me to transport a live moose; straining the paddle shaft, I thrashed half an acre of lake surface into a froth as I backwatered and fled.

Usually I had the lake to myself. During occasional flat calms, I drove the canoe hard, the only sounds the drip of my paddle and the purling wake. When the wind blew, I surfed on the crests of the waves. I learned that a paddler, his paddle, and his canoe can be one. I had discovered solo canoeing.

Often I wished I'd had a more appropriate canoe. Canted to port, two-thirds of the hull was out of water, so that much of the time I had to fight the wind. Getting back to camp was sometimes a chore. Too, the Kennebec weighed 80 pounds, more than twice the weight of many modern solo canoes.

There is considerable variance among these, but all require that you paddle from amidship, either kneeling or seated. Some have sliding seats, pedestals, or merely a thwart against which to lodge your derriere when kneeling. Technically, paddling with a single blade from amidship is not as efficient as propelling a tandem canoe with two paddles, one on each side. A solo canoe tends to turn away from the paddle, although skilled solo paddlers can easily counter this.

Solo canoes are divided roughly into three categories: sport, cruising, and white-water. The specifications often overlap, so that the distinction among them may be one of use or inclination rather than design.

Solo Sport Canoes

The solo sport canoe is primarily a day-tripper, a vehicle for the canoeist who looks upon paddling as an end in itself, who considers swinging the paddle and making the canoe dance the sole reason for being on the water. Being a flat-water craft, the solo sport canoe usually has a straight keel line, possibly with a slight uplift at each end. Despite this design, it is maneuverable. Simply cant it so that one rail is down, and you can turn it within its own length; if you enjoy that sort of thing, you can even make it fishtail. Dwight Rockwell, observing a canoeist doing just this, put it well: "He handles that thing like a downhill skier handles his skis."

Whether you're looking for maneuverability or good tracking, your choice of lengths ranges from 10½ to 16½ feet. However short or long, all solo sport canoes are narrow-beamed: seldom more than 30 inches, often as little as 26. Midship depths are shallow, 10 to 12 inches, while bow and stern depths may differ within the same canoe — perhaps 1½ to 3 inches greater at the bow to help fend off headwind chop.

A fine entry at the waterline is characteristic; hence most solo sport models create little more turbulence than a spoon stirring a

Jensen-design solo model

cup of tea. Of course, if you ply your paddle hard enough, you can leave a sudsy trail. All in all, if your paddling has been confined to stodgy two-seaters, the lines of a solo sport model may startle you just a dite. These are minimal canoes. When I first viewed the Lotus Canoe Company's Dandy, Mike Galt, its designer, was quick to notice my reaction. "Intimidating, isn't it?" he said. Yes, indeed!

Solo Cruising Canoes

A solo cruiser's demeanor is usually a bit more staid. Lightly laden, it will run fast and true, but it's really intended to carry some cargo, a limited camping outfit, for example. Its lines are similar to those of the sport model, only more ample; length runs from 12 to 17 feet, and midship depths, 11 to 15 inches. Beam is not greatly increased, however, rarely exceeding 31 inches. Since the cruiser is expected to handle dusty waters as well as a flat calm, bow height may be 1 to 3 inches greater than the stern's. Like the sport model, the cruiser is at its best running on an even keel; you may have to

WE-NO-NAH CANOES

Mike Cichanowski, owner of We-no-nah Canoes, paddling the Solitude solo model

divide your outfit into two packs, one stowed aft, the other forward.

The cruiser adapts beautifully to day trips, or just "fooling around" on a local bayou, but you needn't hesitate to invade the backcountry for a week or ten days. While the sport model is pretty much limited to flat water, the cruiser, properly handled, isn't fazed by an occasional rocky pitch. Obviously, it won't carry the luxury outfit that can be stowed in a high-volume two-seater. But if you minimize your outfit and keep weight and bulk down, your solo cruiser will be perfectly at home along remote canoe routes.

Solo White-water Canoes

One word characterizes the solo white-water canoe: maneuverability. The better models can pirouette like a ballerina and sidestep like a running back. Ranging from about 14 feet up to a bit over 16, they are somewhat beamier than their sport or cruising counterparts — as wide as 36 inches at the gunwales and 33 at the

4-inch waterline. They are deeper, too, anywhere from 13 to 15 inches, and they may be a bit bulgy in the ends to provide lift over the haystacks. All are well rockered. Because of this, you probably won't enjoy paddling one on flat water. They have only one aim — to run the rips. While they may not be specifically designed as racing or slalom canoes, many of them qualify for sanctioned competition. Because of the need for added strength and durability, they weigh somewhat more than the sport or cruising models — 40 to 70 pounds.

Some General Solo Thoughts

When you start shopping for a solo canoe, you'll be faced with tough decisions. Each designer is convinced that he has come up with the near-ultimate canoe. Trouble is, they don't seem to agree among themselves.

For instance, the DY Special, a marathon racer built by the Sawyer Canoe Company and designed by David Yost is fast and maneuverable, and has won its share of trophies. The DY Special is easily identified by its extreme midship tumblehome. Mike Galt canoes, built by the Lotus Canoe Company, are long and slinky and definitely flared. "As a tumblehomed canoe is loaded," Galt has written, "its invariably ugly shape is pressed down in the water and it acquires the paddling characteristics of a barge."[1] While you're torn between the philosophies of David Yost and Mike Galt, along comes Pat Moore, who's been winning gold medals since his high-school days. His design for the Proem 85, produced by the Blackhawk Canoe Company, has 6 inches of flare in its forward quarter, an inch of tumblehome amidship, and half an inch of flare in the stern quarter!

With whom, then — figuratively speaking — do you want to paddle: David Yost, Mike Galt, or Pat Moore? Frankly, I would, as graciously as possible, decline to compete against any of them. Nonetheless, I lean a bit toward flared hulls.

Most designers agree on one point: they incorporate either a shallow arch, or a shallow or rounded vee. Especially in shorter

---

[1] *Canoe Magazine* (March 1981).

canoes, these bottoms will seem a bit tricky at first, but you'll soon learn to live with them. Remember, these are frisky canoes, not poky freighters.

The shorter a solo canoe, the more it likes to stray. Keeping it on course requires some concentration. Some of them are also "tender," even skittish, requiring that you sit as low as possible, virtually in the bilge. A more tolerant model will permit a semi-kneeling or even a high-kneel position. Among white-water models, where unhampered freedom of movement is required, a pedestal seat seems best.

Solo paddling generally involves solo toting, making weight a consideration. Few single-seat canoes are unduly hefty; 60 pounds is the upper extreme. More typical weights are in the 35- to 45-pound range, and ultralight versions in Kevlar® weigh as little as 25. While a flyweight model is enticing, keep in mind that fragility increases as weight decreases. Paddling a 25-pound canoe is a delightful experience, but ramming a rock with one is not.

Whatever type of solo canoe attracts you, don't be deterred by the image projected by a few super-paddlers who seek to elevate solo canoeing to the level of playing first violin in the Vienna Symphony Orchestra. Solo canoes require skill, but that skill is within reach of anyone who can handle a tandem canoe with some degree of confidence. Just do what comes naturally. The canoe will do the rest.

Women in Solo Canoes

Couples with an adequate budget might consider a pair of solo canoes. The appeal of this strategy is that each person is an entity, independent yet companionable, neither having to answer to the other. It's not dinner by candlelight, but as two canoes slip along side by side, the melody of rippling waters can bring two kindred spirits closer together.

And why shouldn't the individual woman have her own solo canoe? During the preparation of this book, I scanned small mountains of canoeing literature, catalogs, magazines, and advertisements. Incredibly, only twice did I encounter any serious mention of women handling canoes on their own! One of these appeared in the November 1980 issue of *Canoe Magazine*—an article by Sally Sharrard, describing the successful running of Alaska's Fortymile River by seven women. The other item was a pamphlet written by Molly Stark, issued by the Sawyer Canoe Company, entitled *Solo Canoeing for Women*.

Stark calls her Sawyer DY Special "the wings of my world," and she adds: "I can paddle my own canoe, thank you." The pamphlet is aimed at selling Sawyer canoes, naturally, but the sales pitch is thoroughly unobtrusive. Instead, it stresses solo paddling by a woman. "You can learn to do it very quickly . . . and spend the rest of your life getting better and better at it." Solo paddling calls for finesse: "Don't think about pulling the paddle through the water," Molly writes. "Pull the canoe up to the paddle." She paddles in a sitting position with a bent-shaft paddle, and switches sides frequently. She is outspoken about her technique. "A lot of self-styled 'experts'," she writes, "will tell you that you're wrong. 'Real' canoeists don't switch sides. Neither do they sit down. Neither do they paddle with bent shafts. And what the hell are you doing out there by yourself, anyway, honey? Your place is in the bow of a bruisewater, taking orders. Ignore this jazz."

Any woman who is hesitant about paddling her own canoe should read *Solo Canoeing for Women*. It destroys myths about women's dependence on male guidance. Molly concludes: "It's your canoe. You can work out in it, spoon along and look at the birds in it, race it, go camping in it, go fishing in it—anything you want to do. It's as much a medium of personal expression as paint and canvas. If you're uncomfortable with anything I've told you about paddling, do it your way. There won't be anybody in the stern shouting at you."

Canoeing needs more Molly Starks on the waters.[2]

[2] I tried to obtain a photo of Molly Stark paddling her solo canoe, but was unable to do so. Also, in researching I could find no other writings by Molly. In fact, her writing is suspiciously like that of Harry Roberts, who writes copy for the Sawyer Canoe Company. Nevertheless, whether Harry or "Molly" wrote the foregoing, I heartily endorse the sentiments!

Chapter 22

~·~·~·~·~

Freighters and Trippers

EXCEPT IN MAINE AND IN CANADA, high-volume canoes — 20 feet and longer — are rarely seen these days. "Freighters" persist in the Pine Tree State among guides, a few sportsmen, and some downriver rough-water racing paddlers. In the Canadian North, they supplement bush planes in hauling freight and in making long-distance recreational trips. Those used commercially are usually boosted along by outboard motors.

Big canoes are reassuring and comfortable; even with a small mountain of gear aboard, there's still plenty of leg room. However, when canoes are 20 feet or longer, you don't trot over a portage with one. Few of them weigh under 100 pounds.

Few recreational canoeists, even those undertaking extensive cruises, truly need a freighter. You can probably get along very nicely with one of the many "trippers," which range from 16 to 18½ feet and often weigh well under 85 pounds. But the choice should be made carefully.

There are four requirements for a tripping canoe: adequate capacity, reasonable weight, versatility, and durability. Effortless paddling, on the other hand, is *not* a reasonable expectation. Advertising copywriters are fond of making "light work" of a three-day trip. Truth is, no wilderness tripper "paddles like a dream" when loaded to anywhere near its capacity. Pushing half a ton of canoe, gear, and people with a pair of 5-foot paddles in no way resembles gliding over a bit of flat water in a 12-foot solo cruiser. An extended trip involves hard work — a delightful form of hard

The Sawyer X-17, one of the faster trippers. Note ample freeboard despite two-week outfit aboard.

work, that's true—but you can bet there will be days when your shoulders and arms will ache. So as not to close the subject on a dismal note, I should add that there will also be days when a tail wind or a swift current will lend a helping hand. On the whole, though, discount all "easy-to-paddle" claims.

Any tripper worthy of the name is capable of hauling somewhere between 900 and 1,200 pounds, and it must do it with adequate freeboard—no less than 6 inches. You can be sure that, in general, an 18-foot model will outperform a 16-footer. It will carry the load more gracefully, it will paddle a bit more easily, and it will remain drier in sloppy going. Conclusion: bigger is better.

As usual, exceptions can be made. A few 16-foot trippers are designed with extra depth amidship, among them the Mad River Explorer and the L. L. Bean Touring model (the latter made by Mad River). Each of these is 15 inches deep, and thus is capable of greater loads than conventional 16-foot canoes.

Chart C

Representative specifications of freight canoes

LENGTH	HULL SHAPE*	CENTER DEPTH	FABRIC**	WEIGHT
19′	SA	19″	W/C	150 lbs.
19	FB	15	F	115
20	FB	14	W/C	108
20	FB	12	W/C	95
20	FB	13	W/F	104
20	FB	13	Strip	75
20	SA	14	Rx	104
20′8″	SA	16	F	130
21	RV	18	W/C	185
22	FB	15	W/C	130
22′8″	SA	25	F	450
25	SA	19	F	300
25	SA	19	W/C	235

Note: While some of the above canoes qualify as to length, no canoe with a center depth of less than 14 inches can rightfully be considered a freighter.

* FB = flat bottom; RV = rounded vee; SA = shallow arch.
** F = fiberglass; Rx = Royalex®; Strip = stripper; W/C = wood/canvas; W/F = wood/fiberglass.

During a long-distance jaunt, chances are you'll encounter a river where there seems to be a mandatory portage around every bend. Here, needless weight is just cause for cussing. Of course, you could cut down on weight by choosing a 16-foot model with a 12-inch depth. You'd probably save 15 pounds, but chances are, you'd wind up repenting while salvaging gear from your swamped, shallow 16-footer! A Kevlar® hull effects a considerable saving in weight without endangering the outfit, but its cost is higher. If Kevlar® is beyond your means, stick with the bigger canoe and take turns toting it, or use a two-person carry.

Versatility is vital, too. A long trip almost always involves a variety of water conditions, so a tripper should be at home on a windy lake, a swiftly flowing river, and in a brawling pitch. Rocker is nearly mandatory in swift water, though it's a nuisance on a lake. So, compromise. Settle for a slight rocker, or at least some uplift at the ends.

© R. R. NORMAND

A pair of canvas-covered E. M. Whites, traditional guide models, ready to go

Long trips are hard on canoes. They get dragged up on gravel bars; now and then they bump a rock; once in a while they are dropped unceremoniously at the end of an arduous carry. Obviously, durability is important.

If you're a wood-canoe buff, you'll probably argue that a wood-and-canvas or wood-and-fiberglass canoe is perfectly suited to backcountry trekking. And you would be absolutely right. After all, until Grumman came along, wooden canoes managed to survive on virtually every waterway in North America. So, if you have a penchant for wood, by all means go with it. Just be careful out there.

On a more pragmatic note, most of today's trippers are of aluminum, fiberglass, Royalex®, or Kevlar®. I've omitted polyethylene because it requires a keel to stiffen the bottom. I want no keel on

Kay and Jim Henry in the Mad River Voyageur on Ontario's Missinaibi River

my tripper! I would not completely discount aluminum trippers, though I'm a mite skeptical about the shallow midship depths of some of them. Nonetheless, I'd rate aluminum models acceptable because of their fore and aft fullness. They are stodgy, but they ride out rough water well.

If its cost doesn't make you cringe, Kevlar® is the best overall choice. In terms of weight/durability ratio, it cannot be matched. As pointed out earlier, however, no canoe is indestructible, so common sense is required, even in a Kevlar® model. On a rough portage, what a delight it is to tote 50 pounds instead of a shoulder-gouging 80.

Royalex® is heavier than Kevlar®, but the price is right—about half. Too, the ruggedness of this fabric is reassuring. A hundred miles back in the puckerbrush, Royalex® enhances a paddler's confidence.

Fiberglass will withstand tremendous abrasive abuse and a considerable degree of impact shock. I've seen fiberglass canoes bounce off rocks and show little more than a few scratches. However, if your fiberglass tripper should crunch just a bit too hard against a rock, the damage can be severe and difficult to repair in the field.

Perhaps the best-known among wilderness travel canoes, the Old Town Oltonar / Royalex® Tripper

As for proprietary lay-ups, I would want to talk with the builder regarding the exact "ingredients" and the manner in which they were assembled. I'm sure that any of the leading builders who turn out trippers from proprietary lay-ups has in mind that a tripper, by its very nature, is going to take something of a beating.

There are wilderness waterways where the worst abuse your canoe undergoes will occur when you pull it up on a sandbar. But I can recall very few such benign waters in my own experience. My canoes, over the years, have been scarred and sometimes battered by rocks, ledges, bridge piers, half-sunken logs, and even rusty drift-pins protruding from abandoned log dams.

The following charts include only specifications for canoes that are designated by their manufacturers as "wilderness trippers." Some qualify in every sense of these words, and you may have

MAD RIVER CANOE/JAMES A. HENRY

It's not always smooth water! Mad River canoes on the North Fork of the Koyokuk River, Brooks Range, Alaska

difficulty choosing among them. Others are models that qualify only marginally, and among those, you can make your own judgments by comparing specifications. The charts are not intended to be the final word governing your decision. They are nothing more than a starting point in the search for your ideal tripper.

Few canoeists can afford a separate canoe for each phase of paddling — white water, cruising, fishing, or family picnics. While there is no all-around canoe, some of the better tripping models come close. Lightly loaded, they are a delight to paddle, since they draw so little water. For downriver cruising, they slip around the bends nicely, and as fishing craft, many are stable enough to stand in. All in all, if you're limited to one canoe for general recreation (and possibly an annual two-week trek!), a tripper is a good choice.

Two caveats come to mind, though. One, when lightly loaded they are highly susceptible to wind; two, don't expect to win any races. Remember, they are workhorses.

Chart D

*Representative specifications for 16-foot trippers
(including models up to 16½')*

HULL SHAPE*	CENTER DEPTH	FABRIC**	WEIGHT
SV	15"	Rx	75 lbs.
SV	15	F	68
SV	15	KV	57
FB	13	W/C	68
FB	15½	F	82
SV	15	Rx	72
SV	15	KV	57
SV	15	F	68
SA	14	F	75
SA	14	KV	62
SA	14½	F	65
SA	14½	KV	50
SA	15	PL	67
RB	14½	KV	50
RB	14½	F	70
SA	13½	W/C	70

* FB = flat bottom; RB = round bottom; SA = shallow arch; SV = shallow vee.
** F = fiberglass; KV = Kevlar®; PL = proprietary lay-up; Rx = Royalex®; W/C = wood/canvas.

Chart E

Representative specifications for 17-foot trippers
(includes models up to 17½')

HULL SHAPE*	CENTER DEPTH	FABRIC**	WEIGHT
SV	15″	F	75 lbs.
SV	15	Rx	85
SA	14	F	75
FB	13⅛	Al	75
SV	15	Rx	82
SA	15	F	80
SA	15	KV	66
SA	13	Strip	80
SA	14	KV	58
FB	15	Rx	83
SA	13	Rx	80
SA	14½	PL	69
SA	13	F	75
SA	13½	W/C	75
SA	14½	F	72
SV	14½	F	78

* FB = flat bottom; SA = shallow arch; SV = shallow vee.
** Al = aluminum; F = fiberglass; KV = Kevlar®; PL = proprietary lay-up; Rx = Royalex®; Strip = stripper; W/C = wood/canvas.

Chart F

*Representative specifications for 18-foot trippers
(includes models up to 18½')*

HULL SHAPE*	DEPTH	FABRIC**	WEIGHT
SA	13"	PL	65 lbs.
SA	13	KV	50
SA	15½	F	75
SA	15½	KV	60
SA	14	F	85
SV	15	Rx	78
SV	15	KV	64
FB	13½	W/C	95
FB	13⅛	Al	85
SA	14	PL	65
SA	14	KV	61
SV	14½	Rx	87
SV	14½	KV	77
SV	15	F	83
SV	15	KV	72
SA	13	Strip	85
FB	15	W/C	85
FB	13	W/F	86
SA	14½	PL	55
SA	15	PL	67
SA	15	PL	78
SA	13½	W/C	80
SA	15	F	55
SA	15	KV	50
SA	13½	F	65
SA	13½	KV	47
SA	15	F	70
SA	15	KV	50
SA	14	F	66
SA	14	KV	50

* FB = flat bottom; SA = shallow arch; SV = shallow vee.
** Al = aluminum; F = fiberglass; KV = Kevlar®; PL = proprietary lay-up; Rx = Royalex®; Strip = stripper; W/C = wood/canvas; W/F = wood/fiberglass.

Chapter 23

.·~.·~.·~.·~.·~.

Hunting and Fishing Canoes

SPORTSMEN'S MAGAZINES occasionally discuss the canoe as a medium for hunters and fishermen, but publications devoted specifically to canoeing have long neglected sportsmen. This is unfortunate, for although no one knows how many anglers and hunters use canoes, certainly the number must run into the thousands. The types of canoe they use can be divided into three categories: the pack canoe, the pond or car-top model, and the guide's canoe.

Pack Canoes

The pack canoe is a solo craft, not intended for tripping, although an overnight jaunt is not out of the question. It is designed primarily to be carried to otherwise inaccessible waters, generally for fishing or hunting, though its use certainly isn't limited to these. If its weight exceeds 40 pounds, it hardly qualifies as a pack model. The 40-pound limit may at first seem stringent, but not when you consider that you'll probably also be carrying a paddle, fishing tackle, life vest, anchor rope, rain parka, lunch, miscellaneous

OLD TOWN CANOE CO.

Old Town's 18½-pound pack model, introduced in the mid 1970s, has been replaced by a more versatile 12-foot Oltonar / Royalex® model weighing 33 pounds.

necessities, and perhaps even a camera. Your total load could well add up to 50 pounds, considered hefty even by backpackers who use sophisticated packframes.

The foremost exponent of these little canoes is Bart Hauthaway, who not only builds them but uses them. His fishing exploits have already been cited. He is also an ardent hunter (with a bow and arrow), and he has packed out deer in his peanut-shell pack models. "The Coast Guard," he says, "might not approve, but it sure beats hauling out overland. And a freezer full of deer meat (no New Englander calls it 'venison') is my idea of Social Security. Paddler, 155 pounds; deer, 90 pounds; canoe, 17 pounds, 10 ounces." Nothing could more eloquently describe the feasibility of small canoes.

The relatively few canoes included in Chart G may prompt you to ask: What about lapstrake cedar canoes? And solo cruisers? If weight were the only criterion for a pack canoe, these would adapt nicely. However, hunting and fishing is hard on canoes, and to subject a cedar lapstrake to such use would inevitably damage a rather expensive craft. As for the lighter-weight solo cruisers, a few may be stable enough, but generally, they will prove a mite skittish. Of course, there's no law against using either of the above if you see fit.

Chart G

*Pack Canoes**

MANUFACTURER	MODEL	LENGTH	BEAM	CENTER DEPTH	FABRIC***	WEIGHT
Old Town	Pack	12'	32"	11¼"	Rx	33 lbs.
Voyageur	Trapper	12	22	12	F	30
Voyageur	Scout	12	32	12	F	39
Hauthaway**	Pack	10½	27	11	F	19½
Hauthaway**	Bucktail	10½	28	11½	F	22½
Hauthaway**	Rob Roy	10½	29	12	F	27½
Hauthaway**	Sugar Island	12	27	10½	F	27½
Hauthaway**	Nomad	12	31	12	F	35
Hauthaway**	Nessmuk	10½	27	9½	F	21
Hauthaway**	Rushton	12	27	10½	F	30

* Because so few pack canoes are available, specific manufacturers and models are identified.
** In his search for the ultimate small canoe, Bart Hauthaway is not averse to modifying specifications. The seven models listed were among his offerings at this writing.
*** F = fiberglass; Rx = Royalex®.

Pond Canoes and Car-Toppers

Curiosity once led me to hike the 2-mile trail to Maine's Russell Pond, where I found a wealthy man's private fishing camp. The caretaker insisted that I spend the night. "There's no one here but me," he said. "We can catch us a mess of trout in the garden." I assumed the "garden" was a nearby stream pool. But no. It seems the logging company, in raising the water level in the pond for the log drive, had flooded out the summer's vegetables. The garden had been fenced to keep deer out, and now the wire mesh protruded above the water a foot or so. We opened the gate and paddled in. "The trout come in to feed on drowned worms," the

MAD RIVER CANOE/JAMES A. HENRY

Snook fishing in the Florida Everglades in a Mad River Explorer

caretaker explained, "but they'll take flies." And they did! We caught and released dozens, keeping only a few for supper. That day saw two firsts in my life. I had never before caught trout in a cabbage patch; nor had I ever seen a canoe like the one we used.

It was a canvas-covered two-seater, 12 feet long, with a beam of at least 40 inches. The flat bottom extended well to the sides and into each end. It definitely was "tubby." "The boss thought these little canoes would be just right," the caretaker said, "especially since they had to be carried in over the trail." He went on: "The boss likes to stand when he's casting, and these canoes are steady as a raft, even if they don't paddle handily. Makes no difference, though; the pond isn't very big." I had met my first pond canoe, and the caretaker's words had pretty well described their function. Only a few months later, I ran into Grumman's then-astounding 44-pound 13-footer. Today, pond canoes are everywhere.

LINCOLN CANOES/SAM HOSSLER

The Lincoln Sportsman can be carried to remote waters for big fish.

They are light enough to be carried some distance, capable of medium-range loads, and their initial stability is remarkable, due mostly to their unusually wide beams. While a 36-inch width is common in 17- and 18-foot canoes, many of the much shorter pond models are up to 44 inches wide.

There are dozens of 14- and 15-foot two-seaters that might qualify as pond canoes, except that they weigh up to 70 pounds. Ideally, one partner should be able to carry the canoe and the paddles without risking damage to his sacroiliac, while the other partner totes whatever gear is necessary for the day's outing.

Fishing from these abbreviated canoes calls for coordination. Spin fishermen or bait casters may safely cast simultaneously, if they bear in mind that hooking a partner in the ear may bring about harsh words. Fly fishermen, because of their long backcasts, are somewhat more limited. It's best for the stern man to act as "guide," paddling and holding the canoe while the bow man does the fishing.

There's hardly a canoe/fly fisherman who does not stand while casting, or wish he dared. While most fish are hooked within 50 feet, there are days when a longer cast is necessary. Standing in a wide-beam, flat-bottom pond canoe is not a crime. If it helps your fishing, do it. Wear a life jacket, if that adds to your confidence; it won't interfere with your casting. Incidentally, sponson-equipped canoes are of dubious value for adding stability. If you rock the craft violently enough for the sponsons to contact the water, you're doing something wrong and the canoe will almost certainly pitch you overboard. Depend on smooth casting techniques, not sponsons.

Chart H

Representative specifications for pond canoes and car-toppers

LENGTH	BEAM	HULL SHAPE*	CENTER DEPTH	FABRIC**	WEIGHT
11'4"	44"	SA	13"	F	60 lbs.
11'4"	44	SA	13	KV	50
12	44	FB	12	Al	48
12	40	FB	13	F	55
12	39	FB	12	W/C	52
13	37	FB	12	F	60
13	37	FB	13	W/C	58
13	35⅜	FB	12⅞	Al	58
13	39	SV	15	KV	56
13'2"	41	FB	12½	PL	39
13'4"	35	SV	15	F	58
14	35	FB	13	PL	45
14	35	FB	13	F	55
14	35	FB	13	KV	38
14	38	SA	12	F	58
14	39	SV	15	KV	49
14	44	FB	12	Al	58
15	35	FB	12⅛	Al	55
16	34	FB	13	KV	48

* FB = flat bottom; SA = shallow arch; SV = shallow vee.
** Al = aluminum; F = fiberglass; KV = Kevlar®; PL = proprietary lay-up; W/C = wood/canvas.

Hunting from a canoe calls for "time-sharing." The bow man does the shooting, the stern paddler acts as his guide. "Jump" shooting for ducks in a marsh requires both shooting and paddling skill. The "guide" eases the canoe along stealthily. Splashing or paddle-drip is verboten. "Puddle" ducks, such as mallards, will literally erupt into the air at close range, requiring quick reflexes.

THE COLEMAN CO. INC.

Setting out duck decoys on a misty morning

Squirrel hunting with a shotgun or a scope-sighted .22 rifle is not difficult; especially with a .22, however, a combination of quiet paddling and good marksmanship is necessary. Even deer hunting is feasible, particularly as twilight approaches and deer drift to the waterways. The steadiest shooting position results from sitting on the floor; just forward of the bow seat is best. No matter how carefully the paddler manages the canoe, there's a certain amount of "jiggling," enough to throw a shooter's aim off the mark. Sitting on the bow seat would magnify the problem. Only one gun should be kept at the ready, and this one always in the bow, with the safety

SAWYER CANOE CO.

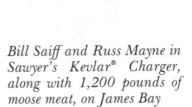

Bill Saiff and Russ Mayne in Sawyer's Kevlar® Charger, along with 1,200 pounds of moose meat, on James Bay

on. The stern paddler's gun should remain unloaded until it is his turn to move into the bow position.

Hunting from a canoe need not involve shooting. Observing and photographing wildlife at close range can be just as exciting and rewarding. Over the years, my wife and I have approached just about every species that exists in our area, often within canoe length. We've watched ruffed grouse budding in overhanging birch trees, and innumerable beaver have splashed us in their headlong dives. We've followed lowly muskrats as they etched silvery vees on evening waters, and we've lost count of the deer we've surprised. Incidentally, for comic relief, sneak up on a black bear. We've seen a number of them almost turn themselves inside out in hasty retreat. A bear cub up a tree is fun to watch, but stay in deep water. Mama is probably close by, and she can be downright ornery if she thinks her offspring is in danger.

Several times we've caught up (by paddling for all we were worth!) with families of otters, alternately diving or sailing along with their heads held high. We've admired a mother raccoon as she waddled along a muddy bank, followed by seven tiny puffs of fur.

MAD RIVER CANOE/JAMES A. HENRY

"Hunting" doesn't necessarily mean shooting. These canoeists watch a cow moose with her calf at close range in Ontario.

Perhaps the most magnificent animal is the moose; since it delights in feeding on lily pads with its head underwater a good part of the time, it is easy to approach. Here again, be careful. A 1,200-pound moose with 5-foot antlers is unruly company in a canoe.

Birdwatching too is rewarding, especially during the early summer, when songbirds haunt the lakeshores and streamsides. Binoculars bring them in close for identification.

Guides' Canoes

Guides' canoes are multi-purpose craft. They are ideal for fishing on big waters likely to whip up a froth; they double as small freighters; and they are also suited to long-distance tripping. Generally flat-bottomed with a touch of tumblehome, they run from 18 feet up to 20 or 22. They are heavy, weighing from 80 to 100 pounds or more; therefore, as a rule, they are based at fishing camps. Quite often, manufacturers omit the bow seat, since many guides prefer to provide a folding canoe chair with backrest (see chapter 8). An old woods partner of mine explained why. "I like my sports [short for 'sportsman'] to stay where I put 'em. With a folding seat, I can put 'em where I want 'em. Makes for steadier goin' and better trim." Actually, such a seat is far more comfortable than the traditional bench seat, especially when provided with a cushion.

A few manufacturers turn out 16- and 17-foot models with a shallow-vee bottom, which they label "guides' canoes." No self-respecting guide would haul turnips in one! Guides prefer bigger canoes, and they want a flat bottom for initial stability.

When fishing for smallmouth bass, I like to stand, and ease my canoe along slowly with a 6-foot paddle. Our bass waters are as clear as good Russian vodka, so usually it's easy to spot the fish in 6 to 8 feet of water. Once I've sighted a fish, I back off a bit, note its location, wait a few minutes, then cast to it. The technique is productive, if unorthodox. But I want a big, steady canoe under me.

Although guides' canoes are subject to hard use, a surprising number of them are canvas-covered, albeit the canvas is a heavy grade and often backed by extra ribs. (Old Town now fiberglasses its guides' models.) My 18-foot Kennebec did yeoman service for 13 years until, in a moment of weakness aggravated by a touch of greed, I sold it for a few dollars more than it had cost me. There was a bit of canvas rot along one gunwale, and one plank was cracked slightly. Other than that, old *Head Winds* was sound.

True guides' canoes are relatively few — few enough to warrant listing them by name:

Donald Fraser Canoes, Ogilvy Special, wood/canvas, 18, 20, and 22 feet;

Island Falls Canoe Company, E. M. White Guide, wood/canvas, 18½ and 20 feet;

Leavitt Quality Craft, Eagle, rib/plank/fiberglass, 18 feet 5 inches;

William V. Miller & Son, wood/canvas, Miller, 18 feet; Moore, 20 feet; Gallop, 20 feet.

Old Town Canoe Company, Guide, rib/plank/fiberglass, 18 and 20 feet;

Ranger Canoe Company, Sportsman, fiberglass, 19 feet;

Fred Reckards, Templeton, rib/plank/fiberglass, 20 feet;

White Canoe Company, Guide, fiberglass, 18 feet 3 inches; Cruiser, 19 feet 11 inches.

Chapter 24

∿∙∿∙∿∙∿∙∿∙∿

Competition

Citizens' Races

IF YOU'RE COMPETITION MINDED, but don't feel that you're ready for the regional and national championships, consider entering "citizens' races." In some parts of the country, these are held almost every weekend during the early part of the canoeing season. I know a couple who travel up to 150 miles every weekend to enter a race. Their living room looks like a trophy shop.

Citizens' races are not "sanctioned"; that is, they are not governed by the rules established by the American Canoe Association or the United States Canoe Association. Almost any type of canoe is permitted, except that racing hulls may be banned; if allowed to compete, their paddlers collect no trophies.

Some of these races were once little more than free-for-alls, but increasingly, sponsors — usually the local chamber of commerce or a service club — are bringing about some semblance of order, so that competition will be fair. "Classes" are evolving. Among tandem canoes, these include teams of a man and a woman; two men or two women; father and son; mother and daughter; and juniors, usually defined as those under 16 years of age. Where solo canoes also compete, separate classes exist for men, women, and juniors.

These races are hardly basic training for the Olympics, although many a championship paddler got his start by beating out 100 other entries in a hometown race. In general, they are merely fun events, with much splashing and an occasional spill. The prize is a secondary consideration, the excitement of racing the prime motivation.

This doesn't mean that you should not take this type of racing seriously. If you want to acquire valuable experience (and perhaps collect some trophies and medals), don't handicap yourself with a

BILL RIVIERE

A typical mass start of a citizens' race

pusher. Get yourself a modern design with a fine entry that's sleek and fast, though not a racing model, which might automatically disqualify you. And, if you've mastered the bent-shaft paddle, take a tip from champion marathoners. They use 'em!

Citizens' races are usually of modest length, perhaps 3 to 5 miles, and they may involve one or more easy portages, quite often around dams. The two-person carry is preferable to the one-man on-the-shoulders portage, since time is a factor. A critical point is the launching after a portage. Many paddlers have spilled trying to launch and board simultaneously. It's not unethical to scout the portage beforehand, to determine how it can be quickly and efficiently accomplished.

Seldom seen nowadays — a war canoe race in Maine

Take a cue from the experts. Carry a spare paddle or two and, if the weather is warm, don't forget drinking water. Paddling under a hot sun is dehydrating.

Marathon Racing

The next step up in competition involves sanctioned races — local, regional, or national — run under the rules set up by the American Canoe Association, the United States Canoe Association, and the International Canoe Federation.

The United States Canoe Association was organized in 1963 to foster flat-water amateur marathon racing, for which it has established four classes of eligible canoes: tandem cruisers, solo cruisers, standard canoes, and aluminum canoes.

In setting up the cruiser classes, the intention was to create a class of racing canoes that would also be suitable for general recreation; these canoes became known as "competition cruisers." However, they have evolved into a distinct racing craft, actually too tricky for most recreational purposes.

Tandem "competition cruisers" are specifically restricted to a maximum length of 18½ feet; a beam at the 4-inch waterline of not less than 14.375 percent of the length; the widest point must be no more than 1 foot fore or aft of center; the minimum bow depth, 16 inches; minimum center depth, 11½ inches; minimum stern depth, 11½ inches; and outwales must be no wider than 1½ inches. Self-bailers are banned. (These are devices built into the bilge at the stern that, when opened while the canoe is under way, suck out water.) Sponges or plastic hand bailers are allowed. Spray covers, which in effect convert an open canoe to a decked canoe, are banned.

A tandem cruiser may be shorter than 18½ feet, but it must still comply with the proportional beam requirement. However, since length is advantageous, virtually all tandem cruisers used in competition take advantage of the full allowable length.

WE-NO-NAH CANOES

Mass start of a solo marathon

Solo competition cruisers are governed by the same specifications, but few paddlers want an 18½-foot canoe for solo racing.

We-no-nah, which has specialized in marathon racers with its Jensen designs, offers a solo marathon model that is 16 feet 7 inches long, with a 4-inch waterline beam of 29½ inches (within the USCA specifications). A number of other firms produce similar solo marathon models, as well as tandem models.

When the USCA recognized that these solo and tandem competition cruisers were really racing machines, rather than recreational boats, it established the Standard Canoe class. Maximum length is 18½ feet; the beam may be no less than 15 percent of the length, with the widest point within 1 foot of center; minimum bow depth, 16 inches; minimum center depth, 12 inches; minimum stern depth, 16 inches; outwales no wider than 1½ inches; and no spray covers permitted. These dimensions come closer to equalling those of an actual recreational canoe.

How about the thousands of aluminum-canoe owners who would like to compete? They need not go up against the standard canoe or the competition cruiser. The USCA has established an aluminum class, for which the cruiser specifications have been modified slightly. Aluminum now races against aluminum. Since they are mass produced, aluminum models are subject to more lenient restrictions.

Marathon distances are regulated, too. USCA rules stipulate minimums of 20 kilometers (12 miles) for men's events, 15 kilometers (9 miles) for women and junior racers. Some marathons have involved distances that required three days to cover! More typically, they are one-day events. No matter what the distance, women may not be required to compete against men.

In 1980, the International Canoe Federation introduced "ICF" races to the United States. These are now administered by the American Canoe Association. The canoes are of radical design, among the fastest of all marathon craft. There are two classes: ICF tandem and ICF solo.

Tandem models may be no longer than 21 feet 4 inches, and must be at least 29½ inches wide at some point, not necessarily at the waterline. Solo specifications limit hulls to 17 feet, with a beam of at least 29½ inches somewhere along the hull. These beam requirements have permitted the introduction of radically asymmetrical canoes. In neither class is a minimum depth stipulated; self-bailers are allowed.

BILL RIVIERE

*Wabash Valley's 17-foot Dyna
C solo marathon model*

Although it is of European design, it's interesting to note that the American-built We-no-nah ICF tandem racer, of fiberglass/Kevlar®/PVC-core construction, took first and second place in the 1982 World Cup races in Luxembourg! We-no-nah's ICF solo model has yet to be tested in competition at this writing, and it is currently the only ICF solo racer built commercially in the United States. Undoubtedly, as interest in this type of racing grows, other builders will produce them.

The "Pro Boat"

The "pro boat," as the name implies, is raced by paid professionals. Yes, they get cash prizes, and some are paid simply to paddle. None of them makes enough at racing to permit posh living, but they are a breed apart. Their races are not sanctioned by any major canoe organization; in fact, pro boats are banned from USCA competitions.

The specifications for pro boats include: maximum length, 18½ feet; at least a 27-inch beam at the 3-inch waterline; gunwale beam of at least 33 inches. There is no minimum depth, self-bailers are

BILL RIVIERE

Not the classic lines of a traditional canoe—but fast!

permitted, and spray covers may or may not be allowed, depending upon the sponsors of the race. In fact, sponsors pretty much make up their own rules, although some abide by USCA regulations except for hull dimensions.

Pro boats are not playthings. Great skill is required to handle them. The demand for them is quite limited, and only two firms, We-no-nah and Sawyer, build them on a production basis. Others who produce them on a limited scale are Al Camp, of Camp Woodworking, Otego, New York; Jensen Canoes, of Minneapolis, Minnesota; and Everett Crozier, of Voyageur Canoes, Marinette, Wisconsin.

Slalom

Slalom is probably the most exciting of canoeing competitions, at least from the spectator's point of view. It is also probably the most demanding of a paddler's skill at precise maneuvering. Slalom is run on a white-water course that may be half a mile long and may include 25 to 30 gates. A gate is simply a pair of poles hung from an overhead wire, somewhat resembling the gates a slalom skier must negotiate. In white-water slalom, however, a racer must negotiate some of the gates by paddling upstream! Since it is a timed event, penalties can hurt. A 5-second penalty is assessed against a paddler who touches a gate, a 50-second penalty against one who fails to pass through it. There are other technical rules that keep slalom interesting.

Following are the classifications of paddlers for slalom racing. (OC-2 stands for Open Canoe, two persons; OC-1, Open Canoe, one person.)

OC-2 — two male paddlers

OC-2 Mixed — one man, one woman

OC-2 Junior/Senior — two paddlers, one 16 or under, the other 25 or over

OC-2 W — two women

OC-2 Master — two paddlers 40 years of age or over

OC-2 Junior — two junior paddlers

OC-1 Short — one male paddler in a short canoe (13½ feet)

OC-1 Medium — one male paddler, medium canoe (15 feet and over)

OC-1 W Short — one woman, short canoe

OC-1 W Medium — one woman, medium canoe

OC-1 Master, Short — one master paddler, short canoe

OC-1 Master, Medium — one master paddler, medium canoe

OC-1 Junior — one junior paddler, any length canoe

If the foregoing seems terribly complicated, take heart. It isn't. Essentially, the classifications divide competitors into men and women, adults 25 or over, juniors 16 and under, and masters 40 and over. Paddlers in each of these groups have a choice of racing in a "short" canoe or a "medium" (15-foot and over) canoe.

Specifications for slalom canoes are not complex. Beam at the 4-inch waterline must be at least 14.375 percent of the length; depth must not exceed 15 inches; the outwales must be no wider than 1½ inches; and the decks no longer than 36.

Virtually every builder of specialty canoes produces slalom models within the required specifications. Such boats are rockered, incorporate the maximum possible depth, and often feature some fullness fore and aft. Of course, *any* canoe whose design meets the regulations may compete, but it will likely be outclassed by canoes built specifically for slalom. Favorite fabrics are Royalex® for its durability, and Kevlar® for its light weight.

Downriver Wildwater

This is a hell-bent-for-leather kind of race, with no gates. The object is to navigate Class III (or rougher!) rapids over a course ranging from 8 to 25 miles long. Not every foot of it must be white water, of course, but race officials try to use sections of rivers that are predominantly rough water. The entire course must be navigable, although it may include one portage.

In neither slalom nor downriver racing are there established records like those in competitive sports where precise course measurements *are* possible — track and field, for example. Since slalom and downriver courses vary in length and are run on different waters from year to year, there is no basis for comparison.

However, both slalom and downriver are timed events. Depending upon the race committee's decision, a downriver competition may get under way with a mass start — everybody off at once — or, if river conditions don't permit this, canoes may be started at intervals.

Following are the classifications of paddlers for downriver racing:

OC-2 Short — two male paddlers in a 15-foot canoe (length not to exceed 16½ feet)

OC-2 — two male paddlers in a canoe longer than 16½ feet, up to and including 18½ feet

OC-2 Mixed — one man, one woman, any canoe up to 18½ feet

OC-2 Junior/Mixed — one junior paddler, one senior, any canoe up to
  18½ feet
OC-2 W — two women, any canoe up to 18½ feet
OC-2 Master — two paddlers, 40 years of age or over
OC-1 Junior — single junior paddler
OC-1 — single senior paddler
OC-1 W — single woman paddler

In some instances, both slalom and downriver events may be
held. This is known as a "combined race." Any tandem paddlers
who enter both events may not change partners, and must use the
same canoe in both events. A single paddler may not change
canoes.

The foregoing are, of course, only the most pertinent aspects of
the regulations. There are many more details in the rules, copies of
which are available from the American Canoe Association and the
United States Canoe Association.

The Nationals, the World Championships, and the Olympics

These are the ultimate competitions. National championship
races, popularly known as "The Nationals," may be sanctioned by
the American Canoe Association, the United States Canoe Association, or the American Whitewater Federation. The American
Canoe Association, for example, annually elects committees which
oversee flat-water paddling, slalom and wildwater, open canoe,
and poling events. Both men's and women's divisions are included.
The United States Canoe Association, which generally sponsors
flat-water competitions, has a similar committee organization. The
American Whitewater Federation, as its name implies, deals primarily with wildwater and slalom events. All three organizations
may also sponsor divisional or regional competitions, a paddler's
first step toward national and international racing.

World Championship events include both flat- and white-water
races, and are sanctioned by the International Canoe Federation.
In recent years, Americans have done well in the World Championships. In 1979, the American Canoe Association slalom and
wildwater teams won the slalom events at Jonquierre, Quebec.

And in 1983, Americans dominated the competition at Merano, Italy. Alas, not so in recent Olympics.

Relatively few paddlers get to compete in the Olympics, and these are the cream of the world's canoeists. Events are limited. In the kayak division, men and women compete separately over a 500-meter (550-yard) course and a 1,000-meter (1,100-yard) course. In the open canoe division, however, there is no women's competition. It's strictly for men in solos and tandems, again over 500- and 1,000-meter courses.

An early Olympic paddler in the beloved "Peanut." Today's Olympic canoes are arrowhead-shaped deltoids.

Canoeing was introduced at the Paris Olympics in 1924, but only as a demonstration event. It became an official competition at Berlin, in 1936, the year that the American Canoe Association became a member of the International Olympic Committee. Since the 1950s Olympic canoeing has been dominated by Europeans, particularly eastern Europeans; the last time an American won a medal was at the Tokyo meet in 1964! Americans had high hopes at Los Angeles in 1984, but they latched on to only one medal: a bronze, won by Greg Barton, of Homer, Michigan, in the one-man 1,000-meter kayak race.

For a brief, but well-detailed history of Olympic canoeing, see Eric Evans' piece in the 1983 edition of the *Coleman Guide to Camping and the Great Outdoors*. As a follow-up, see Evans' article *A Wide-Open Games*, an in-depth report on the Los Angeles kayak and canoe events.[1]

Poling

Since its inception in 1965 at Times Beach, Missouri, competitive poling has been sanctioned by the ACA. Instead of marking the course with gates hung from overhead, buoys — a minimum of 12 but not more than 20 — are strategically spotted to establish a course through Class I, II, or III rapids. The course may be anywhere from 30 to 60 yards long. Class III rapids are pretty heady stuff for polers, and only competitions of major importance are held in such rough waters. The events are more likely to take place in Class I or II waters, in order to attract more participants.

The buoys are dispersed singly; they do not form gates. Instead they are color-coded, to indicate whether a poler must pass to the right or to the left, upstream or down. There is always one buoy that a poler must circumnavigate, and at least one reverse buoy, which the poler must pass by dropping downstream stern-first. Depending upon water conditions, it can be an exciting competition for both polers and spectators.

As in slalom, penalties are assessed to any poler who touches a buoy; navigates one in the wrong direction, or from the wrong side; does not make a complete 360-degree turn around the circle buoy; or fails to navigate within 36 feet (or two canoe lengths) of any buoy.

[1] *Canoe Magazine* (December 1984).

The pole may be of any length or material, and a spare may be carried. Canoes are standard "cruising" types (not to be confused with the USCA "competition cruisers"), but may not exceed 20 feet in length or 38 inches in width.

Classes include men's and women's singles, men's doubles, juniors, and sometimes expert, intermediate, and juvenile.

Getting into Competition

To enter any of the many rather informal citizens' races, you have only to fill out an application, pay a small fee if one is required, and sign a form releasing the sponsors from any responsibility in the event of mishaps. Some races are even more informal than this. You have only to show up!

Becoming a competitor in a sanctioned event takes a little more doing. For some events, you may have to be a member of the ACA, the USCA, or possibly the American Whitewater Affiliation. Such memberships are to your advantage, since you will receive announcements of racing events and news regarding the latest developments in racing canoes and techniques. The same is true of joining a local club.

Some competitions include novice, intermediate, and expert levels. No matter which you seek to enter, you'll need an official application blank, which is most easily obtained from a sponsoring club. Blanks are not distributed except to known competitors or through clubs. Hence, the importance of joining.

Specialize! Your chances of winning both an important flatwater marathon and a slalom event are virtually nil. The degree of expertise that exists among competition paddlers is so high that no one can afford to dilute training efforts. Decide what type of competition interests you most, and devote yourself exclusively to it.

Obtain an appropriate canoe. And don't skimp on one that might be "good enough." Buy top-of-the-line. This holds true for paddles, too, as well as other related equipment.

Compete as often as possible, even though at the outset, you know you'll probably finish among the also-rans. Training and practice are imperative, but unless you acquire actual competition experience, your training will probably be for naught. Should there be competitions in your area that you're not qualified to enter, attend as a spectator.

Get to know other racers, either through club membership or at competitive events. You may make the acquaintance of a gold-medalist who will be willing to give you some tips, perhaps even coach you a bit.

Canoe racing is a grueling sport. Keep yourself in top physical condition.

Public Awareness of Canoe Racing

Compared to other participant and spectator sports, canoe racing gets little attention from newspaper and television sports reporters. I saw no press reports of the June 1983 World Slalom Championships, held in Merano, Italy, despite the fact that American paddlers dominated the event. Even the 1984 Olympic canoe races got scant attention.

However, at the local level, there is a growing consciousness of the sport in the news media. For example, Maine's 17th annual 16½-mile Kenduskeag Stream Canoe Race was reported by both the Portland (200 miles from the scene) and the Bangor (in the neighborhood) papers. They listed the winners in all 17 classes, and pointed out that more than 600 canoeists took part before 15,000 spectators lining the streambanks. That's a better crowd than attends many a big-league baseball game!

Chapter 25

~·~·~·~·~

Paddles

DESPITE TODAY'S EXTENSIVE CROP of well-crafted and functional paddles, many canoeists still slosh around with ill-chosen, misbegotten blades that have all the life and grace of a peavey handle.

Admittedly, choosing the right paddle involves some study of function and design. A paddle should be fitted not only to the paddler but also to his canoe. Unfortunately, the selection process is hampered by conflicting theories about the manner in which a paddle should be chosen. There is much debunking of the old-time formulae, while some of the "new thinking" is not without fault.

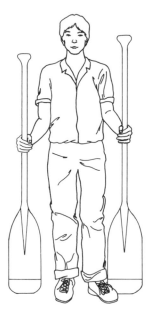

The old formula: stern paddle should reach to the eyes; bow paddle to the chin

Length

The traditional formula for determining proper length requires that the paddler stand erect. The correct paddle for stern use is supposed to reach from the floor to his eyes; for bow use, to his chin. Note that this rule addresses the overall length of the paddle.

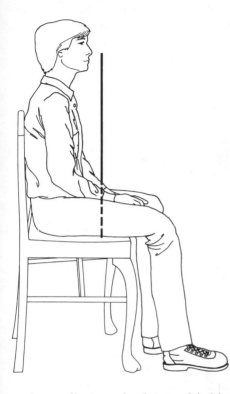

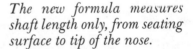

The new formula measures shaft length only, from seating surface to tip of the nose.

According to the latest thinking, proper length is determined with the paddler sitting erect, on a bench, for example. The "base shaft length" is the distance measured from the bench's surface to the tip of the paddler's nose. This rule, you'll note, designates only the shaft length. For tandem paddling, you're supposed to deduct 1 inch; for solo work, add 2 inches; for white water, add 3.

According to the latter formula, my "base shaft length" is 29 inches. I've stirred pancake batter with spoons longer than this! Proponents of either formula accept their versions as gospel, when in fact, neither is universally applicable.

Applying the traditional formula, floor-to-eye while standing, a paddler could well come up with a 66-inch paddle. Used aboard one of the new low-slung performance canoes with low-set seats, this paddle would get in its own way. Decidedly the wrong choice.

On the other hand, the most commonly used canoes are still the so-called recreational or family craft, in which the stern seat is at gunwale level, roughly 9 to 10 inches above the water. Applying the "new thinking," I must add the length of the blade, possibly 22 inches, to my basic shaft length of 29 inches, for a total paddle length of 51 inches. When I'm perched in the stern seat with this paddle, I can dip only 12 inches of my 22-inch blade. To fully immerse the blade, I have to lean out awkwardly.

ELEANOR RIVIERE

The author with three of his paddles, a standard laminate, a bent-shaft, and a 6-foot Maine guide model

Obviously, no one paddle is suitable for all canoes. If you become serious about canoeing, you'll eventually own several paddles. In the meantime, how do you determine the proper length for your first one? Or perhaps you already own a paddle with which you're not happy, and you want to upgrade. The first step is to discard the theories, both the old formula and the "new thinking." Use them as guidelines perhaps, but don't be bound by either.

Visit a riverside dealer or rental livery and ask to rent a few paddles, each a different length, possibly in increments of 2 inches. Don't expect the dealer to supply you with an assortment of his best $65 paddles. He will probably provide you with battle-scarred veterans (renters are hard on equipment); but at this stage, you're not concerned with high-performance refinements, only length.

Paddle about for an hour or more, trying the different lengths. Be sure that the blade is totally immersed, and possibly an inch or so of the shaft. As you stroke the paddle, try to keep your upper hand no higher than chin-to-eye level. This should provide good leverage. And while you're on the water, paddle in different positions — the bow, stern, and solo at midship. Paddle while on both knees, and in the high-kneel position. If a paddle propels you effectively at the various boat positions and body stances, *and* you can paddle comfortably with it, that's about as close to a correct paddle as you can get.

Note that a new element has been introduced: comfort. Neither of the formulae considers this. They are a bit too arbitrary. The fact is that a technically "correct" paddle that is uncomfortable to use is a noxious instrument.

If there's no waterside dealer close by, there are alternatives. Perhaps a friend owns an assortment of paddles (for example, I keep three or four "loaners" on hand) that he might lend you, along with a bit of advice. Don't simply walk into a canoe shop and buy a paddle because it "feels good" as you heft it on the show-room floor!

The paddle you eventually choose will be at its best for only one or two types of canoe. Should you switch from a recreational model to a solo canoe, or to a white-water boat, the selection will have to be repeated, although your original basic tests will make the process much easier.

Materials

Among the one-piece paddles (as opposed to laminates), the most commonly used woods are maple, ash, and spruce. Maple is the heaviest and its use is declining for that reason, but it is tough, virtually unbreakable under most paddling conditions. Ash is con-siderably lighter, yet quite durable. Ash and maple share a desir-able characteristic: they are somewhat limber, ash a bit more so than maple. This flexibility absorbs the slight shock that is trans-mitted to the arms and shoulders as each stroke is initiated. The shock may seem imperceptible when you start out fresh in the morning, but during a long haul with an overly stiff paddle, you'll soon feel little twinges of pain in the shoulder joints. Ash or maple won't eliminate this problem completely, but will alleviate it.

Experienced cruisers invariably test a paddle's flexibility by rest-ing the blade on the floor and holding the grip in one hand so that the paddle is at an angle. They then bear down on the middle of the shaft with the other hand. Too flexible a paddle will be "mushy" or rubbery in the water; too stiff, and you might as well use a pine board. Flexibility can be enhanced by thinning down the shaft at the throat and below the grip, but if this is overdone, it can weaken the shaft and perhaps lead to a break.

Spruce is somewhat stiff and brittle, but it is light, and therefore popular among women who might find the heavier ash or maple blades tiring to use. Children, too, find spruce easier to wield. It's a good choice for recreational canoeing, though few experienced trippers will rely on spruce for an extended cruise.

Thanks to today's waterproof adhesives, it's among the laminated models that you will find the most sophisticated paddles. Not only are the laminates rugged, they are remarkably light, some as little as 20 ounces! Admittedly, some laminates are of crude construction, better suited to whacking backsides during freshman-hazing week, but the better grades approach being the ultimate paddling tool.

GRUMMAN BOATS

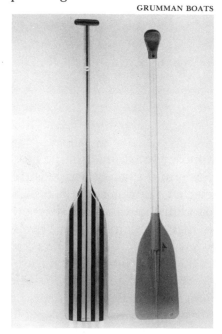

An inexpensive but durable laminate and an aluminum-shafted ABS plastic blade

A wide variety of wood is used in laminates, including eastern spruce, redwood, basswood, cherry, mahogany, eastern cedar, pine, western red cedar, and walnut. Manufacturers disagree among themselves as to which is the best combination, but each aims at producing durability and light weight. Ultimately, most laminated-paddle users make their choice according to the design and finish, rather than wood content. The paddle business is highly competitive and there are countless models from which to choose. Among the better-known brands, you can't go far wrong.

Not surprisingly, synthetics show up in paddles, too, especially in the blades. Various injection-molded plastics are used, along with fiberglass-reinforced polyester or epoxy. The latter is quite durable. Heat-formed sheet plastics are generally crude. A recent introduction was a 16-ounce bent-shaft graphite paddle. Exceptions to my low opinion of synthetics might include some of the sophisticated combinations that mate a fiberglass or Kevlar® blade to a fiberglass shaft; this pairing was adapted from pole-vaulting designs. All in all, though, in the symphony orchestra of canoeing, synthetic paddles are the fiddles; wooden blades are the violins.

Blade Shapes and Sizes

The makers of one-piece paddles stick pretty much to the long-revered Maine Guide and Beaver-tail blades, although the square-tipped Sugar Island style persists. Laminated blades are either square-tipped or oval, and, on the whole, somewhat shorter but wider than the traditional patterns. For instance, one of my Maine Guide paddles has a 31-inch blade that measures 7½ inches wide. Laminates rarely exceed 24 inches, but they may be as wide as 10 inches.

A marathon racer is likely to insist on the largest possible blade, since he needs the ultimate purchase and has the brawn to handle it. A white-water canoeist also wants ample blade surface, for high braces and for dipping into aerated water. The north-woods tripper, who has a heavy load to move, likes a big blade, too. But for general recreational paddling, there's little need for these muscle-wearying tools. Shorter and narrower ones will do the job without wearing out the paddler.

Square tip or oval tip? Here again, look to the marathoner. He dips his blade with machine-like precision squarely into the water. Too, he seeks to keep his shaft as close to vertical as possible. He makes no pretense of being graceful. The square tip "plunks," even splashes, but it offers more bearing surface, and hence each

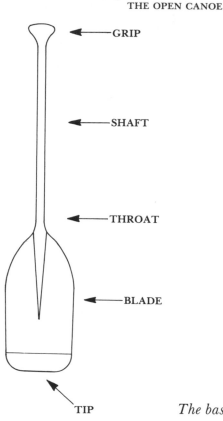

GRIP

SHAFT

THROAT

BLADE

TIP

The basic parts of a paddle

paddle thrust is more forceful. On the other hand, the recreational paddler is less precise, his pace more leisurely. Should he not dip his square-tip paddle squarely into the water—at an angle—the paddle will tend to twist. The oval blade, which slips in with nary a slurp at almost any angle, is easier and more graceful to use.

Until recently, little thought was given to the configuration of a paddle blade's surface. Aiming for ultimate speed, ease of paddling, and general efficiency, some manufacturers now produce a "dihedral" blade shape that directs water to the side of and around the edges of the blade in a smooth flow, creating little turbulence. The aeration and "gurgling" created by a flat-surface blade are eliminated, or at least minimized. "Dihedral" is usually associated with aviation, where the term refers to the gentle upsweep of a plane's wings from the fusilage to the wingtips. Applied to a paddle, it refers to a slightly built-up ridge that runs down the center of the blade and tapers to its edges. In other words, the blade is noticeably thicker along its spine than at its edges.

DIRECTION OF THRUST

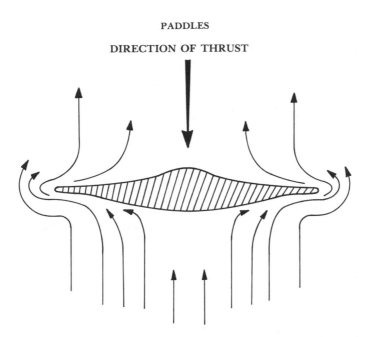

Cross-section of a modern paddle blade, showing smooth flow of water around it

While paddle dihedral has suddenly come into prominence, it is nothing new. Examine almost any of the one-piece "traditional" paddles and you will see a definite dihedral configuration. On the other hand, I own a supposedly up-to-date laminated paddle whose blade is absolutely flat.

Dihedral is built into the "power face" of the blade; that is, the face that pushes the water. On the backside of the blade, innovators have come up with "foil." This resembles a rounded ridge that runs from the shaft to approximately halfway down the blade. What dihedral does for the power face, foil does for the reverse side. Cavitation, which causes a highly aerated semi-vacuum, is minimized, and so is turbulence, which creates drag. You can observe the efficiency of a dihedral/foil blade by first sculling with a flat blade. The paddle will quiver erratically. The paddle with a foiled surface, on the other hand, slips through the water smoothly. Not all foils are alike, so you may have to try out a number of them before finding one to your liking.

The improvement in blade performance brought about by dihedral/foil is a subtle one; if you're relatively new to paddling, it probably won't impress you greatly. In fact, unless you're quite skilled and sensitive to the feel of a paddle, dihedral/foil doesn't amount to a hill of beans. But if you're seeking the ultimate paddling tool to match your highly refined paddling skills, opt for dihedral/foil.

Some manufacturers finish their blades with one or more coats of spar varnish, which actually does little to protect or reinforce it. Other makers go the last mile for utmost quality by coating the blade with resin and fiberglass cloth. This adds a bit to the cost, but it's worth every penny, especially for white-water use. Among square-tip paddles, you may occasionally run into a blade with a hardwood or fiberglass tip—a nice touch that protects the blade.

Shafts

Laminated paddles may or may not have laminated shafts. Most often, a laminated blade is wedded to a solid-wood shaft—ash is a good choice.

Paddles whose blades are made of synthetics—such as the various plastics—often have an aluminum shaft, about which the less said the better, except that these are just plain ugly.

Wooden shafts may be oval or round. The choice is yours, and opinions differ as to which is better. Structurally, there is probably little difference. Feel is another matter. You may be more comfortable with an oval shaft, or conversely with a round one. Personal preference dictates.

Among the laminated shafts, it's not unreasonable to seek a bit of flex, for the same reason that old-time paddlers "sprung" their ash and maple paddles. You'll find that some paddles combine a rather stiff blade with a slightly flexible shaft, or the entire paddle may flex noticeably.

Grips

Grips get little attention from the average paddle purchaser: if he likes the paddle itself, the grip is incidental. It deserves a closer look. There are three basic types: the Maine Guide, the pear or palm, and the T. The Maine Guide, found mostly in one-piece paddles, is flat-topped and flared downward to blend into the

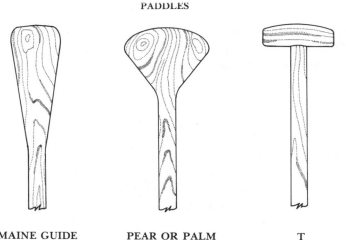

MAINE GUIDE   PEAR OR PALM   T

Paddle Grips

shaft. This flare is thinned to provide flexibility. The pear or palm grip is probably the most versatile, since it does not lock the paddler's hand into one position. This is my objection to the popular T grip. While the T affords the best control (it provides good hand and thumb leverage for changing the paddle's pitch), the fixed positioning of the hand is tiring. I find that my wrist, especially at the point where the ulna bone joins the hand (that little "bump" on the outside of the wrist), begins to pain me if I paddle with a T grip for more than half an hour or so. With the pear or palm grip, I can rotate my arm enough to shift the position of my hand, yet retain control. How many other paddlers may be plagued with this problem, I have no idea.

Most grips can be altered for a better fit. All it takes is a rasp for changing the contour, and sandpaper for a smooth finish.

Weight

The lighter your paddle, the less energy you'll dispense over a given distance. Competition paddlers, especially, like the fly-weights with which they can easily attain a racing beat of 70 strokes or more per minute. But their paddles are chosen from among the ultra-sophisticated designs, which are inherently expensive. An ultra-lightweight paddle in a low price range will probably end up as kindling for the evening campfire. If you want to save a few dollars, accept a few extra ounces. Even then, if you shop carefully, you can buy a reasonably light but sturdy paddle. Ned Sharples comes right to the point: "There is no need to use a paddle weighing more than 2½ pounds," he says.[1]

Critics of one-piece paddles often object not only to their length but also to their weight, a judgment apparently based upon the big maple 6-footers used by guides of another era. In truth, some of the one-piece paddles are not only beautifully crafted, but also lightweight. Shaw and Tenny, of Orono, Maine, produces a pair of 5-footers — the "1897" model, weighing under 2 pounds, and the Penobscot, at slightly less than 2½ — both well within Ned Sharples' specifications.

When buying any paddle, check not only the weight, but also how it is distributed. Balance it at the throat, just about where your lower hand grasps the shaft. The blade should feel noticeably heavier than the shaft. This makes for easier paddling, since the blade will tend to drop into the water by itself, or at least with minimal assistance.

The Bent-Shaft Paddle

There are still diehards who scorn the bent-shaft paddle. They should take a second look at it. First, though, consider what happens when you draw a conventional straight-shaft paddle through the water. As you initiate the stroke, power is thrust downward, and as you complete the stroke, power is thrust upward. This causes the canoe to bob or "porpoise" — imperceptibly when you're dawdling, but noticeably when you apply power strokes. The straight-shaft paddle is fully efficient only at mid-stroke, when the blade is perfectly vertical and is thrusting water back on a horizontal plane.

When a bent-shaft paddle is first thrust into the water, it too thrusts its power downward — of no special advantage at this point. However, almost immediately the blade attains a vertical position, and it remains there throughout most of the stroke. In other words, it directs its thrust horizontally much longer than a straight-shaft paddle does. This drives the canoe ahead with minimal bobbing, resulting in an efficiency increase of up to 10 per-

---

[1] *Canoeing and Kayaking, Canoe Magazine* (1983).

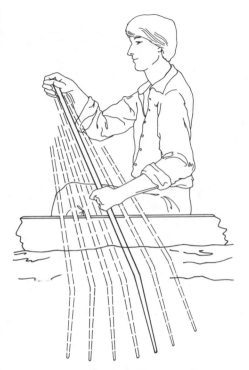

A bent-shaft paddle blade remains vertical through most of a stroke.

cent, according to Eugene Jensen, who devised the bent-shaft in 1971.

The bent-shaft paddle is at its best where a minimum amount of steering or course-changing is required. Marathon paddlers, who use short, quick, "chop-chop" strokes for speed rather than control, are probably the strongest boosters of the bent-shaft. It adapts well to touring on unobstructed waters, where quick maneuvering is unnecessary.

The degree of bend varies from as little as 5 degrees to 18. The greater the bend, the more efficient and longer-lasting are the power strokes. But there's a catch: the greater the bend, the greater the loss of directional control. That's why many paddlers, who want the best of both while "free-styling" on flat water, will choose a 5- to 7-degree bend. They get efficiency *and* better control.

There is on the market at least one paddle that has a double bend—a 14-degree angle on the blade, and another 14-degree bend in the shaft—but it's strictly a marathon paddle.

Bent-shaft paddles are invariably laminated, and their weight rarely exceeds 25 ounces. This tells us something. They are not

A double-bent shaft marathon paddle

Stowe Canoe Company's Beavertail, Otter Tail (Loutre), and Course paddles

meant for dawdling! They are high-speed, flat-water tools that will get you from point A to point B in the shortest possible time.[2]

Bob Hartt, whose Stowe Canoe Company, of Stowe, Vermont, produces the Mansfield canoes, has adapted a straight-shaft paddle to an ancient Passamaquoddy-pattern blade.[3] Its widest point, 6 inches, is located just below the throat and it narrows to 4¼ inches at the tip. Thus the bulk of the paddle's thrust is provided by the upper half of the blade. This, Bob says, has much the same effect as a bent-shaft paddle in reducing porpoising. He calls the paddle "Loutre" (Otter Tail). My tests of the paddle revealed that porpoising continues, though probably at a slightly reduced rate. I was much more impressed by his "Course" paddle, a square-tip reminiscent of the Sugar Island style. At slightly under 2 pounds, it is a delight to wield, driving my Prospector with ease. But, alas, the canoe porpoised noticeably.

[2] The January/February 1981 issue of *Canoe Magazine* includes a detailed evaluation of bent-shaft paddles based upon actual paddling tests. The October 1982 issue similarly evaluates the straight-shaft models. In each instance, specific paddles and manufacturers are identified and the test team's reports omit no details.

[3] See p. 81, Adney and Chapelle's *Bark Canoes and Skin Boats of North America*.

Chapter 26

·~·~·~·~·~

Paddling

MEANDERING DOWN THE SACO RIVER RECENTLY, watching the sandy bottom slip by, I was overtaken by a solo paddler driving his lean canoe at racing speed. He pulled alongside and we chatted.

"You're driving that canoe pretty hard," I said.

"I'm trying out a new stroke I read about," he replied.

I didn't enlighten him. His "new stroke" was a minor modification of the time-honored inverted sweep or hook. He did it well and was soon out of sight, his tiny wake wavering only slightly.

Watch any skilled paddler, whether he's negotiating a brawling rock garden or "free-styling" on a quiet backwater, and you'll notice that he makes dozens of moves per minute, employing deft turns and twists of his paddle. No two moves are exactly alike. Yet each one, if not a full-fledged paddle stroke, is a modification or a combination of one or more of the so-called standard strokes. Nor are they necessarily performed rhythmically. Each is adapted to the immediate situation.

On the other hand, a pair of paddlers cruising along on unobstructed waters, or eating up the map during a wilderness trip, will paddle in unison, with the bow paddler setting the pace. They will make few modifications of the standard strokes.

Some of the standard strokes — the bow rudder and the J stroke, for example — are little used nowadays, especially among highly skilled paddlers in white water. In fact, they have been termed outdated and useless. This is somewhat overstating the case. Of the more than 65 variations of paddle strokes, every one, at some point during its execution, involves at least partial use of the scorned old-time standards.

In fact there is a mistaken belief that some paddle techniques, notably the so-called "leaning strokes" such as the high braces, are "modern" — developed recently. This might be said of the Duffek stroke, introduced by Milo Duffek, a noted Czechoslovakian slalom racer, in 1953. The Duffek is difficult to describe with a typewriter, but it is essentially a turning high brace that is indeed a marked improvement over conventional braces. However, as C. E. S. Franks writes, " . . . it is not strictly accurate to call this style 'modern', for many Indian bands in northern Canada had used the techniques of leans for centuries." [1]

Whether your inclination is toward white-water running, wilderness tripping, solo "free-styling," marathon racing, or just plain paddling on a local mill pond, the basic strokes are a means to an end. Once you can execute them without a second thought, it's easy to move on to more complicated and sophisticated paddling.

Cruising Stroke

Whether you use it in the bow or the stern, this is the easiest of all strokes to learn, its sole function being to drive the canoe forward. The blade is brought forward, dipped, and drawn back along a

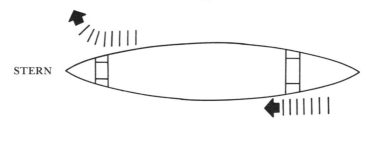

J STROKE   CRUISING STROKE

path that parallels the keel line, not the gunwale. This is the favorite stroke of tandem paddlers using bent-shaft paddles, since every

[1] C. E. S. Franks, *The Canoe and White Waters* (Toronto: University of Toronto Press, 1977).

bit of energy and power is directed at driving the canoe, not steering it. When it is applied in unison by marathon paddlers, surprising speeds can be attained. However, if one paddler plies more powerful strokes than his partner, the canoe will tend to turn off course slightly. Contrary to the old-time belief that switching sides is "uncanoemanlike," switching over every now and then will keep the canoe tracking straight and true. Marathon paddlers do it all the time.

J Stroke

Traditionally, the stern paddler has used the J stroke to counter a canoe's tendency to turn. He compensates with a backward sweep of the blade, twisting it and pushing away from the canoe, thus forming a J. This brings the bow back in line. However, it also slows the canoe and makes it difficult for two paddlers to synchronize their efforts. While the stern paddler is "J-aying," the bow paddler is already returning his blade to the water. Thus, the bow paddler must slow his beat to allow the stern paddler time enough to complete the J. Of course, if tandem paddlers are merely idling along, the J stroke can't do much harm. But for efficient, let's-cover-the-miles tandem paddling, the cruising-stroke techniques are far superior.

Pitch Stroke

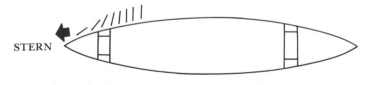

STERN

PITCH STROKE

The pitch stroke is started conventionally, but as the blade passes the hips of the stern paddler, it is gradually turned to form a rudder that, as it sweeps back, terminates with the flat of the blade parallel to the keel line. Unlike the J stroke, no side pressure is applied (although it could be, of course). It is important that the blade be kept fully immersed. It is withdrawn from the water in its "feathered" position, thus offering little wind resistance as it is brought forward. The pitch stroke, like the J, is a bit time consuming, although a skilled paddler can set a fairly fast pace with it.

Sweep Strokes

The greater the degree of rocker in a canoe, the more efficient are the sweep strokes. The full forward sweep is effected by reaching forward with the paddle in much the same position as that of an oar — as nearly horizontal as possible. It is then swept in a wide arc just below the surface until it returns to the side of the canoe. A full reverse sweep is identical, except that the blade starts its arc in back of the paddler and progresses to a point in front of him. Tandem

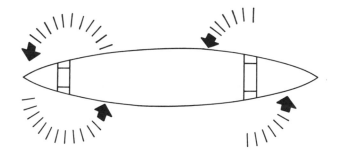

UPPER: FULL FORWARD SWEEP   UPPER: FORWARD HALF SWEEP
LOWER: FULL REVERSE SWEEP   LOWER: REVERSE HALF SWEEP

paddlers, each executing a full forward sweep on the same side of the canoe, will send it into a wide turn away from the paddles. However, a forward sweep at the stern and a reverse sweep at the bow, on opposite sides of the canoe, will cause it to pivot within its own length. A solo canoeist poised amidship can pivot the canoe in either direction with a forward or reverse sweep. The so-called half-sweep and quarter-sweep are simply abbreviations.

194

Inverted Sweep

To effect the inverted sweep while kneeling or seated amidship, the paddler reaches out with his blade some 45 degrees off his bow and draws the blade toward him. As it approaches the canoe's side, he then swings the blade away from it, in an exaggerated J-stroke motion. A modification is the hook stroke. By reaching out over the gunwale with the shaft as nearly vertical as possible, the pad-

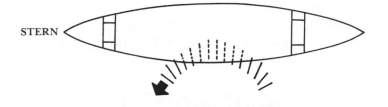

INVERTED SWEEP OR HOOK

dler sweeps the blade *under* the canoe, rather than alongside it and then outward. Depending upon how far under his craft he drives the blade, he can cause the canoe to turn slightly or sharply or simply to forge straight ahead. Tricky as it may seem, once you master it, you'll never be without the inverted sweep, hook, or call-it-what-you-will stroke.

Hold or Jam Stroke

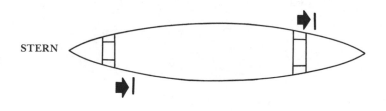

HOLD OR JAM STROKE

The hold or jam stroke "applies the brakes"; it can be executed in tandem or singly. The paddlers literally jam their paddle blades into the water at right angles to the canoe, in a vertical position.

This will stop the canoe's forward momentum quickly at slow speeds, but it requires four strong arms and wrists if the canoe is well under way.

Backwater Stroke

The backwater stroke simply entails reversing the cruising stroke. You paddle backward. It's a natural follow-up to the jam stroke: once the latter has slowed the canoe sufficiently, the backwater stroke brings the canoe to a full stop, even reverses its direction. It's not a commonly used stroke, but comes in handy in tight quarters when combined with other strokes.

BLUE HOLE CANOE CO.

Stern paddler initiating a draw stroke to realign canoe with current on the Rio Grande River

Draw Stroke

No white-water paddler's repertoire is complete without the draw stroke. In fact, without it, many a rough-water run would prove disastrous. The paddler reaches out at approximately a right angle from the canoe (though the angle can and does vary) and, with the flat of the blade facing him, draws it directly and forcefully toward the canoe. Especially in wild water, it is often performed as a quick series of choppy draws, rather than a single long pull. The bow paddler can guide the bow around a midstream rock with a draw stroke, while the stern partner pulls his end about to follow. The situations in which the draw stroke is useful are numberless.

George Walsh (bow) and Ed Menders, winning the national USCA short-class white-water race on the Esopus River in an old Sawyer Canadian. Note positions of hands as Walsh reaches for a cross-draw.

A skilled white-water paddler can execute a draw on one side of the canoe and then immediately — without shifting the position of his hands on the paddle — effect a cross-draw on the opposite side. When you see a paddler successfully executing a cross-draw in a difficult white-water situation, you are watching a master at work.

Of course, the draw stroke is not limited to use in wild water. It can be very effective in a lake traverse when wind and waves are running high. There, keeping the canoe headed on course can be difficult, and invariably the J stroke falls down on the job. But a well-executed draw will do it.

Push Stroke

The push stroke is the reverse of the draw, although it's not as easy to perform. The blade is dipped close to the gunwale, its face parallel to the keel line (more or less) and, held vertically, is pushed away from the canoe. It's not a gracious maneuver, and requires considerable brawn. It's of dubious value, except in combination with other white-water strokes. A far better maneuver is the draw stroke on the opposite side.

Pry Stroke

For a quick change of course, the pry stroke is effective. In white water, though, it can also be dangerous. As the name implies, the paddle is used to pry the canoe to one side. The blade is dipped with its face parallel to the keel line (again, more or less) at a point just in front of the paddler. Using the gunwale as a fulcrum, he pulls the shaft inboard so that the blade is thrust outward. Not only does this call for a rugged paddle, but there is also the possibility that the current or a rock will lock the blade against the canoe's side or, worse yet, sweep it under — so that the paddler must either release the shaft and lose his paddle, or hang on and possibly get flipped. The pry stroke is for experts who have learned to use it judiciously. On flat water, of course, the pry stroke poses few problems; but then, you rarely need it there.

Low Brace

The low brace serves two basic purposes: it keeps the canoe from slipping sideways, at least to some degree, and it stabilizes the canoe even when it is tilted almost to the gunwale. The paddler leans out and extends the paddle in a horizontal position as far as possible, so that the flat of the blade bears down on the water's surface. If a low brace is held for more than a moment or two, the blade will sink. In that case, simply "scull" it back to the surface. The low brace can be used in an emergency — when the canoe seems about to tip — or it can be used as a holding stroke. It's a frequently used stroke in white water. Properly done, your lower hand will grasp the shaft, knuckles up; your upper hand the grip, palm up.

High Brace

If there is one stroke that's mandatory in white water, it's the high brace. The paddler reaches out from the canoe as far as possible, holding the grip hand high above his head, and the blade in sculling position. Quite often the canoe is tilted toward the side of the

Bow paddler draws hard to his left to pull the Blue Hole OCA model's bow away from rock at lower left.

brace. As the paddler bears down hard on the water's surface, the paddle may be sculled to keep it from sinking. The high brace can be used simply to stabilize the canoe, or to initiate a turn.

Especially in white water, the brace strokes are likely to be used in combination with other strokes, the sweep, for example. A good illustration might be two paddlers running downstream in boisterous water. As they approach an eddy on the right, they decide to "eddy out," or slip into the eddy for a respite. Some knowledge of hydraulics is called for. A large boulder above the eddy compresses the main flow of water, accelerating the current. At the same time, water pressure below the boulder is diminished, so that the main current spills over into the quieter water. This creates the eddy, in which the water actually flows upstream. If the main stream is running at 5 to 6 knots, the eddy's upstream movement may be at only 3 knots. Between the two currents is the "eddy line." If the canoe crosses this line without proper guidance, one end will be thrust downstream rapidly while the other is caught in the slower

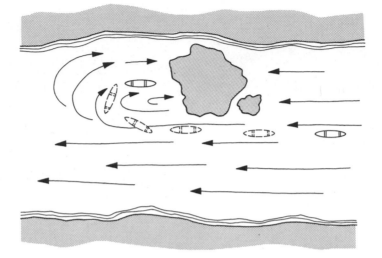

Eddying out. Canoe reverses direction as it enters the eddy.

eddy current. The canoe could well get out of control. In slow currents this is not serious, but in the present white-water situation, catastrophe hovers.

Coming down the right-hand side of a turbulent sluice, the paddlers first slow their canoe as much as possible. The bow paddler then executes a draw stroke on the right to pull the canoe's bow into the eddy line, following which he applies a high brace to pull the canoe into the eddy itself. The stern paddler is not along merely for the ride, however. As the canoe starts to enter the eddy, he applies a strong forward sweep on the left. In this position, he is also ready to go into a low brace to stabilize the canoe, if need be. Thus, with the use of a draw, high brace, sweep, and possibly a low brace, the canoe slips quickly into relatively quiet water, with its bow pointing upstream. Clearly, individual skill is required, but even more important is coordination between the two paddlers.

"Peeling out," or leaving that same eddy, also calls for synchronization. The canoe, pointed upstream, is slanted into the heavy flow in a ferry position, angled across the line of the current. The bow paddler executes a hard draw stroke on the right, and both paddlers lean somewhat downstream to minimize the current's grasp. As the canoe crosses the eddy line, the bow paddler combines draw and high brace strokes, which pull the bow downstream. The stern paddler executes a low brace to steady the craft. Once in the main current, the bow paddler goes into a series of quick cruising strokes — not for added speed, but rather for steerageway — while the stern paddler maintains a low brace, and is ready to apply a pry stroke to keep the stern from swinging too far out into the main current. Peeling out is an exciting maneuver, and like eddying out, it calls for synchronized precision.

Indian Stroke

Also known as the underwater stroke, the Indian stroke is "drip-less" and therefore silent. It is simply an underwater recovery in which the blade is not lifted out, but rather feathered and brought forward, edge first, parallel to the gunwale. The blade is then turned underwater for the next stroke. If you enjoy sneaking up to observe wildlife at close hand, master this stroke. It works.

Sculling Stroke

The sculling stroke might well be called the slowpoke version of the draw. It can be executed repeatedly, without withdrawing the blade from the water, to pull the canoe to one side. It is initiated

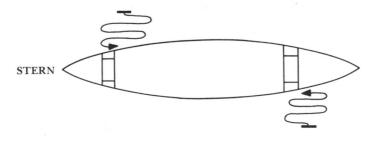

STERN

SCULLING STROKE

much like the draw stroke, with the blade parallel to the gunwale; but instead of drawing the blade directly toward the canoe, the paddler zigzags it back and forth, with first one edge leading, then the other, and each movement under pressure.

Bow Rudder

As the name implies, the bow rudder enables the bow paddler to turn the canoe. It is generally a flat-water maneuver. The turn can be made more sharply if the bow rudder is accompanied by a full forward sweep at the stern, on the opposite side. The bow paddler thrusts his blade into the water at an angle (which can vary) off the bow, and extends the blade as far as possible, while holding its face vertical (like that of an oar). His lower hand should be in back of the paddle shaft, so that it can provide bracing against the blade pressure. All in all, the bow rudder is not an exciting move and is rarely of great value. A draw stroke is quicker and more efficient.

The foregoing strokes are basic; the sophisticated variations that are possible are almost beyond counting. As Bill Mason stated in *Path of the Paddle,* "in fact, all the strokes can be used in a variety of ways and in endless combinations with other strokes."[2]

[2] P. 41.

Chapter 27

~·~·~·~·~·~

Reading White Water

WHITE WATER IS VERSATILE. It's congenial and cooperative, con-
niving and cantankerous, always beautiful. Next to running a
pitch, I most enjoy watching it, examining its quirks, plotting hypo-
thetical courses. No two sets of rapids are alike—in fact, a given
pitch may vary from day to day, sometimes from hour to hour. I
listen to tumbling waters, too. Sometimes the sounds are friendly
and inviting. Then there are rapids that give off a tumultuous roar
that grows ominously as you approach. White water expresses a
variety of moods, ranging from come-on-and-ride-it's-fun to I-
dare-you-to-try-me!

I frequently appraise rapids from the roadside, making hypo-
thetical runs that are invariably successful. I never hit a rock, never
deposit paint on a ledge, never gouge the hull. Plotting an actual
run, though, is another matter. I like to scout the rips from two
levels. From a high bank I can usually get an overall view, possibly
of the full length of the run. But this can be deceptive. Rips often
appear easier to run than they really are; height tends to flatten the
pitches. So I also go down to water level, where, if the rapids seem
somewhat rambunctious, I'm not averse to walking the entire
length. Here, I obtain a more realistic view of how a given pitch fits
into one of the grades established under the International River
Classification System:

Class I—Moving water with a few riffles and small waves. Few or no
  obstructions.

Class II — Easy rapids with waves up to 3 feet, and wide, clear channels that are obvious without scouting. Some maneuvering is required.

Class III — Rapids with high, irregular waves, often capable of swamping an open canoe. Narrow passages that often require complex maneuvering. May require scouting from shore.

Class IV — Long, difficult rapids with constricted passages that often require precise maneuvering in very turbulent waters. Scouting from shore is often necessary, and conditions make rescue difficult. Generally not possible for open canoes.

Class V — Extremely difficult, long, and very violent rapids with highly congested routes that nearly always must be scouted from shore. Rescue conditions are difficult, and there is significant hazard to life in event of a mishap.

Class VI — Difficulties of Class V carried to the extreme of navigability. Nearly impossible and very dangerous. For teams of experts only, after close study and with all precautions taken.

MAD RIVER CANOE/JAMES A. HENRY

A not-so-gentle chute

Classes IV, V, and VI are considered navigable only in kayaks or covered canoes, and the ability to perform the Eskimo roll is mandatory.

The American Whitewater Affiliation recommends that "if rapids on a river generally fit into one of the classifications, but the water temperature is below fifty degrees F., or if the trip is an extended trip into a wilderness area, the river should be considered one class more difficult than normal."

White-water paddlers in the American West, where kayaks and covered canoes are widely used, tend to downgrade western pitches a little. For example, a Class III rapids in the East would earn only a II in the West. Even in the East, though, some writers of river guides have reclassified the classifications. You can frequently find a pitch rated "Easy Class II," for example. Easy for whom? Joe Paddlecanoe, who placed third in the wild-water championships last year, or his cousin Waldo, who bought his first canoe last week?

This is not a how-to-run-rapids book; moreover, if you can handle Class IV or V water, you've no need for an instruction manual. But if your range runs from Class I through Class III, don't accept river-guide descriptions literally. A rise in water might alter a Class II run into a Class III invitation to disaster. On the other hand, a summer drought may convert a Class IV run into a bony passage that you probably can negotiate, albeit at the risk of leaving considerable paint on the rocks.

Scout each set of rapids individually and thoroughly. A cursory glance followed by the famous last words "Looks easy. Let's go!" is not enough. Once you're committed, there's no turning back; so know exactly the course you will follow. If you're paddling tandem, be sure that you and your partner agree on that course and on any possible alternate route.

Ideally, the bow paddler does the "guiding." His view is clearer. It's ludicrous for the stern paddler to act as "captain," shouting directions to the bow. In a tight spot, there simply isn't time for a consultation. An expert in the bow finds the "hole," heads the canoe into it, and the stern paddler sees to it that his end follows.

Single Obstructions

Among the obstructions encountered in almost any river or large stream are rocks, boulders, ledges, stumps, gravel and sandbars, bridge abutments, and "dead heads" — sunken or partially sunken logs left over from river-driving days. Such obstacles create chutes, pitches, sluices, drop-offs, eddies, waves, souseholes, and any number of combinations of cross-currents. For your initial attempts at white-water running, choose a river where obstructions are well spaced, standing waves are small, and drop-offs minor.

One of the "trail signs" is riffling of the water's surface in the form of a V pointing upstream, which indicates a rock or other object, barely submerged, at the apex of the V or a very short distance upstream of it. A similar V pointing downstream signifies that the current is flowing between two submerged, or semi-submerged, obstructions. A wide, smooth V generally affords safe passage.

At the other extreme is heavy flow of water over rocks and boulders of varying sizes, distributed pretty much over the entire river bed. While the aforementioned V's on otherwise smooth water are easily negotiated even by novices, the rapids created by a high-volume flow over many rocks call for skill generally beyond the scope of beginners. Stay in moderate water at first.

The leisurely turns typical of lake paddling have no place in swiftly flowing water; the current continues to carry a canoe downstream even as it is turning. This could bring you up broadside against the rock you're seeking to avoid. Keep the canoe

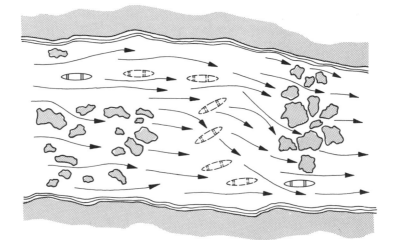

Ferrying from left to right bank

aligned with the current. When an obstacle looms ahead, slide the canoe sideways with draw strokes.

Learn to "ferry." In a downstream run, angle the canoe about 30 to 35 degrees and backpaddle. The current will then strike the upstream side of the canoe and thrust it toward shore, but you must apply paddle power to prevent the current from also carrying you downstream too far. The upstream ferry is even easier: simply continue paddling while keeping the canoe at an angle, and again, the current will "set you over."

River Bends

River bends are deceptive. The current is obviously swifter and deeper on the outside of the bend. But to complicate matters, as the main current strikes the outside bank, it sets up cross-currents that may be deflected back into the mainstream or rolled under. Trying to negotiate a bend of this sort by following the outside channel will almost certainly get you swept directly into the outside bank. The sharper the bend and the more powerful the current,

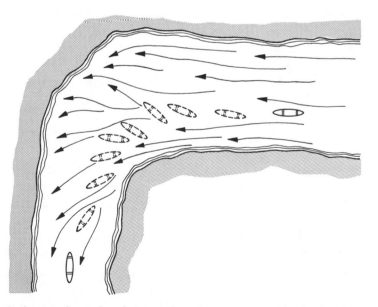

Negotiating a sharp bend. Note that the canoe avoids the outside of the bend.

the more likely this is to happen. Worse yet, at the lower end of the bend you may run into a "sweeper" or "strainer"—a tree that has fallen into the water with its roots still firmly implanted on the shore. The current plunges under a sweeper, and should you run into it, chances are very good that you will be rolled over and swept under, possibly even trapped among the submerged branches. Remain as far *inside* a bend as possible, even at the risk of running aground on a sand spit.

Riffles

You may scrape off a little paint here and there, but riffles are usually delightful runs. The waves are small and the water slips over a shallow bottom, usually gravel. Riffles are often free of major obstructions, but it's not unusual for them to be more or less littered with rocks protruding above the surface, yet still allowing ample passageway. Most riffles are low-water, summertime phenomena, completely buried during the high water of springtime runoff. The shallow water of the summer months makes paddling difficult, however, since the blades repeatedly strike bottom. I've seen canoeists run such rips by using their blades as poles—sacrilegious behavior of the lowest order! In such water, dip your paddles only partially, just enough to maintain steerageway, but not at the expense of chewing up your blade tips. Better technique is to bring the paddles inboard, and to snub with a setting pole.

Sluices or Chutes

These are swift runs of comparatively large volumes of water constricted into a narrowing channel, generating awesome power. A chute itself is often free of obstructions, since the force of the water has prevented the accumulation of obstacles. Usually the surface is smooth, with an almost polished look. As water slips by the point of constriction, the power is released; the fast-running flow strikes the relatively slow water below, thus setting up "standing waves" or "haystacks." Depending upon the size of the chute, the volume of water, and the gradient, the haystacks may be no more than a foot high or they may tower 4 to 5 feet! If evenly patterned and

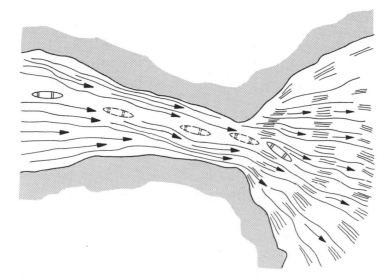

Running a sluice. It is important to avoid broaching in this situation.

regular in form, haystacks indicate deep water. Any noticeable break in the pattern, or any irregularity, is a sure sign of an underwater obstruction.

Sluices themselves are not difficult to run, if you keep the canoe aligned with the current. Speeding up the craft beyond the current's rate will maintain steerageway, but when you strike the haystacks, you'll probably "submarine" instead of riding up over them. The least you can expect is a lapful of water, and even swamping is possible. Paddle only enough to keep up steerageway, while concentrating on keeping the canoe aligned.

The tremendous power of a good-sized sluice drew respect from old-time river drivers as they shepherded logs down to the mills. When a driver slipped and fell in, which happened often, rescue was usually impossible. When a logger drowned in this manner, it was said that "he was sluiced!" They buried him by the river and hung his boots on a tree over the grave.

Drop-offs and Souseholes

These are among the greatest hazards of white-water canoeing. Whenever a substantial volume of water flows over an obstruction

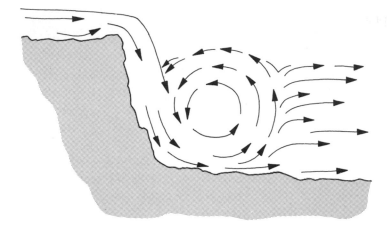

Reversal below a sharp drop-off in heavy water

such as a dam or ledge, a "reversal" is created. As water plunges downward, it strikes the bottom, then is forced upward in a circular motion; in effect, a wheel of vertically circulating water is created. What's more, a reversal is highly aerated, affording little purchase for a paddle and very little buoyancy for a canoe. Some reversals, particularly at the foot of dams, are big enough to engulf a canoe and its paddlers, and keep them spinning around and around until finally ejected into the current, the canoe a battered wreck and the paddlers beyond rescue.

A true sousehole differs somewhat from a reversal, in that the flow of water may come from several directions — from upstream over an obstruction, from the sides, and even from downstream, where rocks break up and shift the flow. As in a reversal, the water is greatly aerated. A small sousehole presents no serious hazard, but on a larger stream where flow exerts great power, a sizable sousehole can develop. Escaping from one may be difficult.

Eddies

While running white water is exhilarating, it is also quite tiring. Eddies are good "pit stops," not only as respites from hard paddling, but also for leisurely appraisals of what lies ahead. Eddies

Blue Hole Model MGA heading into a sousehole on the Rio Grande River. It made it!

were described briefly in chapter 26, along with the techniques of using the high and low braces, the sweep, and the draw strokes.

If you intend to "eddy out," you'll have to make a quick appraisal before leaving the main stream. An eddy that's too small to accommodate your canoe's circular swing into it can become a trap. Also, if it is dotted with rocks, proper maneuvering within the eddy will be next to impossible. Once you're committed to eddying out, it's difficult to change your mind.

Lining and Tracking

The need for lining downstream often arises during an extensive canoe/camping cruise. You arrive at a pitch too rough to be run, but you dread the thought of unloading all that gear and strug-

A tricky bit of navigating . . .

And a dousing. Both paddler and canoe escaped unharmed.

gling over the portage. Get out the rope! I used to carry two 50-foot lengths of ¼-inch manila for this and other camping purposes, but I've switched to nylon. It doesn't rot. Manila does.

How you line the canoe down depends, of course, on the availability of a passable sluice close to shore. This is not the powerful sluice described earlier, but one just large enough to accommodate the canoe. Attach the line to the tow ring or to the bow seat and guide the craft down, letting the current do the work. You merely keep it from running away, with a tight hold on the line. You may have to get your feet wet, although if you're lucky, you can perform the task while remaining on dry land.

If no such convenient streamside passage exists, you can resort to "rock hopping" in midstream, and possibly even wade a bit. If this seems an unpleasant prospect, consider the alternative — the carry trail and all that weighty gear.

Tracking upstream isn't quite as simple. Here the current works against you. Also, if you try to walk along the shore while towing the canoe, you'll have little control over it; almost certainly, it will repeatedly bump into rocks, and perhaps even hang up. Generally, wading and hopping from rock to rock is a more practical approach.

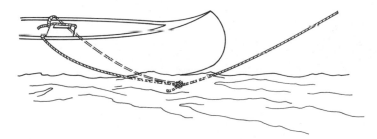

Towing harness or bridle for upstream tracking

Attaching the line to the tow ring or to the bow seat works badly, since pressure on the line forces the bow down just enough so that it "hogs" and weaves about. Instead, rig a towing harness by running a short piece of line from one side of the bow seat, under the canoe, to the other side. Tie the tow line to this piece at the keel line. Pressure on the line will now tend to lift the bow, and the canoe will track like a faithful Plott hound.

While wading, you can keep a steady pressure on the line by placing it over one shoulder and leaning into it as you work upstream. However, if you use it when hopping from rock to rock, this technique can spill you. Pull the line only when you're firmly implanted on one rock, and slack off a bit when you step to another.

As a rule, lining and tracking are practical only when you encounter relatively short rapids. To attempt either on a long set of pitches is often more difficult and tiring than making the portage.

This chapter, like the preceding one, deals only with fundamentals. It is not intended to be a white-water manual. The books listed in the bibliography are strongly recommended—and so is instruction from an experienced white-water paddler.

Chapter 28

⌒⌒⌒⌒⌒

Poling

When I arrived at Grand Falls on Maine's Dead River, I found the pool crowded, a dozen fishermen fruitlessly thrashing the water. Dropping downriver a bit and turning up into Spencer Stream, I poled against the shallow current for about an hour, to the mouth of Little Spencer Stream. Here, on a spit of land, I pitched camp, and nearby, proceeded to catch foot-long trout. I could have filled a packbasket! During the ensuing three days, I had that part of the river to myself.

Poling is often thought of as a competitive event, but there's more to it than bucking the rapids for a medal. It opens up waterways not usually considered "canoeable." Chances are that within half an hour of your home, there is a meandering stream too shallow for paddling. Such streams frequently wander away from highways into tiny bits of semi-wilderness, where minor riffles intersperse stretches of slow-moving water. Poking along these with a pole, it's easy to imagine that you're exploring waters where no man has passed.

There are practical applications, too. Many times my partner and I, upon arriving at the foot of rapids, have split up. One of us hoisted a pack to his shoulders to lighten the canoe and walked the carry trail, while the other maneuvered the craft up through the rips with the setting pole. I'm not sure that we actually saved time and energy, but it certainly broke up the monotony of upstream paddling.

Then, too, there's the delight of poling for poling's sake. The speed and ease with which you can propel a canoe always surprises a first-timer. In paddling, some of the energy expended is dissipated by the fluidity of the water. Not so with a pole, since the bottom of the stream has no "give." Every ounce of energy applied moves the canoe forward. Nor is brute strength required, until you tackle heavy rapids. And downstream poling can be exciting. Here the pole joins forces with the water to drive the canoe at exhilarating speed. In shallow water, either upstream or down, a pole will easily outrun a paddle.

Just how "tippy" does a canoe become in running water when you stand in it? Surprisingly, the force of the current tends to steady it. And, of course, the pole has a reassuringly stabilizing effect. Since poling is most effective in less than 2 feet of water, a spill need not be catastrophic. Getting to shore quickly is not usually difficult, nor is salvaging the canoe.

Avoid using a canoe equipped with a keel, if you want the utmost maneuverability. A shallow-arch or shallow-vee bottom is a bit unsteady at first, but you'll soon learn to position your feet to counter its teetering. If yours is a flat-bottom model, so much the better. This type of canoe tends to slide up and over the oncoming current, and it "sets over" or ferries readily. While it's not my favorite paddling canoe, I've found that the 18-foot flat-bottom Grumman with a river keel outperforms any other canoe I've ever poled.

Poles

Despite the fact that competition polers heap scorn upon my setting pole, I stick with it. (I've no idea where the term "setting pole" originated. It's been my experience that while using one, I do mighty little "settin"!) It's actually a logger's "pick pole" of ash, and was originally 14 feet long. During the days of log drives, pick poles were rigged with a sharp spike and a hook, somewhat resembling a yachtsman's boat hook. River drivers sorted logs with them, either pushing or pulling the logs into the correct sluice or boom. For canoe poling, Snow and Nealley, of Hampden, Maine, equips the pole with a soft-iron shoe that grips rocky surfaces without slipping. I used mine for several years before deciding that its 14-foot length was a nuisance when I carried it in one of my 16-foot canoes. So, I shortened it to 12.

A good friend who does a great deal of downriver canoeing, including running a few rips now and then, does his poling in a sitting position — with a hoe handle! I've run a number of streams with him, using my 12-footer. He gets along just as well with his hoe handle as I do with my professional pole — sometimes better!

Various types of "shoes" have been devised for poles, including the addition of a steel spike: blunt-ended, about ½ inch in diameter, and up to 12 inches long. A short spike — preferably no longer than 3 inches or so — is acceptable, but anything longer can well become lodged in a crevice, leaving the poler the choice of parting

BILL RIVIERE

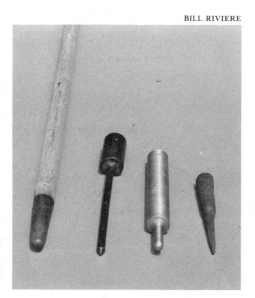

Canoe-pole shoes: author's pole with soft iron shoe at left; long spike can lodge in a crevice; short spike is acceptable; logger's spike, also acceptable

with his pole or parting with his canoe! Where the bottom is soft or muddy, a metal shoe offers poor purchase, since it sinks too far into the mud. In Okefenokee Swamp, for instance, polers attach a pair of curved sticks, 8 to 10 inches long, to form a fork that effectively keeps the pole from driving into the soft bottom.

Along northern canoe routes, it's not unusual for canoeists to cut makeshift poles of spruce, tamarack, or whatever is at hand. Especially among competition polers, however, new concepts in pole design have evolved. More than 90 percent of competition polers have switched to aluminum. Wooden poles survive only among traditionalists.

In their book *Canoe Poling*, Al, Syl, and Frank Beletz[1] suggest the use of a 12-foot, 1⅛-inch-diameter draw tube of 6061 T-6 aluminum, weighing between 2½ and 3¼ pounds, considerably lighter than any of the wooden versions. Such aluminum poles are plugged at each end, so they will float. The Beletz brothers also suggest that colored stripes be painted at 1-foot intervals along the pole, to help determine the water's depth. Since aluminum clings to rocky surfaces, a metal shoe is not an absolute necessity, although a steel shoe or spike does offer a better grip. The Beletz brothers also have developed the Sylvester pole, a 12-foot model weighing 3 pounds, which can be dismantled for carrying. Incidentally, although the Beletz book stresses competition poling, it is probably the best general publication on the subject, and is certainly must reading if you're serious about learning to pole.

The latest innovation in canoe poles is a two-piece, 14-foot fiberglass unit joined by a threaded brass ferrule. This does away with the nuisance of toting a 12- to 14-foot pole, but little else can be said in favor of it. The pole flexes readily — too much so, in fact. As a result, it is slow in directing the thrust against a stream bottom. Its "shoes" are plastic tips that tend to slip on smooth rocks or ledges. What's more, the fiberglass is susceptible to fraying when repeatedly rubbed against rocks, thus weakening the pole. All in all, this design is acceptable for recreational poling in an easy set of rips, but I would rule it out for serious work or competition poling.

Learning How

Naturally, before attempting to wield a pole, you should have acquired some skill with a paddle — enough so that you feel at home in your canoe. For your initial attempt, seek out a lakeshore with a firm bottom and a gradual drop-off; a swimming beach during the off-season is ideal, preferably one sheltered from the wind. A single passenger, seated on the floor aft of the bow seat, will help stabilize the canoe, and enable you to take a position just

[1] Al, Syl, and Frank Beletz, *Canoe Poling* (St. Louis: A. C. MacKenzie Press, 1974).

forward of the stern seat. If you're alone, stand back of the center thwart.

You don't have to poise gingerly over the keel line. Stand with your feet as far apart as possible, and face about 45 degrees off the port side, assuming you're right-handed. If you're left-handed, reverse the stance. Whether your pole is of wood or aluminum is immaterial at this point.

There are several strokes possible, but for starters, use the basic hand-over-hand, or "climbing-the-pole," technique. Grasp the pole about midway of its length, with your hands about 18 inches apart. Drop the end into the water, just back of your station and as close to the canoe as possible, until it strikes bottom. Apply a light backward thrust, as if trying to drive the pole into the lake bottom. As the canoe moves ahead, continue the pressure, using the hand-over-hand motion, "climbing the pole" until your hands reach its top. Go into a slight crouch and apply a final, firm shove. This last move is important: it will maintain headway when you tackle swift currents.

Although your initial pole thrusts may be gentle, perhaps even a bit hesitant, be prepared for a burst of speed you've never experienced while paddling. A canoe propelled by a pole is a lively craft; hence the need for the semi-crouch, to prevent the canoe from darting out from under you.

When your hands reach the top of the pole, lift it smartly out of the water with an upward and forward flip, sliding your hands back down to mid-pole position. Take another purchase and repeat the process, always striving for a smooth, rhythmic beat.

Keep the canoe's path parallel to the shore, in depths running no more than 18 inches or so. If the canoe tends to turn in one direction, or skids sideways a bit, alter the thrust of the pole. Practice this until you're able to keep the craft on a reasonably straight course. Next, try "snubbing."

Snubbing slows the canoe or brings it to a stop. Reach forward with the pole for a firm bite on the bottom, as close to the canoe as possible. As the pole strikes bottom, lean into it, flexing your knees. At slow speed, this will bring the canoe to an abrupt stop. At greater speeds, or in a fast downstream current, you may have to snub several times before coming to a standstill, or else the pole will tumble you over backward. Practice snubbing until you can perform it smoothly and confidently.

Poling Upstream

Next, seek out a shallow, slow-moving stream, relatively free of obstructions. Even in a slow current, keep the bow pointed upstream until you get the "feel" of running water. A short practice session here, and soon you'll be ready to tackle a stretch of water where Nature has strewn a few rocks about. Drop your pole into thrust position and hold the canoe while you plot your course.

Your first inclination may be to stick to the main channel, but this is not necessarily the easiest route. The mainstream may be too powerful or too deep. In this case, work your way upstream to one side, in somewhat shallower and less powerful flow. Take advantage of boulders, which create eddies that will carry you upstream. Stop often to determine your next move. Working from eddy to eddy is one sign of a skilled poler.

ELEANOR RIVIERE

The author poling up through Walker's Rips on Maine's Saco River

You will have discovered by this time that it's not absolutely necessary to keep the bow pointed directly upstream, as it was during your initial trials. Now that you've acquired a bit of skill and confidence, you can ferry from side to side, or around obstructions. Ferrying with a pole is identical to ferrying with a paddle. Point the canoe diagonally into the current, and apply only enough pole pressure to keep the current from pushing you downstream. Water pressure on the upstream side of the canoe will set it over.

As you move into swifter water, more powerful pole strokes are required, often at an accelerated pace. Because a canoe is so beautifully streamlined, the current cannot get a firm grip on it. It follows that so long as you exert a greater pressure on the pole than the current applies against your canoe, it will make headway. However, a good poler recognizes a superior force when he meets it. When you find yourself losing ground or at a standstill despite brute-strength effort, you're in water too powerful to be overcome. Try another channel, or graciously acknowledge defeat. It happens to all of us!

Downstream Snubbing

During downstream running "on the pole," let the current do most of the work. Do more snubbing than poling. In fact, during your first few downriver runs, pay more attention to guiding your canoe than to making headway. Keep the canoe at slightly under the current's speed, in order to maintain absolute control. If your canoe does not do exactly what you intend, you're probably running too fast. The more rocks there are, the more slowly you should run, so that if you do strike an obstruction, it will be a gentle bump. Striking a rock while poling at high speed will likely toss you out.

If it's not too deep or too rough, take advantage of the main current for travel with minimal effort. Incidentally, it's best to have the canoe slightly bow-heavy. This frees the stern from the grip of the current, so that you can set the stern over easily to follow the bow into a clear passage.

If your route suddenly becomes impassable, don't make a hair-trigger decision to change it. Snub to a full stop, and appraise the possibilities of other channels. If the flow is a mite strong, it's considered cricket to wedge the canoe gently against a rock, to help hold it while you search for another passage.

Bear in mind, too, that when you change your course with a

diagonal traverse, your canoe will automatically be borne down-stream, so that while you're trying to avoid one rock, you may strike another. The ferry, or diagonal traverse, is an apt move only if there's plenty of room. If not, snub to a dead stop and thrust the canoe straight sideways; in other words, cut square corners.

Variations on the Pole

While the hand-over-hand, or "climbing-the-pole," technique is probably best for precision work, especially in tight quarters, there are other strokes.

The so-called quick-jab method is effective in a swift, powerful run. The quick-jab calls for a single sharp push against the bottom, followed by a quick lift of the pole barely out of water, and then jabbing again. The position of your hands on the pole does not change.

Some of the "newer" strokes are not possible with a wooden pole, due to its weight, but they are effective when performed with an aluminum pole. The quick-jab, for example, is especially effective with aluminum, since there is less weight to lift. It's also possible to execute the hand-over-hand stroke on alternating sides of the canoe. This is less feasible with a wood pole, since its weight makes for a cumbersome series of strokes.

The "windmill" stroke is easily performed with an aluminum pole. After each thrust, the pole is twirled or rotated, so that first one end, then the other, is thrust against the bottom. This is usually executed on one side, although there is no reason why it cannot be alternated from side to side.

An aluminum pole can also be used like a kayak paddle, useful if you suddenly find yourself in deep water. From either a standing or sitting position, the ends of the pole are dipped into the water on alternating sides. Obviously the pole lacks the blades of a kayak paddle, but the metal shaft provides enough purchase to propel the canoe. It's an especially effective stroke during a downstream run.

All in all, once you have mastered the hand-over-hand stroke, the quick-jab, and the snub, you're well on your way to becoming a competent poler. I have used the kayak stroke on occasion, and I'll concede that it's better than hand-paddling. As for the windmill, it strikes me that it is easier and quicker to use the quick-jab or even the hand-over-hand stroke than it is to twirl the pole like a 12-foot baton.

In this chapter I have touched only upon the bare essentials of poling, but it should be enough to get you started. Even better, study the Beletz book thoroughly, and then take to the shallows with your pole. Like fly casting, the basics can be acquired in a very short time. You can then spend a lifetime perfecting your technique.

Poling doesn't necessarily mean endless hours of bucking relentless currents until your shoulder and neck muscles twist themselves into painful knots. At times, poling can be hard work. But every now and then, you'll come upon a swift downstream run that literally dances over a gravel bottom, with nary an obstruction in sight. Point the bow into it and drive the pole, drive it hard!

Chapter 29

~·~·~·~·~

Toting

IT OFTEN SEEMS THAT MY CANOE spends more time on my shoulders or on my truck than it does in the water. It rides from my barn to one river or another, where — almost inevitably — I tote the canoe over portages that range from a short lift over a beaver dam to a couple of miles over a trail that would stymie a pack mule. And every time, I vow that I'll find an easier method. I'm still looking.

Car-topping

In the past, lashing canoes atop automobiles posed some problems. For instance, how do you carry an 18-foot canoe on a 1937 Dodge convertible? It took a bit of contriving. We lowered the cloth top, and rested the canoe on the windshield frame and on the open rumble-seat cover. Tied snugly fore and aft, the canoe rode securely.

ELEANOR RIVIERE

The author's 18-foot Kennebec traveled hundreds of miles on a 1937 convertible without mishap.

BILL RIVIERE

The going was slower on a 1931 coupe, but it got there!

My struggles with car-topping have involved a number of vehicles: a 1931 Oldsmobile coupe, a 1934 Chevrolet sedan, an interim family wagon or two, a 1967 Jeep Commando, a Border Patrol squad car, and a couple of International Scouts. The basic problem has been that, more often than not, I've had to load alone. Single-handedly getting a canoe atop some of the older models verged on an Olympic weight-lifting event. In later years, when I switched to Jeeps and Scouts, their high profiles aggravated the problem. Those high lifts, especially at the end of a long day's paddling, were sometimes a bit torturous.

A second problem originated with the various car-top carriers I tried. Some of these perched on suction cups or rubber pads, the carrier held in place by adjustable straps that hooked onto the rain gutters. Others had "feet" that attached directly to the gutters, locked in position by various and sundry clamps. On smooth highways both types of carriers worked quite well, but once I ventured onto rough backcountry roads where bouncing was unavoidable, every one of the carriers either broke free or seriously damaged the gutters. The latter, in fairness, were sometimes to blame: some of the gutters were rather flimsy.

It was a no-win situation, until I acquired a low-slung mini–pickup truck. The cap over its bed is only about 4 inches higher than the cab. I had carrier bars welded at each end of the cap. Total height: well below eyeball level. Loading and unloading, even when I'm alone, is easy. Despite some rough-and-tumble backroad travel, the carrier bars remain solidly intact. Tying down is simplified, too. Using heavy-duty elastic shock-cord, I lash the canoe directly to the carrier bars. Since these are almost 7 feet apart, there is little tendency for the canoe to pivot. For added

BILL RIVIERE

Elastic shock-cords secure canoe to both the carrier and the truck. End tie-downs used in windy weather

security, I lash the canoe with another set of shock-cords, this time directly to cleats on the truck's bed. Usually this is adequate, but when it's windy, I also tie down each end to the bumper with nylon cord.

GRUMMAN BOATS

Foam blocks cushion the canoe; straps tie it down securely.

Despite my early problems with car-top carriers, they are not without merit. There are two basic types, the cushion and the crossbar. The cushion model consists of four foam blocks that fit over the gunwales and then rest directly on the car's top. A pair of over-the-canoe straps, which hook into the rain gutters or the door frames, hold the canoe and foam pads in place.

Crossbar carriers may be equipped with rubber or foam pads, the carriers held in place by straps attached to the rain gutters or door frames. Another type has "feet" that lock mechanically to the rain gutters. How well these hold depends on the design. Those that rely solely on the tension or upward pull of straps against the gutters are generally unreliable, since they may be dislodged as bouncing occurs on a rough road. A two-piece mechanical clamp that locks to the rain gutter from above as well as below is much more secure. The crossbar carriers, too, are equipped with straps with which to lash the canoe. Whatever type you buy, be sure the straps are nylon, not cotton, which deteriorates rapidly.

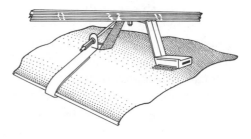

Crossbar carrier with rubber-coated "feet" held in place by gutter straps. Not always a secure arrangement.

Gutter-clamp or rubber-footed units are available minus the crossbar, so that you can build your own carrier, possibly one wide enough to carry two canoes. You have only to attach your own crossbars, at whatever length you want them.

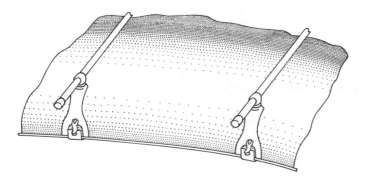

Crossbar carrier with "feet" locked mechanically to rain gutters

Gunwales riding on bare crossbars can be marred, even broken, especially on wood-trimmed canoes. You can provide padding by attaching a strip of indoor/outdoor carpeting, to metal crossbars with an epoxy adhesive, or to wooden crossbars with brass or copper nails.

No matter how well your carrier adapts to your car, if your canoe is not properly lashed, it could end up by the roadside in a heap. Worse yet, it could turn into a 75-pound javelin, plunging through another motorist's windshield.

Carriers that come equipped with only a pair of over-the-canoe tie-down straps might lead you to believe that's all the lashing you need. Not so. For highway travel, especially on windy days, tie down the ends with inverted-V lashings, by running each line from the canoe to the ends of the bumper, not to the center. This will keep the canoe from twisting or pivoting on the carrier bars. Otherwise, a crosswind gust or the blast of air created by a large truck can thrust the canoe out of alignment with the car. This not only causes greater drag or air resistance, it may also loosen the center tie-downs, or strain them to the breaking point. During a long haul, stop often to check the carrier and the lashings.

Camping gear can be carried in the inverted canoe, thus freeing space in the car for passenger comfort. However, don't assume that the duffel will remain dry in a rainstorm just because it's "sheltered" by the canoe. Water will be carried by the flow of air over the roof, so that within a few miles, the duffel gets a soaking. Wrap it in a waterproof tarp, or load it in wetpacks.

Portaging

Into every canoeist's life must come a portage, or two, or three . . . Few extensive trips are without one or more carries, over a ridge between two lakes, around a dam or a nasty set of rips. But a carry, no matter how arduous, can be a welcome break from the monotony of a lengthy paddling session. Body muscles need a change of pace; so does the spirit.

As you approach a set of rapids — when you first hear their rumble, or when they seem at hand on your map — look for the take-out spot. It is usually a natural landing, possibly a small beach or sloping ledge with signs of human activity, such as campfire ashes, cut poles, even litter. Along busy canoe routes, there may be signs to indicate the take-out. Old-time portages were marked by a "lob-tree," a tall evergreen whose uppermost branches had been cut away so that the bare trunk protruded into the sky, visible from some distance. Regrettably, lob-trees have disappeared.

About as rough as a portage trail can be, yet this canoeist handles it well alone

Blow-downs may obstruct a little-used portage trail, so the first person across should carry an axe. The length of a carry can be estimated on your map, using the scale—1 inch to 1 mile, for instance. However, since trails wind and twist with the terrain, add about 25 percent to the "scale" length. Some maps designate distance in "chains," which are a surveyor's measurement equal to 66 feet. Contour lines on a map will indicate the amount of climbing and descent that may be involved.

Carrying Yokes

Most yokes consist of a hardwood crossbar attached to the gunwales at midship by means of bolts and thumbscrews. The cushioning pads may be fixed or adjustable. Increasingly, manufacturers are installing permanent yokes in place of a center thwart, usually a hardwood crosspiece curved to fit around the neck and on the shoulders. This type generally lacks padding. Some built-in yokes are not sufficiently curved for a comfortable fit, and may press on the cervical rather than resting the weight on the shoulders. The problem can be solved by using a wool shirt or sweater as padding.

I have yet to encounter a commercially made yoke that is completely satisfactory. For a short carry, I'm satisfied with an ordinary center thwart as a yoke, cushioned with a sweater or shirt. For lengthy toting, the best possible yoke consists of a pair of paddles, lashed so that the flat of the blades rests on the shoulders. It takes mere minutes to rig, and it's only logical that the paddles should earn their keep ashore as well as on the water. Otherwise, they are a nuisance to carry. This type of improvised yoke works only with a center thwart. Lacking one, paddles can be lashed to the forward and the stern thwarts if these are not too far apart. However, in this case the paddle shafts, rather than the blades, will rest on the shoulders, requiring considerable padding.

The Tump Line

The tump line has been maligned by those who have never given it a fair trial. Fur-trade voyageurs using nothing else could carry a minimum of two 90-pound "pieces," and there are recorded instances of three or even four being trotted over the portages. Granted, they were professional packers who exulted in outdoing each other — much to the delight of the fur companies.

An occasional tump line appears on the American market, but it's invariably little more than a toy, too short to be practical. The original version, still in use in Canada, consists of a headband up to about 3 inches wide, generally of leather, to which is attached a pair of 6-foot leather thongs. I have heard that nylon webbing is also being used. The thongs are used to lash two or more packs together so that they will ride on the packer's back. He swings the load upward, rests the headband atop his head, and takes off with the load. The tump line directs the weight along the spinal cord, a far more efficient method than dangling the weight from the shoulders.

The tump line is also used for carrying canoes. Bob Cockburn, of Fredericton, New Brunswick, who guides extensive Canadian

BOB COCKBURN

Paddles rigged as a carrying yoke. Note tump line hanging below blades.

canoe trips, writes: "I regularly carry a 17-foot double-ribbed, wood/canvas canoe over some of the longest and most demanding portages in Canada. I could not do so were I not using a tump line."

Bob rigs all of his trip canoes with a carrying bar of cedar or pine, which is lashed securely to the center thwart. A pair of paddles is inserted into this lashing, and the tump-line thongs are laced into the gunwale apertures, leaving the headband slack. Thus, when the canoe is lifted, the band rests on the packer's head and the paddles rest on his shoulders; weight can be shifted from one to the other, or distributed equally between them.

My touting of the tump line for portaging a canoe is probably an exercise in futility. Except for my own, I have never seen one south of the Canadian border.

"Throwing" the Canoe

Experienced wilderness trekkers never lift a canoe. They "throw" it. Here's how it's done. Roll the canoe onto its side, with the interior facing away from you. Reach down with one hand as far as possible to grasp the center thwart or the yoke. Now, all in one smooth, continuous move, shove the canoe forward with your knees and, using both hands, propel the craft with an upward motion so that it rolls into an inverted position. Duck your head into the yoke or into place along the center thwart, and allow the canoe to drop gently to your shoulders. With one arm extended along each gunwale to balance the canoe, you're ready for the carry.

For a two-person carry, the lift is relatively easy. With the canoe right side up on the ground, one canoeist stands by the bow seat, the other at the stern, both on the same side. At a signal, each bends down and grasps the canoe, one hand on each gunwale; in unison, they lift the canoe, rolling it over as it rises. Once it is overhead, they lower it so that the forward edge of a seat rests on the back of each one's neck. Frankly, this can be a miserable carry unless ample padding is used. Each carrier can, of course, lift the canoe to relieve pressure. But even at best, it's not a comfortable carry.

MEYERS INDUSTRIES

These youngsters easily transport their Sportspal canoe with a two-person carry.

Two persons can also carry the canoe right side up, the ends resting on their shoulders. With a keelless canoe and a bit of padding, this makes for a fairly painless carry. A keel, however, will cut into the shoulders. Depending upon how much weight the packers can handle, some gear can be left in the canoe. A partially loaded canoe can also be carried with one person at each end grasping the edge of the deck as a handle.

Except in the case of an unusually heavy canoe or an extremely rough portage trail, the two-person carry is far from ideal. It's difficult for two people to synchronize their footsteps, and the uneven rhythm of each person's stride causes the canoe to bounce

MAD RIVER CANOE/JAMES A. HENRY

Four people can portage a loaded canoe for short distances.

erratically, jarring each paddler repeatedly. Coordination perfect enough to avoid this is virtually impossible.

Even a lone packer quickly learns that a "bouncy" stride has a jarring effect, as the canoe bobs up and down. You can alleviate this somewhat by walking with "swivel hips"—adopting a slinky, smooth stride.

Periodically there appear on the market various folding carriers, rigged with bicycle-size or smaller wheels. If the carry trail happens to be a gravel road, well and good, but I've yet to see such a rig work satisfactorily on a rough trail.

Any canoeist in good health should be able to "throw" and portage a recreational canoe, of up to 75 or 80 pounds, single-handedly. And with today's ultra-light tripping models, a one-person carry should pose even less of a problem. However, there is no place for heroics on a portage trail. Don't overdo it. Heed the warning signals—shortness of breath, or pain in the shoulders, neck, or chest. Lug the canoe alone only if you can do it gracefully. Keep the pace moderate, and the rest stops frequent. During a long haul, swap loads with your partner. You don't have to be miserable to enjoy a canoe trip.

Chapter 30

~·~·~·~·~

Learning How

MY EDUCATION IN CANOEING was a classic example of how not to learn and, subsequently, how not to teach.

My only textbook was *Deep River Jim's Wilderness Trail Book,* published by *Open Road for Boys* magazine. Deep River Jim advised on how to trap muskrats, how to build a campfire in the snow, how to catch peepers on a balmy June evening, how to recognize woods noises at night, and even how to build a log cabin. Jim also dashed off some rather skimpy observations on the subject of canoe cruising. And I treasured his words — particularly when, at age 14, I was finally allowed to use the family Old Town all by myself during our annual two-week vacation. Unlike Deep River Jim's typewriter perambulations, my "cruising" was limited. I had to stay within sight of the cottage.

I had just turned 17 when a dream job came along — canoeing instructor at a nearby camp for underprivileged boys. "Can you handle a canoe well enough to teach?" the camp director had asked.

"Oh, sure," I had replied. "I've done quite a bit of paddling."

It was not really a lie, but it fell far short of the full truth. Nonetheless, that was the extent of the interview and I got the job. I taught canoeing two hours a day. At least I then had my certificate as an American Red Cross Senior Life Saver. But as for my expertise as a canoeing instructor, it could justly be said that I was highly unqualified. The kids were shortchanged by a self-appointed "expert," while the camp director was grossly negligent in not checking my credentials.

Youngsters attending most summer camps now receive at least adequate instruction and supervision. The luckier ones fall into the hands of true experts and blossom into potential world champs.

Unfortunately, this cannot be said for the general canoeing public. Whenever I venture onto popular canoe waters, I run into paddlers who don't paddle; they flail. They zig when they want to zag. In white water, they point their canoes downriver and hope the rocks will get out of the way. Luckily, most of them escape any bodily harm; but their canoes take a beating.

Today's tough hulls are not substitutes for expertise. In addition, skill makes for fun. Just as in any sport, the better you are at it, the more you enjoy it. The pleasure derived is in direct proportion to your ability to make your canoe do exactly what you intend. Bobbing through a rocky set of rips surely and adeptly, that's canoeing! Easing stealthily to within camera range of a deer standing in a reflected sunset, that's canoeing! But you gotta know how.

With the help of one of the dozens of instructional manuals, teaching yourself is not difficult. It will just take a little time. Two novices, working together, are better than one. Mutual criticism will help you both to progress rapidly. Stick to the easy stuff; leave the fancy maneuvers for later.

One-on-one instructions are ideal. You will learn more quickly from a friend or relative who has had a few years of experience. Don't be shy about asking someone to teach you. Most of us who have attained some degree of paddle skill enjoy displaying it and passing it along.

Canoe clubs often schedule training sessions that range from the elementary to competition levels. Beginners' classes are frequently open to the public for a small fee. Canoeists are a gregarious lot, and most clubs want to see their membership grow. Teaching newcomers nurtures this growth. If there is no club in your area, check with the local chapter of the American Red Cross. Its water-safety programs often include canoeing.

Public school systems have moved into canoeing, too. Many high schools' adult-education programs schedule evening sessions. Sitting in as an observer, I watched Peter Brawn, a 12-year-veteran Maine guide, conduct such a course. It included three two-hour evening classroom sessions at Westbrook, Maine, High School,

LINCOLN CANOES

Small groups allow an instructor to give individual attention.

during which he used copious amounts of chalk to explain canoe types, paddle strokes, and the foibles of running water. He drew on his prodigious store of canoeing anecdotes, some amusing, some downright dramatic, to illustrate various points. A fourth evening was spent in canoes in an indoor swimming pool, where classroom theory was put to practice. The course concluded with two one-day trips on nearby rivers. None of the students had become an overnight expert, but each was well on the way to competence.

There are also commercially operated schools. Don't be put off by the commercial aspects; the instructors are often topnotch professionals and national champions. You'll probably learn more quickly from them than from anyone else, and you'll be exposed to highly technical paddle skills, something you won't see on your neighborhood millpond. Courses range from one day up to a week, at all levels of expertise.

Often the courses are "packaged," incorporating lodging and meals, equipment, and even local transportation. A discount may be offered if you provide your own gear. Daytime sessions are conducted on the water, while evenings are devoted to classroom instruction that uses movies and slides as visual aids. There is generally a low student-to-instructor ratio — as low as three to one — so that individual attention is possible. If you're a starry-eyed neophyte, these schools will teach you to recognize the bow from the stern and go on from there. If your skills are already advanced, you may even qualify for the American Canoe Association Instructor certificate, an award not easily attained nor casually handed out.

Commercially operated canoeing schools are not numerous, but their numbers are growing. Each of the rivers on which instructions are given might well be called the Tiffany of canoeing waters: the upper Hudson, the Ottawa, the Petawawa, the Nolichucky, the Youghiogheny, the Androscoggin, the Wolf, the Red, the Peshtigo, the Sacandagas, the Salmon, the Sacramento, and the Klamath (see the appendix).

Regrettably, the opportunities for learning to repair canoes are much more limited, even in this era when canoe construction methods and fabric combinations have reached new heights of complexity. In the days of wood-and-canvas, simple tools and a tube of Duco or Ambroid cement were all you needed. Today, with proprietary lay-ups, fiberglass, Kevlar®, and the "near-indestructibles" — Royalex®, polyethylene, and aluminum — repairs are no longer a simple "patch-up" job.

There are several excellent building and restoration manuals from which you can glean repair tips, but using this method, you're on your own in transforming theory to practice. A canoe builder who operates a small shop might be willing to teach you repair techniques, perhaps in exchange for a few hours of labor. Canoe clubs also conduct repair clinics. During the spring months, L. L.

Bean, of Freeport, Maine, conducts clinics during which actual repairs are made.

Perhaps you'd like to build a canoe, possibly a stripper, but you're hesitant about tackling the project. Check your local high school's adult-education department for a program like the one conducted by Gil Gilpatrick (see chapter 14). Or perhaps a local builder will take you on as an apprentice, in return for a bit of assistance in the shop. No harm in asking!

Horace Strong, a Craftsbury, Vermont, builder, offers a nine-day course limited to eight students, who build a 16-foot wood-and-canvas canoe under his direction. Walter Simmons, of Lincolnville Beach, Maine, conducts a similar course in which students produce a lapstrake canoe. At both schools, the students draw lots when the course is completed. The winners take the canoes home.

Learning to paddle, repair, or build canoes is much like running an endless river. Around every bend there is a new revelation, a new idea, a new way of doing.

Chapter 31

~·~·~·~·~

Safety

EVERY YEAR, IN MY HOME STATE OF MAINE, up to half a dozen canoeists lose their lives, usually during the early part of the season,
while either fishing or running white water. Considering the thousands of paddlers on our waters, that's a good record. But not for
the families of the victims, certainly. The record can always be
improved.

Let's face it, though. Canoeing will never be as safe as prayer
meeting. Not that canoes themselves are unsafe. I've never known
one to flip over of its own accord. Somebody flipped it!

Accidents occur within three segments of canoeists: individuals
or unorganized groups who tackle water beyond their capabilities,
or who fail to take adequate precautions during seemingly routine
excursions; organized river-runners, usually members of clubs,
who maintain the best safety records of all; and boys' and girls'
summer-camp trips led by counselors ("trip leaders") who may, or
may not, be thoroughly competent.

Going It Alone

Much of canoeing literature addresses the potential dangers of
running white water with the standard admonishment: "Don't
paddle alone. Three boats is the minimum." But what about flat
water? Are you at risk if you go alone? That depends.

If you're a novice who has wet a paddle perhaps half a dozen
times, the answer is probably, "Yes—you are at risk." And the
bigger the water and the farther you stray, the greater the danger.

On the other hand, if you have some experience under your belt, the risk diminishes as your skill level rises. Only you can make a fair appraisal. Be objective.

I can tolerate my own company; so I relish going it alone, having done so for more years than I like to admit to in print. Yet, I'm ever conscious that I might make a mistake; that I might run into a situation where I'd eagerly trade my lower 10 acres for a helping hand. I've no lack of confidence, but always in the back of my mind lurks a faint nagging. "What if . . . ?" But I go and I enjoy every moment.

No one has the right to dictate whether or not you can paddle alone safely. That determination must be yours. While the following are not hidebound rules, they are certainly guidelines that will help you make that determination:

- Wear a life jacket. It's not a proclamation to the world that you are insecure or that you are incompetent.
- Be at home in the water, as well as on it. If you cannot swim well, don't paddle alone, not even while wearing your life jacket.
- Be able to execute the standard paddle strokes without having consciously to figure them out. Your responses should be automatic.
- Be able to recognize signs of approaching severe weather, especially thunderstorms, which often generate winds that will peel the sod off a root cellar.
- Don't paddle so far on your outward leg that you'll become exhausted during the return. A weary canoeist is not at his best.
- Let someone know where you are going and when you expect to return.
- Carry a spare paddle.

There is a caveat. Even if you can comply with all of the foregoing, cold water adds considerably to the hazards. Wearing a wet suit (more about these later) alleviates that hazard somewhat. Nevertheless, paddling alone on icy waters must rank as foolhardy.

Upwind

Why is it that casual lake paddlers, out for a leisurely cruise, almost invariably head downwind, delighting in the ease with which the canoe travels? When they turn around, they suddenly discover that "the wind has come up." It may or may not actually have risen, but it certainly has a longer sweep when you're paddling into its teeth, and the waves are definitely built up. The return trip is no longer fun; it's a somewhat frightening struggle. Paddling upwind from a starting point makes more sense. The return leg, with the wind, is then an easy one.

The same principle applies to stream paddling from a cottage or other fixed point. Paddle upstream initially. Then, later in the day, when weariness sets in, let the current carry you home.

Wind and Waves

Sooner or later, if you cruise large lakes, you'll run into heavy winds and heaving waves that will toss your canoe around like a beach ball. We tend to think of lakes and large rivers without rapids as "flat" water. In truth, wind-whipped surfaces can be as turbulent as an ornery Class III rapids.

You may choose to challenge whitecapped waves for the sheer excitement they afford. However, if your canoe is heavily laden with a trip outfit, good sense dictates that you seek a lee shore, even at the cost of paddling extra miles to reach your destination. The alternative is a one-sided contest: while you grow weary in the struggle to make headway, the waves do not tire. They just keep coming, and coming . . . Once you're tuckered out, it's easy to make a false move.

If you must work your way upwind, "quarter" into the waves, keeping the canoe at about a 30-degree angle to the combers so that it climbs them "slanchways." There will be no time for the leisurely strokes of flat-water paddling. Short, choppy strokes are necessary. Nor is it feasible for two paddlers to try to dip their paddles simultaneously. In fact, alternating the strokes, one blade always in the water, will hold the canoe on a steadier course and help to stabilize it. Even if you find yourself held to a standstill occasionally, keep digging. Lake winds are gusty, and often interspersed with lulls. It's during these lulls that you'll make headway.

Downwind

Running downwind in heavy seas can be exciting, not unlike dropping through a set of boisterous rapids. Paddle only enough to maintain control. Let the wind and the waves carry you. In fact, you'll discover that when a wave lifts your canoe to its crest, you can hold the canoe there using the stern paddle as a rudder, for a few moments, and surge ahead at surprising speed; you're actually surfing. The wave will outrun you, of course, and drop your stern into the following trough. Now is the time to ply the paddles, since you'll be traveling uphill momentarily. When you've once again been lifted to the crest, go back to steering.

As you progress downwind, the combers will grow larger and more powerful. How long you can continue to ride them depends upon your skill. But don't push your luck. Whether you're surfing downwind, or struggling upwind, it's wise to work your way gradually into the lee of an island or point of land. And, of course, while you're in such turbulent waters, keep your center of gravity low by kneeling, and wear your life jacket.

Cold Water

Canoe-related fatalities often occur early in the season. This is when the rapids are most challenging, the water high and barely a few degrees warmer than the ice and snow from which it originated only a few hours before. A life jacket will probably keep you from drowning should you capsize, but this may be little consolation, since the shock of sudden immersion in frigid waters has been known to cause cardiac arrest. Even if you survive the initial shock, you must extricate yourself (or someone else must haul you out) immediately. Otherwise, you're an instant candidate for hypothermia.

This occurs when the body's inner-core temperature is lowered. The longer the victim is exposed — remains in the water — the more severe the effects. The initial symptom is shivering. If the victim is not warmed, shivering will accelerate, speech become slurred, and incoherent, lack of motor control, and lack of judgment become evident. After a while, shivering will cease. This is a signal that the victim is going into the advanced stages of hypothermia. Unconsciousness may follow. Death occurs when the body's inner-core temperature drops into the low 80s. Cold water affects different people at varying rates, but immersion in 40-degree water can result in death within 15 minutes, or even sooner.

Strangely, swimming or treading water aggravates the condition, since it accelerates the flow of chilled blood from the extremities to the torso. If rescuers trying to reach you are at hand, remain still, floating in a semi-fetal position, knees drawn up somewhat and arms folded across the chest. If would-be rescuers cannot reach you immediately, it's then logical to try to work your way toward them, or to shore.

Since a victim's condition continues to deteriorate after rescue, instant treatment is imperative. Ideally this consists of a warm bath in water heated to 105 to 110 degrees Fahrenheit—an unlikely possibility at streamside. Instead, undress the victim, and place him in a sleeping bag or roll him up in blankets along with one or two other people, also disrobed. In this way, rescuers transmit their body warmth to the victim. They should concentrate on warming the torso, not the legs or arms. If the victim is conscious and able to swallow, give him warm drinks, but under no circumstances administer an alcoholic beverage.

There's a far better approach to hypothermia: prevent it. Wear a wet suit. These vary in design somewhat, but a popular model is made of nylon-backed, ⅛-inch-thick foam that insulates the body against chilling. It also provides some flotation, though not enough for rough water. Wear a life jacket over the wet suit.

Spilling in the Rapids

One of the major dangers associated with swamping in heavy rapids is the possibility of being pinned against a rock by your canoe, or even worse, being held underwater by it. When filled

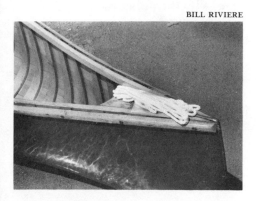

BILL RIVIERE

Grab lines or painters are held out of the way with tape until needed.

243

with water, the craft becomes a projectile whose power to crush is not unlike that of a runaway truck. The moment you spill, get upstream of the canoe; hang onto it if possible, or at least latch onto one of the grab lines with which it should be equipped. If there's a chance you can salvage the canoe without danger to yourself, try to work it toward shore, keeping the bow or stern pointed into the current, never broadside to it.

Should the canoe become solidly lodged, there's no point in further midstream risk. Simply stay with it until another boat can reach you, or until someone can get a line to you. If neither is possible, try to work your way toward shore or toward rescuers, taking advantage of rocks that deflect the forces of the current.

Occasionally, a canoe will float away freely with the current. Hold onto the upstream end and float with it, keeping your feet close to the surface and in front of you. Should you drag your feet, one of them could become lodged between sunken rocks; if the current is powerful enough, it could suck you under and hold you there. Of course, if an obvious danger spot appears below your position, let the canoe go. It's expendable.

If someone else spills, forget about the canoe for the moment. Concentrate on rescuing the paddler, even if there's a chance that his craft will be wrecked. Once the paddler is safe, then try to salvage the canoe.

Life Jackets

I'm inclined to balk at calling a life jacket a "personal flotation device," the official Coast Guard designation. "Life jacket" is less of a mouthful, which helps explain why the abbreviation "PFD" is also in common usage.

Life jackets are classified as Type I, II, III, and IV. The latter is not actually a life jacket, but rather a buoyant seat cushion, which is next to useless except when used as a "life saver" with a throw line attached to it.

The Type I jacket is quite bulky, more likely to be found aboard offshore boats than in a canoe. The Type II is the so-called horse-collar model, with buoyancy chambers located on the wearer's chest and at the back of the neck. It provides sufficient buoyancy,

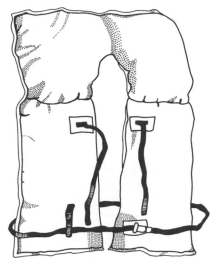

Type II life jacket, best known as a "horse collar"

but affords little protection for the body against rocks, since the back and sides are unprotected. Most practical is the Type III, which encases the upper torso completely, yet thanks to ample armholes does not interfere with paddling. It consists of five to ten layers of foam sandwiched between an outer shell of nylon and a mesh interior lining; the entire unit weighs less than 2 pounds.

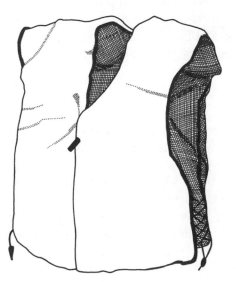

Type III nylon/foam sandwich life jacket

245

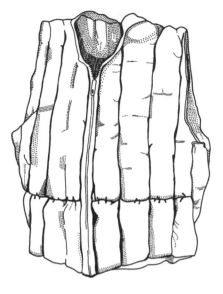

Another Type III life jacket,
with foam-filled compartments

Another Type III model is made of segmented vertical tubes of nylon, filled with polyethylene foam. It weighs about 1 pound, yet provides adequate flotation and protection against rocks. The better Type III styles are "hinged" so that the bottom segment folds upward into the paddler's lap when he is seated.

A properly fitted life jacket should not hamper paddling, yet should be snug and secured so that it cannot slip off. It should be large enough to fit over a wool shirt or jacket in cool weather, and certainly over a wet suit. Choose a bright color—yellow, red, or orange—so that rescuers could spot you readily.

Trip Organization

It's not surprising that canoe clubs have an enviable safety record. Most of them subscribe to the safety code of the national canoeing organizations. All three, the American Canoe Association, the United States Canoe Association, and the American Whitewater Affiliation, abide by essentially the same code.

Especially for river travel, the code mandates that a trip include at least three canoes, and that paddlers be competent swimmers, that they wear life jackets, and that they be sufficiently skilled to keep their canoes under control at all times. The latter includes being able to stop the craft in midstream, or to work it toward shore before reaching a danger spot. Paddling ability may be waived to some degree for training or instructional trips, but in that case, additional qualified leaders or instructors are required.

Trip leaders have considerable responsibility. They must even check footwear to see that paddlers are wearing shoes that protect the feet adequately (for swimming in rocky waters or for walking out for help). Tennis shoes are recommended. Trip participants may be required to carry a knife and waterproof matches, for backcountry emergencies.

Trip leaders also check to see that all canoes are in sound condition. This goes for paddles, too, with a spare in each canoe. Repair kits may also be required, and — when rough water is anticipated — extra flotation. Leaders examine life jackets to be sure that no buckles or tie cords might snag in an upset. They may also disqualify from the trip any canoe whose seats are set too low, thus doubling as "bear traps" for a paddler's heels when he tries to escape during an upset. Bow and stern grab lines are required, at least 8 to 10 feet long, secured on the canoe in such a manner that they will not work loose until needed.

And there's still more required of a trip leader. He should know the river well; or, if it's an exploratory trip, he must be able to read maps accurately. During the trip, his word is law, his decisions final. Unless all members of the party are highly skilled, there's little room for democracy. In making decisions, the trip leader must take into account the varying levels of expertise within the group.

Next in command is the "sweep," the last canoe in a brigade. The sweep sees to it that the group paddles in a compact formation. He never allows canoes to string out so that they become too far apart for mutual assistance. And under no circumstances will a sweep allow a canoe to drop back of him.

If the trip is headed into a wilderness area, a float plan is filed with appropriate authorities. Contact points along the route are established, too, so that communications with the outside are possible.

I've probably omitted a few details involved in the planning and conducting of a club trip, but the foregoing explains why this type of group has such a fine safety record. Nothing is left to chance.

Summer-Camp Canoe Trips

During my guiding days I frequently encountered summer-camp canoe trips. Some were well-organized, orderly groups, closely spaced, the youngsters wielding their paddles like latterday voyageurs. Nor did they seem regimented: there was plenty of banter and shouting, and — whether boys or girls — it was obvious they were having fun. Other groups were having "fun," too, but their canoes were sometimes strung out over a mile of open water, some beyond shouting distance of the counselors, the interior of the canoes so cluttered with loose gear that they resembled floating rummage sales. And, of course, there were the usual "water fights" — kids splashing each other with paddles whenever one canoe managed to approach another.

Camp directors face special problems when planning canoe trips for their charges. Counselors or trip leaders are usually of college age; some may be quite skilled with a paddle, while others are barely out of the novice stage. Some states require trip leaders to be licensed, much like hunting and fishing guides; other states have few if any regulations. To compound these problems, skill with a paddle varies greatly among the participating youngsters. Then, there's the psychological effect of escaping the regimen of everyday camp life, with its many rules. It's easy for the youngsters to bust loose with a certain amount of hell-raising on a canoe trip.

All too often, trip leaders are indifferent to this; they put in their time and draw their pay, rather than directing excess energy into useful channels. My son-in-law and my daughter once went ashore on a Maine river to watch loggers at work, leaving their canoe beached. While they were up on the hillside, they happened to look down, just in time to see a canoe brigade draw up and steal their life jackets, as the trip leaders looked on laughingly! The canoes were later identified as belonging to a well-known and reputable boys' camp.

One solution is for the camp director to put a full-fledged professional guide in charge of canoe trips. Few camps do this, however, being either unwilling or unable to pay a guide's wages. Trip leaders work for much less money.

The alternative is to require that every trip leader have completed a training course such as those offered by the American

Canoe Association. What's more, every member of the trip group should be made to comply, where appropriate, with the ACA safety code. Any serious violation of the code by a trip leader should mean dismissal; any violation by a participant should mean barring him from any future trips. Harsh? Perhaps so, but not when you've watched game wardens dive for the body of a youngster who decided to run the rapids when his trip leaders left their charges alone in order to scout the pitch.

Frankly, I find safety a dull subject, and there are "free spirits" who resent the slight regimentation that safety rules impose. However, no one has guaranteed me that there are clear-running rivers and canoes in the Next Life, so I want to stick around in this one as long as I can.

Chapter 32

·٠ᖭ·᠊ᖭ·᠊ᖭ·᠊ᖭ·᠊ᖭ·

Canoe·Camping Gear

Tents

SLEEPING UNDER AN OVERTURNED CANOE HAS ROMANTIC APPEAL, but it can lead to misery. Either the bugs, the rain, or both will get to you. Modern tents are light, easy to erect, stable, and — if you choose the right size — spacious. There's little logic in doing without one.

Nylon — tough, light, and mildew-proof — is now the standard fabric. Three types are used: rip-stop, taffeta, and coated nylon. Rip-stop has reinforcing threads woven in at intervals of 3/16- to 1/4-inch. It is extremely difficult to tear. Taffeta may sound flimsy. It is not; it is, in fact, probably more abrasion-resistant than rip-stop. Coated nylon is waterproofed with polyurethane or vinyl.

Double-wall tents have solved a problem that has long plagued campers: interior condensation. The human body exudes roughly two pints of insensible perspiration per day. Additional moisture is brought into the tent on rain-soaked clothing, even sweaty socks. All of this moisture vaporizes and floats upward to the tent roof. If the roof is waterproof, the vapor cannot penetrate it and be released. It cools quickly, condenses, and falls back into the shelter as water. On the other hand, if the tent fabric allows these vapors to pass into the atmosphere, it will also allow rain to penetrate.

So the double-wall tent was devised. The shelter itself is made of rip-stop or nylon taffeta that is not waterproof. Vapor passes out through it. The outer wall, a urethane-coated waterproof fly, is draped over the tent, leaving an air space between the two. The outer wall turns back the rain, while interior moisture is dissipated in the air space between the tent and the fly. Unless you're doing your canoe camping in an arid region where it seldom rains, don't settle for anything other than a double-wall tent.

During the era of cotton tents, ground moisture was absorbed into the sewed-in floor, which soon rotted it. Today's sewed-in floors are of vinyl-coated nylon, not only waterproof and rot-proof, but remarkably durable. A European innovation is now commonly available in North American tents: the tub bottom. This is a coated-nylon floor that extends a few inches up the side-walls. It keeps out rain runoff, eliminating the need for "ditching," or digging a runoff trough around, a tent.

But there are still the bugs. Most insect netting will turn back mosquitoes, black flies, deer flies, and moose flies, but not the ubiquitous midges or "no-see-ums." These are tiny, barely visible insects whose sting results in a sharp, burning sensation. A recent development is no-see-um insect netting, the weave fine enough to keep the tiniest insects from penetrating.

As for tent size, you'll need a minimum of 12 square feet per person. That's 2 feet by 6 – hardly luxurious accommodations. You will also need space for packs. Today's tents are rated according to capacity — "two-man," "four-man," etc. — but such ratings can be deceptive. The following chart illustrates this:

CAPACITY	DIMENSIONS	AREA	PER-PERSON AREA	WEIGHT
Two-man	5'3" × 7'2"	37.6 sq. ft.	18.8 sq. ft.	7 lbs. 14 oz.
Four-man	7'2" × 8'9"	62.7	15.7	9 14
Six-man	10'3" × 8'6"	87.1	14.5	17 10

Note that the four-man tent is not twice as large as the two-man version. In fact, the larger the tent, the smaller the space per occupant. For a two-canoe, four-person trip, the four-man version would probably be a poor choice, although its "four-man" designation suggests otherwise. A pair of two-man tents or a six-man model might be better choices. Having to "go outside to roll over" doesn't make for sound rest. A good rule to follow: buy a tent slightly larger than you think you'll need. The extra weight and bulk are trivial.

Suspension systems (they used to be called "tent poles") are usually flexible fiberglass wands or tubular aluminum sections that fit into fabric sleeves on the tent's exterior, eliminating the nuisance of interior poles. These systems flex, to ease tension on the fabric or to take up slack when the wind blows. Fiberglass wands are connected by means of ferrules not unlike those on fishing rods. Aluminum sections are connected with elastic cord, so that matching section A to section B no longer requires trial and error.

Thanks to these ingenious systems, tents are freestanding, requiring neither guy lines nor stakes unless strong winds rise (although the outer wall, or fly, may require short lines and a few stakes). Suspension wands or sections should be carried in a separate bag. Wrapping them directly in a folded tent can damage the fabric.

For generations, the traditional canoe tent has been the Explorer. There's an aura of the North about it, and its very name conjures up visions of faraway places. However, it requires a minimum of six guy lines and a dozen stakes. There are now better tents, lighter and easier to set up.

EUREKA! TENTS

Double-wall A-frame tent

If you are a backpacker as well as a canoeist, you probably own a tent suitable for canoe camping, albeit it may be a bit small. If you're about to buy a tent specifically for canoe camping, consider the A-style. It is freestanding, has ample headroom, and is easy to erect, about as bug-proof as a tent can be, easily ventilated, and available in double-wall construction. Sizes range from two- to six-person.

EUREKA! TENTS

Double-wall dome-style tent

An alternative is the double-wall dome model, somewhat resembling a fabric igloo. It too is freestanding, and provides more space per pound than most other types. It sheds wind superbly. Ventilation may be a minor problem, since most domes are equipped with a ceiling vent that may become partially blocked by the close-fitting outer wall.

The tunnel or quonset-type shelter sheds wind well and provides good headroom. With a door at each end, or with a window at the back, cross-ventilation is facilitated. Form-fitting flies convert the tent to a double-wall shelter.

Sleeping Gear

In his 1917 classic *Camping and Woodcraft,* Horace Kephart wrote: "In selecting camp bedding, we look for the most warmth with the least weight and bulk, for durability under hard use, and for stuff (fill) that will not hold moisture, but will dry out easily."[1] No writer since has better defined a modern sleeping bag.

A sleeping bag does not "make you warm." It regulates the escape of natural body warmth. For this, insulation is required, the thickness of which is known as "loft." Currently, two insulating materials are used, waterfowl down (duck or goose) and polyester. The latter is marketed under various brand names, such as Hollofil II® and PolarGuard®, the registered trademarks of the E. I. DuPont de Nemours Company and the Celanese Corporation, respectively. Not only do these insulations help to contain body warmth, but they also permit the escape of body moisture.

---

[1] Horace Kephart, *Camping and Woodcraft* (New York: Macmillan Publishing Co., 1916, 1917), p. 125.

At first glance, down-filled sleeping bags appear to be the best choice, despite their high cost. Down is "thermally efficient" — that is, it provides the greatest insulation per ounce. It is highly resilient and compressible, and is some 20 to 30 percent less bulky than polyester. However, if your down sleeping bag gets wet (canoes do tip and water slops aboard!), the down filling absorbs water and loses its "fluff"; it mats into globs of sodden follicles, absolutely useless as insulation. Worse yet, it requires several days of warm sunlight to dry it. Should you decide on a down-filled bag, be sure that it is encased in an absolutely waterproof pack.

In assembling a down sleeping bag, the insulation is blown into compartments sandwiched between the inner and outer shells, until proper loft is attained. A polyester bag is manufactured somewhat differently. Polyester is provided to the manufacturer in the form of batts. These are edge-sewn between the bag's inner and outer shells, and sometimes overlapped for added loft. Polyester does not compress quite as compactly as down, but for all practical purposes, a 3-inch loft of polyester will keep you just as warm as a similar thickness of down. And should your polyester bag get a thorough soaking, just wring it out and crawl into it! Despite the dampness still retained, it will keep you warm through a chilly night. A dry bed is preferable, but in an emergency, a slightly moist polyester bag is not a bad second choice. What's more, sunlight will dry it out quickly.

GERRY MOUNTAIN SPORTS

Standard rectangular sleeping bag

There are three basic shapes of sleeping bags: rectangular, mummy, and barrel. Rectangular styles are roomier; you can roll over inside one. But this generous space allows air to circulate about your body, creating a cooling effect. Also, the rectangular bag makes for a bulky bundle. The mummy bag, since it fits more closely about the body, is more thermally efficient. Trouble is, roll over in a mummy bag and it rolls over with you. It's a bit constraining. The barrel type, cut more generously than the mummy, is roomier and roughly body-shaped, yet without the heat-wasting aspect of the rectangular style.

Mummy-type sleeping bag is compact

Sleeping bags are rated: "comfortable down to 20 degrees," for example. They are also divided according to the seasons in which they can be used comfortably: summer, three-season, and four-season. A summer grade will loft up to about 2 inches, suitable down to about 30 degrees Fahrenheit. A three-season bag lofts to about 3 inches, suitable down to about 10 degrees Fahrenheit for use during the spring, summer, and fall. The four-season model is for extremes of cold weather, not likely to be encountered during a canoe trip.

Summer nights in the North can be chilly, so the three-season bag is more expedient. If you run into an unusually warm night, simply leave the bag partially open. Of course, if you're strictly a warm-weather canoe camper, a summer bag will be adequate.

Sleeping-bag zippers are of metal or nylon. Metal is cold, temperamental, and inclined to corrode. Opt for nylon. It's more reliable. Two types are available: the tooth-and-ladder style, in which the teeth interlock; and the coil, which is "self-repairing" and will continue to work despite minor damage.

Pads and Mattresses

Those of us fortunate enough to have known the bough bed will remember how the resiliency of spruce and the Christmas-tree aroma of balsam fir lulled us to sleep. Alas, days of the bough bed are gone. Whatever comfort we enjoy during wilderness nights we must now carry with us.

This can be provided by an air mattress or a foam pad. To do without one or the other of these is false economy. If you choose to sleep on the ground without benefit of padding, be prepared for some miserable nights. Mother Earth's bosom is about as soft and forgiving as a city sidewalk!

With a down sleeping bag, some sort of padding is mandatory. Otherwise, when the weight of your body compresses the down, its insulation value is almost nil. Polyester is also subject to some compression, but less so.

For warm weather, an air mattress is the logical choice. It's comfortable, and far more compact than any of the foam pads. Check it carefully for leaks before leaving home, and carry a repair kit. A self-inflating air mattress is available, which consists of a waterproof nylon envelope encompassing an open-cell foam pad. Open the valve and the foam expands, sucking in air. It inflates to about 1½ inches and weight runs from 1½ to 2 pounds, depending upon whether you choose the 48- or the 72-inch length.

Closed-cell foam pads, which do not absorb moisture, are used extensively by winter campers who sleep on snow; but, since they are only ⅜- to ½-inch thick, they are of dubious value on hard ground. Open-cell foam pads can be up to 2 inches thick, and hence are remarkably comfortable, but their great bulk virtually eliminates them from canoe-trip use. Also, they readily absorb moisture.

Packs

Although the exquisitely crafted Indian-made pack basket has just about disappeared, the commercial variety is still popular in the Northeast and in parts of eastern Canada. It protects fragile items, and that alone probably justifies its use. Waterproof covers are available, but these protect only against rain, not the possibility of a dunking.

Few are Indian-made nowadays, but pack baskets remain popular in some areas.

In the upper Midwest and in Ontario, the Duluth pack has reigned for many years and is still widely used. It consists of a flat canvas envelope (some modern versions have expandable bellows sides), up to 28 by 30 inches, with a generous flap that closes with straps and buckles; it is rigged with both shoulder straps and a tump line. It's a highly flexible pack: you can always jam in one more item. Some newer-design Duluth models incorporate waterproof fabric in the lower third of the pack. This is fine *if* the pack remains upright when there's water sloshing around in the bilge.

Duffel bags are available in waterproof nylon, but since they are equipped with zippers that are certainly not waterproof, these bags, too, will leak.

When using a pack basket, Duluth, or duffel, it's possible to "waterproof" it by lining it with a plastic trash bag. Two bags, one inside the other, better keep water away from equipment, supplies, or clothing. On the whole, though, the trash-bag improvisation is a jerry-rig—not very reliable.

THE COLEMAN CO. INC.

This wet pack is actually two bags in one, with waterproof slide closure.

There are waterproof packs that resemble World War II "wet packs." Some are made of coated nylon, others of plastics such as polyethylene and polypropylene, often in a double-layer construction. They are usually available from outfitters who specialize in canoe-trip and river-running equipment. Some of these are quite small, while others will hold a couple of sleeping bags plus clothing. The larger ones are rigged with shoulder straps.

No serious threat arises if the cooking gear gets dunked, but how about the foodstuffs? Prepackaging these in waterproof plastic bags is an obvious precaution, but despite this, some grub inevitably is spoiled in a watery accident. A further precaution might include the use of the polyethylene replacement for the pack basket, commercially marketed as the "Rec Pac." Its cover is fitted

*Polyethylene "Rec Pac" cover
is gasket-sealed*

with a gasket, so it's reasonably waterproof, and since it is rigged with shoulder straps, it can be portaged readily. If not too heavily loaded, it will float; but should a spill occur, recover the pack as quickly as possible. If submerged — caught under an overturned canoe, for example — it may leak.

The external-frame pack, common on backpacking trails, is frequently seen along canoe routes. The frame may interfere with carrying the canoe, but it is the most comfortable of all packs for portaging supplies and equipment, providing someone else totes the canoe. Also, when the pack is lodged crosswise in the canoe, its frame acts as a bridge, keeping water in the bilge from reaching the contents.

Internal-frame packs are easily stored in a canoe. Equipped with compression straps, they tend to hold the load close to the packer's back, which makes for better balance, a godsend on a torturous carry trial. Nor does the pack interfere with carrying a canoe.

Regrettably, neither the external- nor the internal-frame pack is leakproof — those zippers again!

If I seem to be preoccupied with keeping gear and supplies dry, it's simply because I've spent too many miserable nights in siwash camps where clothing was damp, the flour sack a bag of mush, my sleeping bag clammy, and my general disposition completely averse to any congeniality! The farther from civilization your trek takes you, the more important it is to keep the outfit dry.

While not exactly a pack, the "wanigan" or "chuck box" is a time-honored contrivance. Usually homemade and often fiberglassed inside and out, it houses cooking utensils and part of the grub supply. Some are equipped with shoulder straps, others with

Construction details of a wanigan

rope handles. A wanigan is a boon to a canoe-trip chef who likes to have his tools and supplies well organized and easily accessible upon landing for the night. For a lengthy trip where portages are few, it provides an ideal form of packing. But if arduous carries are in the offing, conventional canoe packs are a better choice.

Cutting Tools

Banish me into the woods for 30 days and allot me only one item, and I'd choose my 3-pound pole axe. With it, I can rig shelter, obtain food, even make a fire. Its 28-inch handle provides a hefty swing that drives the bit deep and true. It's for serious work. No chopping tool will manufacture fuel more quickly and efficiently.

The next best choice is the Hudson's Bay axe, with its 2-pound (give or take a few ounces) head and its 24-inch handle. For its size, it's remarkably efficient, and certainly much safer to use than that most abominable of all woods tools, the hatchet. For cutting firewood or clearing a blowdown from a carry trail, the Hudson's Bay axe is second only to the pole axe.

It may be that you're a bit fearful of an axe. It is, after all, a tool that calls for some skill. In that case, take along a folding saw, preferably the Sven model. Its triangular frame allows for easy sawing of limbs up to 3 or 4 inches thick. The 24-inch blade fits into the handle, out of harm's way for carrying, and the saw weighs barely a pound. There's a thumbscrew adjustment for tightening the blade. The tighter it is, the better it cuts.

BILL RIVIERE

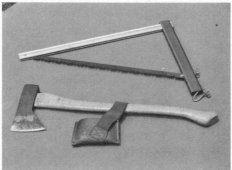

Sheathed Hudson's Bay axe and the Sven saw

Knives have a fascination. There's a mystique about a sharp blade. My favorite knife is a lowly wood-handled, carbon-steel sheath knife that cost less than $5 when I acquired it several years ago. Using a Washita stone (mined in Arkansas and available from perceptive outfitters), I touch up the blade every two or three days when I'm in the field. I manage to maintain a scalpel-like edge. True, the blade has turned an ugly gray, but I'm more interested in cutting efficiency than I am in color. Many knife users insist on stainless steel. Frankly, try as I might, I've never been able to develop a decent edge on a stainless-steel blade. For my money, stainless steel is pretty; carbon steel is practical.

The choice between a sheath knife and a folding pocket model is a matter of personal preference. The sheath knife is ready to go to work the moment you draw it. The pocket knife is slower, since it requires two hands to open, but it provides at least two blades from which to choose. If you'd like an assortment of miniature tools at hand, choose a Swiss army knife. If your inclination is toward a sheath knife, buy one with a blade no longer than 4 inches. Eight- to 10-inch blades are better suited to commando in-fighting than to precise work.

Campstoves

If you're a gastronomical maestro of the canoe trails, you probably prefer to do your cooking over an open fire. The campstove that will match the speed and efficiency of a campfire has not yet been invented, nor can a campstove produce the menu variety possible with flames and glowing coals. The cook-fire comes into its own, too, where large quantities of food are to be prepared—for a multi-canoe brigade involving four or more persons, for example. In this case, your basic tools will consist of an axe and/or a saw, plus one or two asbestos gloves for hot-pot handling.

But the cook-fire is not for all canoe trippers. Unless you limit yourself to corned-beef hash or canned beans and franks, cooking consistently delectable meals over an open flame calls for a degree of skill that is just not native to all paddlers. Hence the popularity of the various campstoves.

If the trip is a leisurely one with no ominous portages in the offing, the famed two-burner Coleman stove is not out of place. Its reliability and ease of operation are well known, and with two burners, you can whip up hot dishes approximating home cooking. There's even a folding box oven that perches atop one of the burners and turns out pretty fair biscuits or a pan of cornbread. However, if you have to lug the Coleman two-burner stove over hill and dale to the next waterway, you'll cuss its weight and bulk, to say nothing of the fuel can that must accompany it.

A pair of small, backpacker-type stoves are a better choice, particularly for a one-canoe, two-person outfit. Their weight is trifling, bulk is minimal, and because of their economy of operation, only a small quantity of fuel need be carried.

The easiest to operate is the Camping Gaz stove, a European import that burns butane gas contained in disposable canisters.

BILL RIVIERE

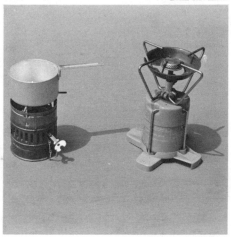

The Svea 123 and the Camping Gaz stoves

You have only to turn on the valve and light it; no pumping, no priming. The stove works well in warm weather, although its burner-head is susceptible to wind. It has drawbacks. At temperatures approaching the low 30s, butane does not vaporize well and produces a spindly flame. And there is the problem of the empty canisters: you'll have to carry them out. All in all, these little butane stoves are fine for a summertime weekend outing, but badly suited to an extended trip.

The Svea 123, which burns white gas or Coleman fuel, will fire up in any weather during which you're likely to be canoeing. It weighs slightly more than a pound, and, as one outfitter states in his catalog, "it takes hardly more room than a can of soup." A ⅓-pint filling of the tank will burn for about 45 minutes, boiling 1½ pints of water in five to six. The stove has long been a backpacker's favorite, even though it must be primed for starting. However, its 4-inch-diameter base rather limits the size of pots that can be used. Too large a kettle may topple, unless it is centered perfectly.

The Coleman Peak 1 stove, weighing about 2 pounds, is equipped with a pressure pump that eliminates the need for priming and assures starting and burning in any weather. Not surprisingly, it burns Coleman fuel or white gas; one filling of its 11-fluid-ounce tank lasts about 1½ hours. Heat output will boil a quart of water in less than four minutes. The burner-head is divided into

THE COLEMAN CO. INC.

The Coleman Peak 1 stove

four quadrants protected by a windshield, so that if the wind should extinguish one quadrant, the other three continue to burn. While the stove itself has a diameter of only 4½ inches, fold-out legs broaden the base considerably.

The fact that you're carrying one of these little stoves does not mean that you're restricted to its use. For a quickly prepared one-pot dish, unlimber the stove. But if more elaborate fare is desired, switch to a cook-fire. Thus you'll allow the riverside chef some flexibility in menu planning.

Chapter 33

~~~~~~

The Canoeist's Library

WHEN IT COMES TO CANOEING LITERATURE, I'm a bibliomaniac. Webster's Third New International Dictionary defines this as "an avid book collector." That's an understatement. I collect not only books, but also pamphlets, brochures, fliers, catalogs, racing programs, magazines, and even building plans. I haunt yard sales, flea markets, and book fairs. If it has to do with canoeing, I latch onto it. It's not as exciting as running wild water, but collecting canoeing literature holds an insidious fascination. Once you start, you'll probably never quit.

Come the biting winds of November, I stack my canoes in the barn, where they remain until the frothy runoff of April. During the interim five months, evenings are spent reading the treasures I've picked up during the summer. Many collectors acquire scarce or rare books solely for the pleasure of possession and display, but that's only half the delight of ownership. Reading them is like savoring a fine wine instead of merely admiring the bottle.

Every winter I reread Thomas Sedgwick Steele's *Paddle and Portage from Moosehead to the Aroostook River,* published in 1882. Steele had a rough trip due to low water, and notes in the foreword that "the reader will perceive in the following pages that a cart, rather than a canoe, might have been used."

Captain Willard Glazier, in his *Headwaters of the Mississippi,* claimed to have discovered the source of that river, a lake that he modestly named Lake Glazier. His 1881 claim is generally discounted. Later, on his way down the river, he swapped his two birchbark canoes for wooden ones, one built by the Racine Boat Company, the other by J. Henry Rushton. This downstream trip resulted in another Glazier tome: *Down the Great River,* published in 1887.

Of more recent vintage (published in 1935 and reprinted in 1965) is Eric Sevareid's *Canoeing with the Cree,* in which the famed journalist describes how he, then 17 years old, and his partner Walter C. Port, 19, paddled from Minneapolis to Hudson's Bay, a 2,500-mile trek that required four months. Even today, many sections of their route are for experts only—or, "you'd better portage!"

Voyages occupy a substantial space in canoe literature: highlights include Alexander MacKenzie's *Voyages from Montreal to the Frozen and Pacific Oceans,* published in 1789 and 1793; Sir George Simpson's *Peace River: A Canoe Voyage from Hudson's Bay to the Pacific,* from 1828; and Nathaniel H. Bishop's *Voyage of the Paper Canoe,* from 1874–75. The MacKenzie and Simpson titles have been reprinted several times, while Bishop's book is generally available in one of the early printings.

A modern-day saga of similar magnitude is recorded in *One Incredible Journey* by Clayton Klein and Verlen Kruger, published in 1985. It describes a 7,000-mile canoe journey by Kruger and Clinton Waddell, from Montreal to Fort Yukon, Alaska, and then down the Yukon River to the Bering Sea.

Then there are the works of the late Sigurd Olson, who lived at Listening Point, near Ely, Minnesota. He wrote *Runes of the North, The Lonely Land, The Singing Wilderness,* and other books that stir a canoeist's soul. Grace Lee Nute, also a Minnesotan, brings to life the fur-trade days in *The Voyageur* and *The Voyageur's Highway,* which contain perhaps the best descriptions of a voyageur's daily stint along early canoe routes. In *The Voyageur,* you will even find the words and music to the songs of the French Canadian crews that manned the fur canoes. Robert E. Pinkerton's 1914 *The Canoe* is a classic, as is Nessmuk's *Woodcraft.*

Not all canoe-related books are devoted to voyages. Nor are you limited to reading out-of-print books. In recent years, there has been a proliferation of canoe books by contemporary authors. They have covered the building, repair, and restoration of canoes; design, paddling, and white-water techniques; canoe-camping and tripping; and the various forms of competition.

Though they are not specifically canoeing books, the "Rivers of America" series, published by Holt, Rinehart and Winston, devotes an entire volume, each by a different author, to each of the major American rivers. My last count of these books was 57, but I'm certain others have since appeared. Granted, my provincialism is showing, but I found *The Allagash,* by Lew Dietz, and *The Kennebec,* by Robert P. Tristram Coffin, difficult to put down — especially *The Allagash,* which is synonymous with "canoe." Even if you do not manage to acquire the entire set (not an easy task, since the series is a favorite of collectors), you can perhaps locate those that cover rivers in your part of the country.

BILL RIVIERE

Part of the author's library. Rockered model at right is that of an Okinawan ocean-going canoe.

A still more recent title is *Allagash,* by Gil Gilpatrick, published in 1983. The book details much of the history of the region, as well as Gilpatrick's experience as a guide on the waterway.

Still another category includes the river guides, most of which are regional. Covering all canoeable waters in the nation in one volume is virtually impossible, at least in adequate detail. I can think of only one exception, and that is *Canoe Canada,* by Nick Nickels. But then, Nick has flown over nearly every square mile of Canada, and has been collecting data for more than 50 years. James C. Makens, in his *Canoe Trails Directory,* came close to compiling a suitable national guide book, detailing major canoe waters on a state-by-state basis.

Since the 1930s, the Appalachian Mountain Club has published and periodically revised its *Guide to New England Canoeing,* which covers just about every bit of flowing water in the region that will float a canoe. Published in 1956, Lawrence I. Grinnell's *Canoeable Waters of New York State and Vicinity* is a much-sought-after, out-of-print title. Also highly collectible is Randy Carter's *Canoeing White Water: A Guide Book to the Rivers of Virginia and Eastern West Virginia,* published in 1967. One of the outstanding works in this field is *Appalachian Waters,* by Walter Burmeister, published in four volumes in 1962. Also in demand is *Exploring the Little Rivers of New Jersey,* by James Cawley, published in 1945.

A great many soft-cover or pamphlet-type guides have been published, all worthy of being added to a serious collection: *Blue Ridge Voyages,* by H. Roger Corbett and Louis J. Matacia; *Missouri Ozark Waterways,* by Oz Hawksley; *Illinois Canoeing Guide,* Illinois Department of Conservation; *Wisconsin Water Trails,* Wisconsin Department of Conservation; *Buffalo River Canoeing Guide,* the Ozark Society; *Michigan Guide to Easy Canoeing,* Michigan Department of Natural Resources; *Canoeing Guide to Western Pennsylvania / Northern West Virginia,* Pittsburgh Council of American Youth Hostels; and *Iowa Canoe Trips,* by the Iowa Conservation Commission.

Many of the foregoing are probably out of date, although some may have been reprinted with updated material. I have cited them merely as a nucleus for a collection. To list all of the currently updated river guides would require a small volume in itself. Such a list, in the form of a booklet, is available free from the American Canoe Association.

For canoeists who are also linguists, an appropriate addition to any collection is *Guide des Rivieres du Quebec,* published in 1973 by the Federation Quebecoise de Canot-Kayak (Quebec Canoe-Kayak Federation).

Another intriguing area of canoe-literature collecting is catalogs. They are not easy to come by. In the first place, they were fragile and readily discarded. The few that remain are prized, and, if offered for sale, often command outlandish prices. Nevertheless, originals keep surfacing in very limited numbers, and occasionally, reprints appear. Thus, you can browse through the 1910 Old Town offerings, which included an 18-foot guide's model for $30! In the 1935 edition, the price had soared to $69. The 1914 Mullins catalog, its illustrations tinted, features poetry and the claim that the Mullins canoe is "unsinkable" because of "buoyancy pads made of an imported material" located in the ends.

Rushton's 1903 catalog depicts the Indian Girl — his first wood-and-canvas canoe — and, of course, all of his then-current lap-strakes, including the Nessmuk. Kennebec's 1914 catalog describes materials and woods used in canoe construction. Canoe interiors, with fine detail, are clearly illustrated in the B. N. Morris 1908 literature. Several of the foregoing are available as reprints from the Wooden Canoe Heritage Association.

These old catalogs and their reprints are extremely helpful to anyone restoring a canoe, since photos and specifications make identification possible, even if the canoe long ago lost its nameplate.

Outdoor periodicals contain canoe information that ranges from the ludicrous (but entertaining!) to enlightening. In the September 1946 issue of *Outdoors,* Chief Henry Red Eagle, of Greenville, Maine, describes "The Fine Art of Canoeing." The Chief, whose ability with the English language fell only slightly short of that of William F. Buckley, Jr., dragged in a bit of synthetic Indian talk: "Canoe is not a toy, or for tricks like standing on head and jump in water. Canoe is for use over lakes and rivers. Injun's way, safe way; white man's way, dam' fool way!" The article is illustrated with a photo of the Chief, a Penobscot, wearing a Sioux war bonnet while standing in his canoe!

One of my treasures is the March 1902 issue of *The Amateur Sportsman.* It contains ads for E. M. White, J. Henry Rushton, and B. N. Morris canoes, but I'm especially captivated by a brief article describing a sectional canoe built by the W. H. Mullins Company, of Salem, Ohio. In part, the article reads: "Made of stamped sheet steel, the 14-foot canoe is 39 inches wide, 14 inches deep, and weighs 95 pounds." The canoe came apart in the center, and the

BILL RIVIERE

Good reading come a winter's night . . .

stern section then nested into the forward half for carrying. Apparently, it preceded the hula hoop and the Edsel into oblivion. It does not appear in the 1914 Mullins catalog.

Another item in the same issue of *The Amateur Sportsman* is noteworthy. E. T. Keyser writes of The Speed Club (apparently of Toronto, although this is not clear). "There are over three hundred members," Keyser notes, "who make a weekly run on Thursday nights during June, July, August, and as far into September as the weather permits. The club has built a large concert stage on the water's edge . . . and we have a first-class musical programme every night of the club run." I showed the item to a friend. "That's class," he exclaimed, "waltzing in canoes to Johann Strauss!"

For anyone interested in early sailing canoes, the June 1887 issue of *Outing, an Illustrated Monthly Magazine of Recreation* carries the "History of American Canoeing," with several drawings of varied sailing rigs of the day, as well as of such famed canoes as the Rob Roy, the Nautilus, and William Alden's Shadow. The author is C. Bowyer Vaux, who also wrote *Canoe Handling* in 1885, a book that became the canoeists's bible of the era, probably because it covered "History, Uses, Limitations and Varieties, Practical Management and Care and Relative Facts." Mr. Vaux overlooked very little! My copy is a second edition, printed in 1888, but this does not detract from the delight it affords on a winter's night when a nor'easter's frigid fingers peel shingles off the barn.

Canoeing went into a slump between World Wars I and II, at least as a general sport. However, it was kept alive among hunters, fishermen, trappers, and campers, and therefore outdoors-slanted magazines continued to cover canoe activities. Although they are no longer published, copies of many of these magazines are not difficult to locate, especially the more popular ones such as *Forest and Stream, Hunting and Fishing, National Sportsman,* and *Outdoors.* And, of course, currently published periodicals have also covered canoeing for many years, among them *Field and Stream, Outdoor Life, Sports Afield,* and *Fur, Fish, and Game.* You can be sure that every new development in canoeing, as it occurred over the years, was noted by these publications.

Other current periodicals logically join the nucleus of a canoe-literature collection, especially those devoted exclusively to the canoe. Ever since 1880, *The American Canoeist* has been published by the American Canoe Association. The American Whitewater Affiliation has distributed *American Whitewater* since its founding in 1954, while the United States Canoe Association has issued its bi-monthly *Canoe News* since 1968. A collection of these, even if incomplete, is a treasure trove.

Perhaps the most important periodical is *Canoe Magazine,* to which I have made numerous references in the foregoing chapters. Not all, but many back issues are still available.

Wooden Canoe, the quarterly publication of the Wooden Canoe Heritage Association, is invaluable for the traditionalists among paddlers, those who prefer wood. A relatively new periodical (first published during the winter of 1979–80), it promises to be of increasing importance in its field. Luckily, all back issues, or reprints of them, are currently available.

As a starting point for building up a canoeing library, check the suggested reading list in the bibliography. It is by no means complete, nor is it intended to be "must reading." Unfortunately, once you start shopping among bookstores, you'll discover that they carry only a few of the most popular titles still in print. On the other hand, the American Canoe Association's Book Service keeps an extensive assortment on hand. The Wooden Canoe Heritage Association has a more limited stock, but only because it deals solely with wooden-canoe literature. You need not be a member of either organization to buy.

When seeking out-of-print books, don't assume that only first editions are worth collecting. Naturally, a "first" is usually more valuable than a subsequent printing, but for reading or research, later editions are just as desirable and less costly.

Start by visiting rare- and old-book shops. Even if one does not have the specific titles you're seeking, it will probably have others just as interesting. The bookseller can refer you to other shops, too.

Dealers who specialize in outdoor subjects and who offer mail-order service seem a logical source, especially since most of them distribute catalogs or for-sale lists. However, this segment of the used-book business comprises licensed inflationaries who will charge you an arm and a leg. Prices are much more reasonable among shops that carry a general stock.

How do you recognize an overpriced book—or a bargain? You'll feel like a babe in the woods at first, but after visiting a few shops and noting prices, you'll quickly learn to pass up a $5 book for which a dealer is asking $15.

Expect to make a few mistakes now and then. I once paid $45 for a copy of Fanny Eckstorm's *The Penobscot Man,* only to run across two copies within a few days, either of which I could have had for $15. It pays to shop around. While looking for Steele's *Paddle and Portage,* I found several copies at $45. I kept looking, and eventually located a first edition at $12. All in all, a "fair" price depends entirely upon how badly you want a specific book.

During a serious search for used books, you can expand your efforts by making up a "want list," which needs only to include the authors' names and the titles. Leave a copy with each shop you visit. Most booksellers will gladly contact a client when they locate a wanted title. Using the mail broadens your search ever farther.

You can obtain the names and addresses of hundreds of book-sellers throughout the United States and Canada in the pages of the *A B Bookman Weekly*, to which many libraries subscribe. Thus you can send out as many copies of your want list as your postal budget will allow.

You'll soon start receiving "quotes." These include the author's name, the title, date published, condition of the book, its postpaid price, and the length of time the dealer will wait for your reply before selling it elsewhere.

Buying a used book through the mail is not the gamble it might appear to be. Of the hundreds I've purchased, only half a dozen or so were inaccurately described; and among the sellers of those half a dozen, all except one refunded my money.

Apart from book shops and mail-order buying, there are other sources close to home: book fairs, flea markets, household auctions, and lawn sales. Book searching is like panning for gold. You'll go weeks without a worthwhile find. Then, suddenly, pay dirt!

So much for books. There is also "paper ephemera" — most often pamphlets. One such item is the Bangor and Aroostook Railroad's annual publication *In the Maine Woods*, first issued about 1900 and discontinued just before World War II. Some issues ran up to 160 pages and included all sorts of advertising related to the outdoors. Several issues describe the Allagash River trip as it was when it started at Moosehead Lake, more than double the length of the trip that now starts at Telos Dam in northern Maine.

A prized bit of ephemera is an 1895 copy of *Forest and Stream's* 48-page booklet, *Canvas Canoes — How to Build Them,* by Parker B. Field. The back cover advertises other publications in a similar vein: *Canoe and Boat Building,* by W. P. Stephens; *Canoe Handling,* by C. Bowyer Vaux; *Canoe and Camp Cookery,* by "Seneca" (Henry H. Soule); and *Two Hundred Miles on the Delaware River,* by J. Wallace Hoff.

The domino theory works in book collecting, too. Find one book, one pamphlet, one catalog, and it will lead to another and another. The search goes on. Collect them and display them proudly on your shelves, but they'll give you the greatest pleasure come an evening by the fire when the weather outside "just ain't fittin'."

Chapter 34

·~·~·~·~·~·~

Afterthoughts

PRODUCING A BOOK ON MODERN CANOEING can be very frustrating. A writer researches musty volumes for historical background, studies new catalogs, reads periodicals, even tucks away bits of newsprint for the latest developments they might contain. There are interviews to be conducted with canoe builders, paddlers, even retail dealers. Too, there are photos to be made or to be obtained from dozens of different sources. In addition, literally hundreds of letters must be written (to say nothing of phone calls) to obtain some minute but vital details. Nothing must be overlooked lest the book be found wanting. Admittedly it's a joyous form of work, one which only a compulsive writer enjoys.

Yet even as my editors and I meticulously edit the manuscript, and even as we read and correct the proofs, the canoe scene changes, much like a sunset as a photographer tries to capture it on film.[1]

For example, who would have thought that Old Town would market a polyethylene canoe? In canoe plants throughout this country and Canada, new design and building concepts continually evolve as the search for the ultimate canoe goes on. Since this manuscript was completed, Blue Hole has come up with its Sunburst, a new white-water solo craft. Mad River has designed and built award-winning canoes that incorporate Kevlar®, Airex®, and

---

[1] Even as I proofread these final words, an unconfirmed but reliable report reveals that the Old Town Canoe Company is negotiating to purchase its neighbor down the street, the White Canoe Company. Similarly, the 25-year-old Lincoln Canoe Company has just been purchased by Saco River Industries of Bar Mills, Maine. The new owner will continue the output of Lincoln canoes.

new resins. Mohawk, not to be outdone, has announced the Scamp, 15½ feet of white-water excitement. As for the Sawyer Canoe Company, keeping up with it is difficult. It turns out new high-performance models seemingly on a monthly basis! If you want to keep abreast of the doings at We-no-nah, you must camp on the doorstep and eavesdrop as the company reaches farther and farther into the field of fast canoes. And just as I wrote that Bart Hauthaway produced only 6 pack canoes, he announced a seventh.

I've cited only a few examples of fast-moving, on-going progress in the industry. No doubt, at this very moment, every canoe builder in North America is planning or working on one or more new models which he hopes will capture the hearts of paddlers and a greater share of the market. Who knows, then, what is waiting in the wings?

I envy John Viehman, editor and publisher of *Canoe Magazine*. He publishes 6 times a year, never more than a few weeks behind the most recent developments in the canoeing world. A book author doesn't have this luxury.

Based upon the developments during the past decade, one doesn't need a crystal ball to predict that the remaining few years in the twentieth century will see some exciting advancements in canoe building.

It's certain that canoes will be lighter, sturdier, faster, easier to paddle, more buoyant, more stable, more maneuverable, and more versatile. The "all-round" canoe probably will never be attained, but don't be surprised if a number of canoes become adaptable to a greater variety of water conditions without sacrificing safety. The already burgeoning interest in solo canoeing will mushroom further, with canoes adapted to the paddler's weight, paddling style, and expertise. Cruising models will part the waters like some of today's racing canoes. The renaissance of the wooden canoe will continue, but modern technology will play an even greater part in the development of paddling fun. This last, in fact, is not a prediction. The transition is already under way. And it will accelerate, of that you can be sure.

Appendix

Canoe Manufacturers

Note: Some canoe manufacturers, notably those operating small shops, seem to play musical chairs. They're here Monday, gone Tuesday, and back on Wednesday under a different name or at a new location. While the following list was accurate at the time of its compilation, some canoe builders listed will have vanished within a few months; others as yet unknown will appear on the scene. If, as time goes on, you want to keep this directory up-to-date, refer to the *Buyer's Guide* included each year in *Canoe Magazine*'s December issue. Also, *Wooden Canoe* puts out an annual directory that not only includes builders of all types of wooden canoes, but also suppliers of lumber and fastenings (sometimes difficult to find) for repairing and restoring wooden hulls.

CEDAR-STRIP CANOES

Carl L. Bausch
Route 1, Box 294
Charlotte, Vermont 05445

Bear Mountain Boat Shop
Box 1041
Bancroft, Ontario
Canada K0L 1C0

Curtis Canoes
Box 38
Hemlock, New York 14466

Custom Canoes
Route 1, Box 216
Carthage, New York 13619

Gillies Canoes
General Delivery
Margaretville, Nova Scotia
Canada B0S 1N0

Bob Hodson
916 South Ioka
Mount Prospect, Illinois 60056

Jensen Canoes
308 78th Avenue
Minneapolis, Minnesota 55444

Doug Jones
Box 29, Route 1
Acton, Ontario
Canada L7J 2L7

Lakeland Canoe
Ste. 297, 7305 Woodbine Avenue
Markham, Ontario
Canada L3R 3V7

Mentha Wooden Boat Company
Route 2, Box 119
Lawton, Michigan 49065

(CEDAR-STRIP CANOES, Cont.)

Morley Canoes
P.O. Box 147
Swan Lake, Montana 59911

Muskoka Canoe
Box 1769
Gravenhurst, Ontario
Canada P0C 1G0

Northern Shadow Canoe
21 Golf Valley Lane
Etobicoke, Ontario
Canada M9C 2K2

Payne Canoe Craft
2401 Virginia Drive
Ottawa, Ontario
Canada K1H 6X2

RKL Boatworks
Pretty Marsh Road
Mount Desert, Maine 04660

Secret Harbor Boatworks
13700 Powerhouse
Potter Valley, California 95469

William Sommerfield
32 Elm Street
Massena, New York 13662

Ned Teachman
Box 293
Port Sydney, Ontario
Canada P0B 1L0

Schuyler Thomson
343 Weekeepeeme Road
Woodbury, Connecticut 06798

Willis Enterprises
Route 3, Curtis Road
Freeport, Maine 04032

CEDAR-STRIP BUILDING KITS

Country Ways
221 Water Street
Excelsior, Minnesota 55331

Mentha Wooden Boat Company
Route 2, 23rd Street
Gobles, Michigan 49055

Old Town Canoe Company
Old Town, Maine 04468

BIRCHBARK CANOES

Beaver Bark Canoes
Route 3, Box 2
Woodruff, Wisconsin 54568

Alexander Comb
Route 1, Box 319
Two Harbors, Minnesota 55616

Ferde Goode
Route 3, Box 2
Woodruff, Wisconsin 54568

Bill Hafeman
Route 1
Bigfork, Minnesota 56628

Tom MacKenzie
525 Orchard Drive
Madison, Wisconsin 53711

Jack Minehart
505 Holmes Drive
Cedar Falls, Iowa 50613

Paul Munninghoff
Route 1
Rhinelander, Wisconsin 54501

Jay Parsons
243 Hendrick Street
Easthampton, Massachusetts 01027

Henri Vaillancourt
Box 199
Greenville, New Hampshire 03048

FIBERGLASS/KEVLAR® CANOES

Allagash Canoe
Francestown, New Hampshire 03043

American Fiber-Lite, Inc.
P.O. Box 67
Marion, Illinois 62959

Anegada Marine
Box 2311
Crystal River, Florida 32629

Apple Line
146 Church Street
Amsterdam, New York 12010

(FIBERGLASS/KEVLAR° CANOES, Cont.)

Badger Boat Builders
Box 97
Couderay, Wisconsin 54828

Blackhawk Canoe Company
937 North Washington Street
Janesville, Wisconsin 53545

Black River Canoes
Box 537
LaGrange, Ohio 44050

Bluewater Canoes
699 Speedvale Avenue West
Guelph, Ontario
Canada N1K 1E6

Cal-Tek Engineering
36 Riverside Drive
Kingston, Massachusetts 02364

Canandaigua Canoe Works
5741 Dalton Drive
Canandaigua, New York 14424

Chicagoland Canoe Base
4019 North Narragansett Avenue
Chicago, Illinois 60634

Chief Manufacturing
428 Richard Road
Rockledge, Florida 32955

Core Craft, Inc.
Box 249
Industrial Park
Bemidji, Minnesota 56601

Cowan Canoes
RR #5
Brussels, Ontario
Canada N0G 1H0

Curtis Canoes
4587 Clay Street
Hemlock, New York 14446

Dolphin Products, Inc.
142 Second Street, West
Wabasha, Minnesota 55981

Easy Rider Canoe and Kayak Company
Tukwila Branch
P.O. Box 88108
Seattle, Washington 98188

Gazelle Products, Inc. (Note: Recently acquired Rivers and Gilman of Hampden, Maine, and now producing Indian Brand canoes.)
P.O. Box 163
China, Maine 04926

Great Canadian
45 Water Street
Worcester, Massachusetts 01604

Bart Hauthaway
640 Boston Post Road
Weston, Massachusetts 02193

Hoefgen Canoe Manufacturer
SR 137, Highway M-35
Menominee, Wisconsin 49858

Indian River Canoe Mfg.
1525 Kings Court
Titusville, Florida 32780

Kellogg and Miller Boat Works
146 Church Street
Amsterdam, New York 12010

Lotus Canoes
7005 North 40th Street
Tampa, Florida 33604

Mad River Canoe, Inc.
P.O. Box 610
Waitsfield, Vermont 05673

Memphremagog Canoe
P.O. Box 466
Newport, Vermont 05855

Merrimack Canoe Co.
Crossville, Tennessee 38555

Mid-Canada Fiberglass, Ltd.
Box 1599
New Liskeard, Ontario
Canada P0J 1P0

Millbrook Boats, Inc.
P.O. Box 14
Riparius, New York 12862

Mohawk Canoes
P.O. Box 668
Longwood, Florida 32750

(FIBERGLASS/KEVLAR® CANOES, Cont.)

Moise Cadorette, Inc.
1710 Principale
St. Jean des Piles, Quebec
Canada G0X 2V0

Montgomery Marine
935 West 18th Street
Costa Mesa, California 92627

Nona Boats
1945 Placentia Avenue
Costa Mesa, California 92627

Nova Craft Canoes
Glanworth, Ontario
Canada N0L 1L0

Old Town Canoe Company
Old Town, Maine 04468

Orion International, Ltd.
3175 Orchard Park Road
Orchard Park, New York 14127

Production Glass and Design
10836 NW St. Helens Road
Portland, Oregon 97231

Quapaw Canoe Company
326 5th Avenue N.E.
Miami, Oklahoma 74354

Rainbow Boat Works
Box 159
Newport, Vermont 05855

Ranger Canoe Company
Route 25, Tenny Mountain Highway
Plymouth, New Hampshire 03267

Saco River Canoe
Depot Street
Bar Mills, Maine 04004

Sawyer Canoe Company
234 South State Street
Oscoda, Michigan 48750

Seda Products
1085 Bay Boulevard
Chula Vista, California 92011

Stowe Canoe Company
Box 207
Stowe, Vermont 05672

Trailhead
1341-2 Wellington Street
Ottawa, Ontario
Canada K1Y 3B8

Voyageur Canoe Company, Ltd.
3 King Street
Millbrook, Ontario
Canada L0A 1G0

Voyageur Canoe Company
Route 2, Box 78
Marinette, Wisconsin 54143

Wabash Valley Canoes
616 Lafayette Avenue
Crawfordsville, Indiana 47933

We-no-nah Canoes
P.O. Box 247
Winona, Minnesota 55987

Western Canoeing, Inc.
Box 115
Abbotsford, British Columbia
Canada V2S 4N8

White Canoe Company
82 North Brunswick Street
Old Town, Maine 04468

York River Industries
Box 1447
Peterborough, Ontario
Canada K9J 7H6

ROYALEX® CANOES

Allagash Canoe
Francestown, New Hampshire 03043

The Blue Hole Canoe Company
Sunbright, Tennessee 37872

Canoes by Whitesell, Ltd.
Box 9839
Atlanta, Georgia 30319

Easy Rider Canoe and Kayak Company
Tukwila Branch
P.O. Box 88108
Seattle, Washington 98188

(ROYALEX® CANOES, Cont.)

Front Royal Canoe Company
Box 473
Front Royal, Virginia 22630

Gazelle Products, Inc.
P.O. Box 163
China, Maine 04926

Mad River Canoe, Inc.
P.O. Box 610
Waitsfield, Vermont 05673

Michi-Craft Corporation
20000 19 Mile Road
Big Rapids, Michigan 49307

Mohawk Canoes
P.O. Box 668
Longwood, Florida 32750

Old Town Canoe Company
Old Town, Maine 04468

Penrod's Canoe and River Adventures
Box 93, RD 1
Summerhill, Pennsylvania 15958

Perception, Inc.
P.O. Box 686
Liberty, South Carolina 29657

Sawyer Canoe Company
234 South State Street
Oscoda, Michigan 48750

Seda Products
1085 Bay Boulevard
Chula Vista, California 92011

Shenandoah Canoe Company
Route 3
Luray, Virginia 22835

Tanana Canoes
2001 Old Greenboro Road
Jonesboro, Arkansas 72401

We-no-nah Canoes
P.O. Box 247
Winona, Minnesota 55987

Western Canoeing, Inc.
Box 115

Abbottsford, British Columbia
Canada V2S 4N8

White Canoe Company
82 North Brunswick Street
Old Town, Maine 04468

ALUMINUM CANOES

Alumacraft Boat Company
315 West St. Julien
St. Peter, Minnesota 56082

Great Canadian
45 Water Street
Worcester, Massachusetts 01604

Grumman Boats
7 South Street
Marathon, New York 13803

Lowe Industries
P.O. Box 989
Lebanon, Missouri 65536

Meyers Industries, Inc.
Box 188
Tecumseh, Michigan 49286

Michi-Craft Corporation
19995 19 Mile Road
Big Rapids, Michigan 49307

Misty River Marine, Ltd.
1 Third Avenue
Bluemenort, Manitoba
Canada R0A 0C0

Norcal Fabricators, Inc.
Box 250
Callander, Ontario
Canada P0H 1H0

Osagian Boats, Inc.
Highway 5 North, Box 213
Lebanon, Missouri 65536

Pro Boat
1605 Warner Road
Mineral Ridge, Ohio 44440

Smoker-Craft
P.O. Box 65
New Paris, Indiana 46553

APPENDIX

LAPSTRAKE CANOES

Carl L. Bausch
Route 1, Box 294
Charlotte, Vermont 05445

John Beltman
Box 37
Lincolnville, Maine 04849

John S. Breiby
3205-A
Wasilla, Alaska 99687

Geoffrey Burke
Box 212
Chocorua, New Hampshire 03817

William Clements
Box 87
North Billerica, Massachusetts 01862

Alex Comb
Route 1, Box 203
Two Harbors, Minnesota 55616

Duck Trap Woodworking
RFD 2, Cannan Road
Lincolnville Beach, Maine 04849

Freedom Boat Works
11423 East Mine Road
Baraboo, Wisconsin 53913

Steve Gurney
52 Edgewood Way
New Haven, Connecticut 06515

Maureen Hayes
184 Scottsville Road
Rochester, New York 14611

Fuat Latif
Route 1, Box 233
Orwell, Vermont 05760

Kevin Martin
RFD 1, Box 441
Epping, New Hampshire 03042

Fred Nagelbach
2748 Ewing Avenue
Evanston, Illinois 60201

James Ritter
Box 697
East Hampton, New York 11937

St. Lawrence Boatworks
65 Bellwoods Avenue
Toronto, Ontario
Canada M6J 3N4

William Sommerfield
32 Elm Street
Massena, New York 13662

Stewart River Boat Works
Route 1, Box 203
Two Harbors, Minnesota 55616

John Stuart
9 Aucort Avenue
Marion, Massachusetts 02738

Jeff Trapp
Box 138
Manitowish Waters, Wisconsin 54545

Woodchuck Shipyard
Route 3
River Falls, Wisconsin 54022

WOOD-AND-CANVAS CANOES

Note: Some of these builders cover their hulls with fiberglass rather than canvas. These are indicated by "F." Others offer a choice, and are indicated by "C or F."

Allagash Canoes (C or F)
Francestown, New Hampshire 03043

Beaver Canoe Corporation
Hazelton Lanes, 55 Avenue Road
Toronto, Ontario
Canada M5R 3L2

Leonard Beckwith
9 Favor Street
Eastport, Maine 04631

John Beltman
Box 37
Lincolnville, Maine 04849

J. W. Brown and Son (F)
2684 Lake Winyah Road
Alpane, Michigan 49707

Canandaigua Canoe Works (F)
5741 Dalton Drive
Canandaigua, New York 14424

Cedarcraft Canoes
R.R. 2, Box 1118
Clearwater, British Columbia
Canada V0E 1N0

Cedarwood Canoes
R.R. 1, Mouth of Keswick
York County, New Brunswick
Canada E0H 1N0

Coldwater Canoe Company
Box 324
Coldwater, Ontario
Canada L0K 1E0

Alex Comb
Route 1, Box 203
Two Harbors, Minnesota 55616

Guy Cyr
Box 33
West Sullivan, Maine 04689

Donald Fraser Canoes
176 Woodstock Road
Fredericton, New Brunswick
Canada E3B 2H5

Freedom Boat Works (C or F)
Route 1, Box 12
North Freedom, Wisconsin 53951

Gates Canoes
Route 2
Middleton, Nova Scotia
Canada B0S 1P0

Great Canadian
45 Water Street
Worcester, Massachusetts 01604

Willard J. Hewey (F)
Lake Annis, Route 1, South Ohio
Yarmouth County
Canada B0W 3E0

Iris Boat Works
Marshfield, Maine 04654

Island Falls Canoe Company
RFD 3, Box 76
Dover-Foxcroft, Maine 04426

Doug Jones
Willowridge Farm
R.R. 1
Baltimore, Ontario
Canada K0K 1C0

Klondike Wood Works
Route 1, Box 19
Lake Linden, Michigan 49945

Leavitt Quality Craft (C or F)
RFD, Box 1549
Hampden, Maine 04444

Miller Canoes (C or F)
Route 1, Plaster Rock
Nictau, New Brunswick
Canada E0J 1V0

Muskoka Canoe
Box 1769
Gravenhurst, Ontario
Canada P0C 1G0

Noth Bay Canoe Company
166 Campbell Avenue
North Bay, Ontario
Canada P1A 1W3

Northern Shadow Canoe
21 Golf Valley Lane
Etobicoke, Ontario
Canada M9C 2K2

OAT Canoe Company
RFD 1, Box 4100
Mount Vernon, Maine 04352

Old Town Canoe Company (F)
Old Town, Maine 04468

Fred Reckards (F)
Box 148
Rockwood, Maine 04478

Red House Canoes
573 Canboro Road, R.R. #5
Fenwick, Ontario
Canada L0S 1C0

Robert Rick
475 Cedar Street
St. Paul, Minnesota 55101

Joseph Seliga
244 East Pattison Street
Ely, Minnesota 55731

APPENDIX

(WOOD-AND-CANVAS CANOES, Cont.)

Hugh Stewart
Box 288
Temagami, Ontario
Canada P0H 2H0

Stewart River Boatworks
Route 1, Box 203
Two Harbors, Minnesota 55616

Strong's Canoe Yard
Craftsbury Common, Vermont 05827

John Stuart
9 Aucort Avenue
Marion, Massachusetts 02738

Ned Teachman
Box 293
Port Sydney, Ontario
Canada P0B 1L0

Temagami Canoe Company
Box 20
Temagami, Ontario
Canada P0H 2H0

Tender Craft Boat Shop (C or F)
67 Mowatt Avenue, #031
Toronto, Ontario
Canada M6K 3E3

Thomson Canoe Works
343 Weekeepeeme Road
Woodbury, Connecticut 06798

Ole Thornbloom
Fleming Route
Box 55
Aitkin, Minnesota 56431

Rollin Thurlow
Box 40
Kenduskeag, Maine 04450

Trapper Canoe Company
911 South Sawyer Street
Oshkosh, Wisconsin 54901

Peter Van Wagner
119 Cragmore Road
Pointe Claire, Quebec
Canada H9R 3K7

POLYETHYLENE CANOES

The Coleman Company, Inc.
250 North St. Francis
Wichita, Kansas 67201

Old Town Canoe Company
Old Town, Maine 04468

Smoker-Craft
P.O. Box 65
New Paris, Indiana 46553

BUILDERS WHO OFFER PROPRIETARY LAY-UPS

Apple Line
146 Church Street
Amsterdam, New York 12010

Blackhawk Canoe Company
937 North Washington Street
Janesville, Wisconsin 53545

Black River Canoes
Box 537
LaGrange, Ohio 44050

Cal-Tek Engineering
29 Pemberton Road
Cochituate, Massachusetts 01778

Gillies Canoes
General Delivery
Margaretville, Nova Scotia
Canada B0S 1N0

Lotus Canoes
7005 North 40th Street
Tampa, Florida 33604

Mad River Canoe
P.O. Box 610
Waitsfield, Vermont 05673

Quintus Enterprises, Inc.
444 Lake Mary Road
Flagstaff, Arizona 86001

Saco River Canoe
Depot Street
Bar Mills, Maine 04004

Sawyer Canoe Company
234 South State Street
Oscoda, Michigan 48750

Voyageur Canoe Company
3 King Street
Millbrook, Ontario
Canada L0A 1G0

We-no-nah Canoes
Box 247
Winona, Minnesota 55987

Noah Whitewater
Maple Springs Road
Box 193B
Bryson City, North Carolina 28713

Canoe Schools

Note: Canoe Magazine continually updates its list of canoe schools, including brief descriptions of each.

John Berry Canoe Clinic
P.O. Box 14
Riparius, New York 12862

Boats and Paddles
P.O. Box 441
Madison, New Jersey 07940

Chattooga Whitewater Shop
Highway 76
Long Creek, South Carolina 29658

Eastern River Expeditions
Box 1173
Greenville, Maine 04441

Equinox Adventures
RR No. 3, 30 Road
Beamsville, Ontario
Canada L0R 3B0

Madawaska Kanu Camp, Inc.
Winter:
2 Tuna Court
Don Mills, Ontario
Canada M3A 3L1
Summer:
P.O. Box 365
Barry's Bay, Ontario
Canada K0J 1B0

Mid-America River Voyageurs
Box 7264
Spencer, Iowa 51301

Nantahala Outdoor Center
Box 41
Bryson City, North Carolina 28713

New England Whitewater Center, Inc.
Box 15
The Forks, Maine 04985

Nolichucky Expeditions, Inc.
P.O. Box 484
Erwin, Tennessee 37650

North American River Runners
P.O. Box 81
Hico, West Virginia 25854

Northern Outdoors
P.O. Box 100
The Forks, Maine 04985

Outdoor Centre of New England, Inc.
8 Pleasant Street
Millers Falls, Massachusetts 01349

River Paths Outfitters
RD 1, Box 15
Confluence, Pennsylvania 15424

Riversport School of Paddling
P.O. Box 100
Ohiopyle, Pennsylvania 15470

Riverwind Kayak and Canoe
Box 2098
Jackson, Wyoming 83001

Saco Bound
Box 113
North Conway, New Hampshire 03813

Whitewater Specialty
Box 157
White Lake, Wisconsin 54491

Steed's Wolf River Lodge, Inc.
White Lake, Wisconsin 54491

W.I.L.D. W.A.T.E.R.S
S. Johnsburg and Glen Creek Roads
Warrensburg, New York 12885

Voyageur School of Canoeing
King Street
Millbrook, Ontario
Canada L0A 1G0

World of Whitewater
P.O. Box 708
Big Bar, California 96010

Canoe Organizations

Note: There are literally hundreds of local canoe clubs in the United States and in Canada affiliated with one or more of the following national groups. To obtain the name of a club nearest you, write to the following:

American Canoe Association
Box 248
Lorton, Virginia 22079

North American Birch Bark Canoe Association
3016 Neola Street
Cedar Falls, Iowa 50613

American Whitewater Affiliation
Box 1483
Hagerstown, Maryland 21740

United States Canoe Association
1818 Kensington Boulevard
Fort Wayne, Indiana 46805

Canadian Canoeing Association
32 Sedgewick Crescent
Islington, Ontario, Canada

Wooden Canoe Heritage Association
P.O. Box 5634
Madison, Wisconsin 53705

Bibliography

Books

Note: River guides are not included among the following, since they now number in the hundreds. A list of them is available free from the American Canoe Association Book Service.

The American Canoe Manufacturers Union, 439 East 51st Street, New York, New York 10022, annually issues an extensive canoe-book listing that includes the "book of the year."

Adney, Edwin Tappan, and Chapelle, Howard I. *The Bark Canoes and Skin Boats of North America.* Washington, D.C.: Smithsonian Institution, 1964.

American Red Cross. *Canoeing.* Garden City: Doubleday & Co., 1977.

Beletz, Al, Syl, and Frank. *Canoe Poling.* St. Louis: A. C. MacKenzie Press, 1974.

Bishop, Nathaniel H. *Voyage of the Paper Canoe.* Boston: Lee & Shepard, 1878.

Bolz, Arnold. *Portage into the Past.* St. Paul: University of Minnesota Press, 1960.

Brenan, Dan. *Adirondack Letters of George Washington Sears.* Blue Mountain, N.Y.: The Adirondack Museum, 1962.

Brosius, Jack, and LeRoy, Dave. *Building and Repairing Canoes and Kayaks.* Chicago: Contemporary Books, 1978.

Davidson, James W., and Rugge, John. *Complete Wilderness Paddler.* New York: Alfred A. Knopf, 1977.

Durant, Kenneth. *Guide-Boat Days and Ways.* Blue Mountain, N.Y.: Adirondack Museum, 1963.

Durham, Bill. *Canoes and Kayaks of Western America.* Seattle: Copper Canoe Press, 1960.

Evans, Jay, and Anderson, Robert R. *Kayaking.* Brattleboro, Vt.: Stephen Greene Press, 1975. Not a canoeing manual, but includes excellent descriptions of white-water technique.

Field, Parker B. *Canvas Canoes: How to Build Them.* New York: Forest and Stream, 1891.

Foster, Thomas S. *Recreational Whitewater Canoeing.* Millers Falls, Mass.: Leisure Enterprises, 1981.

Franks, C. E. S. *The Canoe and White Water.* Toronto: University of Toronto Press, 1977.

Gibbon, John Murray. *Romance of the Canadian Canoe.* Toronto: Ryerson Press, 1951.

Gilpatrick, Gil. *Allagash.* Yarmouth, Me.; DeLorme Publishing Co., 1983.

Gilpatrick, Gil. *Building a Strip Canoe.* Yarmouth, Me.: DeLorme Publishing Co., 1980.

Gilpatrick, Gil. *The Canoe Guide's Handbook.* Yarmouth, Me.: DeLorme Publishing Co., 1982.

Glazier, Capt. Willard. *Down the Great River.* Philadelphia: Hubbard Brothers, 1887.

Glazier, Capt. Willard. *Headwaters of the Mississippi.* New York: Rand McNally and Co., 1892.

Hall, Leonard. *Stars Upstream.* Chicago: University of Chicago Press, 1958.

Handel, Carle W. *Canoe Camping.* New York: A. S. Barnes Co., 1953.

Handel, Carle W. *Canoeing.* New York: A. S. Barnes Co., 1956.

Hazen, David. *Canoe Stripper's Guide to Canoe Building.* Diagrams and plans, available from Wooden Canoe Heritage Association.

Heese, Fred. *Canoe Racing.* Chicago: Contemporary Books, 1979.

Henderson, Luis M. *The Outdoor Guide.* Harrisburg: Stackpole & Heck, 1950.

Hubbard, Lucius L. *Woods and Lakes of Maine—A Trip from Moosehead Lake to New Brunswick.* Boston: James R. Osgood Co., 1883.

Jacobson, Cliff. *Wilderness Canoeing and Camping.* New York: E. P. Dutton, 1978.

Jaques, Florence Page. *Canoe Country.* Minneapolis: University of Minnesota Press, 1938.

Klein, Clayton, and Kruger, Verlen. *One Incredible Journey.* Fowlerville, Michigan: Wilderness House Books, 1985.

Lyon, Robert L. *Who Was Nessmuk?* Wellsboro, Pa.: Wellsboro Chamber of Commerce, 1971.

MacGregor, J. *The Rob Roy on the Jordan.* New York: Harper & Brothers, 1870.

Malo, John. *Canoeing.* Chicago: Follett Publishing Co., 1969.

Malo, John W. *Malo's Complete Guide to Canoeing and Canoe-Camping.* New York: Quadrangle/New York Times Book Co., 1974.

Malo, John W. *Wilderness Canoeing.* New York: MacMillan Publishing Co., 1971.

Manley, Atwood. *Rushton and His Times in American Canoeing.* Syracuse, N.Y.: Adirondack Museum/Syracuse University Press, 1968.

Mason, Bill. *Path of the Paddle.* Toronto: Van Nostrand Reinhold Ltd., 1980.

McDonald, Archibald. *Peace River: A Canoe Voyage from Hudson's Bay to the Pacific.* Reprint of Sir George Simpson's 1828 account. Edmonton, Alberta: M. G. Hurtig, Ltd., 1971.

McNair, Robert E. *Basic River Canoeing.* Swarthmore, Pa.: Buck Ridge Ski Club, 1968. May have been reprinted by other publisher.

McPhee, John. *The Survival of the Birch Bark Canoe.* New York: Farrar, Straus & Giroux, 1975.

Mead, Robert Douglas. *The Canoer's Bible.* New York: Doubleday & Co., 1976.

Miller, Lew. *Build a Stripper.* Camden, Me.: Canoe Magazine.

Morse, Eric W. *Fur Trade Routes—Then and Now.* Ottawa: Queen's Printer, 1969.

Neide, Charles A. *The Canoe Aurora from the Adirondacks to the Gulf.* New York: Forest & Stream, 1885.

Nessmuk (George Washington Sears). *Woodcraft.* New York: Forest and Stream, 1888. Reprint, Dover Publishing Co., New York, 1963.

Norton, C. L., and Habberton, John. *Canoeing in Kanuckia.* New York: G. P. Putnam Co., 1878.

Nute, Grace L. *The Voyageur.* St. Paul: Minnesota Historical Society, 1955.

Nute, Grace L. *The Voyageur's Highway.* St. Paul: Minnesota Historical Society, 1944.

Olson, Sigurd F. *Listening Point.* New York: Alfred A. Knopf, 1958.

Olson, Sigurd F. *The Lonely Land.* New York: Alfred A. Knopf, 1961.

Olson, Sigurd F. *Runes of the North.* New York: Alfred A. Knopf, 1963.

Olson, Sigurd F. *Wilderness Days,* New York: Alfred A. Knopf, 1973.

Phillips, John, and Cabot, Thomas. *Quickwater and Smooth.* Brattleboro, Vt.: Stephen Greene Press, 1935.

Pinkerton, Robert. *The Canoe.* New York: MacMillan Publishing Co., 1914. Several reprints since.

Pinkerton, Robert E. *The Hudson's Bay Company.* New York: Henry Holt Co., 1931.

Riviere, Bill. *Pole, Paddle and Portage.* New York: Van Nostrand Reinhold Co., 1969. Also Little, Brown and Company, Boston.

Roberts, Kenneth G., and Shackleton, Philip. *The Canoe: A History of the Craft from Panama to the Arctic.* Camden, Maine: International Marine Publishing Company, 1984.

Rowlands, John J. *Cache Lake Country.* New York: W. W. Norton & Co., 1947.

Rutstrum, Calvin. *Back Country.* Pittsboro, Ind.: Indiana Camp Supply, 1981.

Rutstrum, Calvin. *New Way of the Wilderness.* New York: Macmillan Publishing Co., 1963.

Rutstrum, Calvin. *North American Canoe Country.* New York: MacMillan Publishing Co., 1964.

Sale, D. G. *Olympic Single Blade Canoeing.* Toronto: University of Toronto Press, 1965.

Severeid, Eric. *Canoeing With the Cree.* St. Paul: Minnesota Historical Society, 1935. Subsequent printing 1968.

Stearns, Bill and Fern. *The Canoeist's Catalog.* Camden, Me.: International Marine Publishing Co., 1978.

Steele, Thomas Sedgwick. *Canoe & Camera—Or 200 Miles Through the Maine Forests.* New York: Orange Judd Co., 1880.

Steele, Thomas Sedgwick. *Paddle and Portage—From Moosehead Lake to the Aroostook River.* Boston: Estes and Lauriat, 1882.

Stelmok, Jerry. *Building the Maine Guide Canoe.* Camden, Me.: International Marine Publishing Co., 1980.

Stephens, W. P. *Canoe and Boat Building for Amateurs.* New York: Forest and Stream, 1885.

Teller, Walter Magnes. *On the River.* New Brunswick, N.J.: Rutgers University Press, 1976.

Urban, John T. *White Water Handbook for Canoe and Kayak.* Boston: Appalachian Mountain Club, 1965.

Walbridge, Charles. *Boatbuilder's Manual—How to Build Fiberglass Canoes and Kayaks.* Penllyn, Pa.: Wildwater Designs, 1973.

Wallace, Dillon. *The Lure of the Labrador Wild.* New York: Fleming H. Revel Co., 1905.

Watters, Ron. *The White Water Book.* Seattle: Pacific Search Press, 1982. Kayak-oriented but excellent descriptions of white-water technique.

Whitney, Peter Dwight. *White-Water Sport.* New York: Ronald Press Co., 1960.

Willis, Melvin. *Build a Wood Strip Canoe.* Freeport, Me.: Willis Enterprises, 1982.

Periodicals

The American Canoeist. American Canoe Association, P.O. Box 248, Lorton, Va. 22079. (Membership publication.)

American Whitewater. American Whitewater Affiliation, Box 1483, Hagerstown, Md. 21740.

Canoe Magazine. Highland Mill, Camden, Me. 04843.

Canoe News. United States Canoe Association, 1818 Kensington Boulevard, Fort Wayne, Ind. 46805.

Che mun. Michael Peak, Box 548, Station O, Toronto, Canada, M4A 2P1.

Wooden Canoe. Wooden Canoe Heritage Association, P.O. Box 5634, Madison, Wisc. 53705.

Glossary

ACA American Canoe Association.

Access point Streamside or lakeshore location where watercraft may be launched or landed.

Aft Toward the stern, or rear.

Aground Bottom lodged on shallows, ledge, rock, or sandbar.

Air lock Suction within a canoe when it is overturned in the water. Makes craft difficult to right.

Amidship The center area of a canoe.

Astern Behind the canoe.

AWA American Whitewater Affiliation.

Backlash Standing waves at foot of a powerful chute or sluice created when fast-flowing water strikes relatively still water.

Backpaddle To paddle backward to slow a canoe or to stop it.

Bail Removing water from a canoe with a tin can, sponge, or plastic scoop made from bleach bottle.

Banana boat Canoe or kayak-type craft with pronounced rocker and high ends, designed for utmost maneuverability.

Bang plate Metal plate on leading edge of cutwater, bow and stern, to protect hull.

Bar Sand or gravel shallows often found on inside bend of a stream.

Beam The width of a canoe at its widest point, at the gunwales, or at the 3- or 4-inch waterline.

Bilge The interior of a canoe below the waterline.

Bilge keel Extra keel, one each side, located just inside the chine, to protect fabric on canvas canoe.

Blade The flat section of a paddle.

Boil   Water swelling upward, usually upon striking underwater object.

Bottom   The underwater section of a hull.

Bow   The front end of a watercraft.

Bowman / bowperson   The bow paddler in a tandem canoe.

Brace   May be high or low; a paddle stroke used to stabilize a canoe. In a high brace, the grip hand is held high, the paddle at an angle in the water, the lower hand applying pressure against the water. In a low brace, the paddle is almost horizontal, the flat of the blade applying a downward pressure against the water.

Broach   Turning broadside to oncoming waves or current.

Bucket seats   Form-fitting seats, usually well below the gunwale.

Buoyancy   The ability to float. Buoyancy may be enhanced by the installation of tire tubes, foam blocks, or air bags.

Cane seats   Wooden-frame seats with woven cane filling.

Canoe pole   Pole used to propel a canoe in shallow water.

Capsize   To overturn.

Carry   A portage where the canoe and/or the outfit is carried around a section of unnavigable water. Also, the route followed.

Center of gravity   The point of resolution of downward forces or weight within a canoe, including cargo and paddlers.

Channel   The course in which the bulk of a stream flows; also, a navigable route among obstructions.

Chine   The curving section of a canoe's sides where they blend or merge into the bottom.

Chute   An accelerated section of a stream, often compressed between two or more obstructions and dropping faster than adjacent currents.

Classification   A rating applied to a stream or section of current describing its navigability.

Comber   A large, powerful wave.

Combination stroke   A blending of two or more basic strokes.

Confluence   The point where two or more streams join.

Course   The route chosen in paddling a canoe from one point to another.

Crest   The top of a wave; in lake-paddling terminology, a "whitecap."

Cross-current   The movement of water at an angle to the mainstream or current.

Cross-draw   A draw stroke in which the paddler switches sides without changing the position of his hands.

Dead man   Log, anchored at one end, afloat at the other, found on streams where log drives have occurred.

Deck   Triangular section fitted between the gunwales at the bow and stern of paddling canoes.

Decked canoe   Canoe with full covering, also known as a closed or covered canoe.

Depth   The depth of a canoe measured vertically amidship from the bilge to gunwale height.

Difficulty rating   Same as *Classification.*

Displacement   The volume of water displaced by a canoe, its cargo, and its crew.

Double blade   Paddle with a blade at each end used to propel a kayak and some canoes.

Downriver race   Also known as "wildwater" racing, a long-distance race through white water.

Downstream ferry   Backpaddling while the canoe is at an angle to the current, which then propels the craft to one side.

Draft   Depth of water required to float a canoe, or the vertical distance between the waterline and the keel line.

Drag   Resistance caused by friction between water and the hull.

Draw stroke   The flat of the blade is drawn directly toward the canoe to pull the craft to one side.

Drift   Moving with the current or the wind without assistance of paddles.

Drop   A sudden pitch or unusually sharp dip in a section of rapids.

Dry pack   Same as a *wet pack;* a waterproof bag that keeps clothing or other items dry.

Duffek stroke   A high brace stroke especially useful when entering or leaving an eddy. Also known as a turning high brace.

Eddy   Section of a current, downstream of a major obstruction, where the water flows upstream, often used as rest stop.

Eddy hopping   Paddling from eddy to eddy, usually to scout what lies ahead.

Eddying out   A 180-degree turn in direction from the main current into an eddy. Entering an eddy.

Eddy line   Fine line between a swift downstream current and the circulating or upstream current within the eddy.

Even keel   Properly trimmed to float in a level position.

Face   A paddle blade's surfaces. The "power face" is the one drawn against the water. Also refers to the sloping surface of a wave.

Falls   Free-falling water, at least part way, over an obstruction. Heavy rapids are also called "falls."

Fast water   Generally conceded to mean rapids, but can be applied to swiftly flowing water without obstructions.

Feather   To bring the paddle forward with one edge leading, thus reducing resistance by water or air.

Fend　To push off, as from a dock or beach.

Ferry　Angling the canoe so that the current, striking the canoe's upstream side, drives the craft toward shore.

Flare　A canoe design in which the beam is somewhat greater at the gunwales than at the waterline.

Flat water　Lake water or river section where no rapids exist. Sometimes a misnomer, since wind can create large waves on so-called flat water.

Flotation　Usually foam built into canoes, to keep them afloat when swamped. Additional flotation may include air bags, foam blocks, even inner tubes.

Following sea　Waves that overtake a canoe from astern.

Fore　Toward the bow, or front of a canoe.

Forward stroke　The basic or "cruising" stroke for propelling a canoe forward.

Freeboard　The vertical distance between the water and the gunwales, measured amidship.

Freighter　Large canoe used for hauling heavy loads.

Gate　Poles hung from overhead wires for a slalom course.

Gauging station　Streamside station that automatically measures water flow in cubic feet per second.

Gilpoke　Lumberman's term for a log protruding into a stream, used to deflect logs during a river drive; a hazard to canoeists.

Grab line　Eight- to 10-foot line attached to each end of canoe for use in case of upset.

Gradient　The average rate of drop in a river, generally expressed in feet per mile.

Grip　Top of a canoe paddle, shaped to fit the hand, which controls the pitch of the blade.

Gunwale　Also known as "gunnel." Strips along the top of a canoe's sides, extending from bow to stern, providing longitudinal rigidity.

Hanging stroke　The high brace stroke and its variations, during which the paddler leans out over the gunwale and literally hangs onto the paddle as the blade is pressured against the water.

Haystacks　Standing waves at the foot of a swift sluice or rapids.

Head　Volume of water or sudden rising of river level as the result of opening dam gates.

Heavy water　Large volume of water in a set of rapids, creating greater-than-average turbulence.

High brace　See *Brace stroke.*

Hog　A canoe is said to "hog" when it is bow-heavy and thus moves forward erratically. Also applies to a canoe whose backbone has been broken, so that the keel line is higher amidship than at the ends.

Holding position   Stopping downstream movement to appraise upcoming passages.

Horizontal line   Looking downstream, the surface of the river seems to drop away with nothing in view but the sky. Indicates a sharp drop-off. Can be very hazardous.

Hull   The main body of a canoe.

Hung up   Aground or caught on an obstacle.

Hydraulics   A term applied to the movements and forces of moving water.

Hypothermia   The lowering of the body's inner core temperature as a result of exposure to cold water or air.

Inboard   Within the inside of a canoe.

Inside bank   The slower and shallower water in the bend of a stream.

Inwale   The inside half of a gunwale.

J stroke   Thrusting the paddle blade away from the canoe at the completion of a forward stroke, used to keep a canoe on course.

Keel   Strip of wood or other material along the bottom center of a canoe, running from stem to stern, designed to reinforce the hull bottom and to minimize drift during lake paddling. A detriment in white water, since it interferes with maneuverability.

Keel line   A design line running from stem to stern along the exact center of a hull.

Knee braces   Supports, designed so that a paddler can lock his knees into position for better control of a canoe during precise maneuvering.

Knee pads   Usually foam, either worn on the knees or attached to the bottom of the canoe for added comfort and protection.

Knob   Same as *Grip;* at top of paddle shaft.

Lead canoe   A trip leader's canoe, leading a group and selecting passages.

Lean   Tipping a canoe to one side during maneuvering or to stabilize the craft.

Ledge   Projecting stratum of rock that confines or partially dams stream flow.

Lee   Section of a waterway protected from the wind.

Left bank   The left side of a stream facing downstream.

Life vest   Personal flotation device worn like a vest, popularly referred to as a "PFD."

Lining   Guiding a canoe downstream through rapids or shallows by means of a rope or line.

List   The lean of a canoe, resulting from improper positioning of its cargo or paddlers.

Lob tree   Old-time portage marker, consisting of tall tree with upper limbs removed.

Low brace   Brace stroke with entire paddle almost flat on the surface of the water. Used for stabilizing a canoe.

Off side   Opposite side of the canoe from that where canoeist is paddling.

Open canoe   Also known as a "Canadian" canoe; not enclosed or fully decked.

Open gunwale   Characteristic of wood-and-canvas canoes; sections between the rib ends are open, permitting quick drainage when the craft is overturned on shore.

Outside bank   The side to which the water is thrust by centrifugal force in a stream bend, usually deeper and swifter than on the inside bank.

Outwale   The outside section of a two-piece gunwale; that portion of the gunwale on the outside of the canoe.

Overall length   Extreme length of a canoe, as opposed to the waterline length.

Paddle sensitivity   A sort of rapport between a paddler and his paddle; a "feel" for its responses to his efforts.

Painter   Same as *Grab line.*

Pear grip   Also known as a "palm" grip, semi-rounded to fit paddler's handhold.

Peeling out   Exiting from an eddy.

PFD   Personal flotation device; a life jacket.

Pick pole   A canoe, or setting, pole.

Pillow   Bulge on surface created by an underwater obstruction, usually a rock.

Pitch   Steep section or sharp drop in a set of rapids.

Pivot   Turning a canoe within its own length.

Planking   Longitudinal strips that form the hull, as in a wood-and-canvas canoe or a stripper.

Poling   Propelling a canoe, usually in a standing position, with a pole, either up- or downstream.

Pool   Still or slow-moving water, usually deeper than surrounding sections.

Port   The left side of a canoe, facing forward.

Portage   Same as *Carry.*

Power face   The side of a paddle blade that bears against the water.

Pry   A paddle stroke that uses the gunwale as a fulcrum to thrust the canoe to one side.

Pudding stick   Derogatory term applied to a poor paddle.

Rapid   Commonly referred to as "rapids" even when singular. Swiftly flowing water, tumbling among obstructions, creating considerable turbulence.

Recovery   Part of a paddle stroke in which the blade is recovered from the water and dipped for the next stroke.

Resistance   Resistance is created as the canoe displaces water at its bow; by surface friction between the hull and the water; and the eddy or suction effect of its wake.

Reversal   A vertical and circular motion of water, usually highly aerated, as it drops over a steep obstruction and flows back over itself.

Ribs   Curved strips that run from gunwale to gunwale to reinforce a hull.

Riffles   Swift, shallow water running over sand or gravel bottom, creating small waves. Could be termed gentle rapids.

Right bank   Right side of a stream facing downstream.

Rips   Moderate rapids.

River rating   Same as *Classification.*

River reading   Appraising river conditions, possible routes, and potential danger spots.

Rocker   Upsweep of the keel line from amidship to each end, a prerequisite for maneuverability in white water.

Rock garden   Navigable rock-strewn set of rapids requiring precise maneuvering.

Rollers   Standing waves forceful enough to roll back upon themselves to some degree.

Rooster tail   A wave formation occurring when two currents come together, forcing water upward in the form of a rooster's tail. Does not provide stable support.

Ruddering   Using a paddle blade strictly as a rudder.

Run   A section of fast water, sometimes rough. Also applied to a passage through rapids.

Sandpaper   Small, choppy waves over shallows, as in a set of riffles.

Scout / scouting   Examining a set of rapids to determine difficulty and best possible passage.

Sculling   A side-to-side movement, edge first, of the paddle blade, similar to a figure 8, usable in many combinations with other strokes.

Set over   Same as *Ferry.*

Setting pole   Same as *Canoe pole.*

Shaft   The handle of a paddle, between the grip and the blade.

Shake out   To rock a swamped canoe back and forth, thus splashing out most of the water.

Sheer   The upward curve of the gunwale line from midship to the ends, best seen in profile from one side.

Shoe keel   Also known as river keel. A shallow, usually rounded projection found on some aluminum canoes. Principal purpose is to hold the two halves of the hull together without interfering with maneuverability.

Shoot To "shoot" the rapids; a term falling into disuse.

Sideslipping When a canoe continues to slip sideways despite also making forward way, as when "eddying out."

Slack water Slowly flowing or still water without rapids.

Slalom A zigzag course with a number of gates on white water. Competitors are timed and must negotiate the gates, some of them upstream.

Slap support An emergency low brace in which the flat of the blade is literally slapped onto the water's surface to stabilize the canoe.

Sleeper Barely submerged rock marked by little or no surface disturbance.

Slough around To veer erratically, out of control.

Sluice Same as *Chute*.

Smoker A particularly violent and hazardous set of rapids.

Snubbing Using a pole to slow or stop a canoe's motion, usually during downstream runs.

Soloing Paddling alone.

Sousehole Highly aerated water flowing into a depression from several directions, with surface level below that of the surrounding surface.

Splash out Same as *Shake out*.

Sponsons Elongated air tanks on the outside of the hull, formerly used to provide secondary stability. Foam pads are now used on some canoes.

Standing wave Same as *Backlash*.

Starboard The right side of a canoe facing the bow.

Stem The extreme front end of a canoe, which cuts through the water.

Stem band Same as *Bang plate*.

Stern Rear section of a canoe.

Stopper A reversal so powerful it may stop a canoe, or slow it markedly.

Stripper Canoe built of thin strips, usually ½- by ¾-inches, assembled on temporary forms and fiberglassed inside and out.

Strainer Fallen tree or other debris through which water flows, but which will hang up a canoe. Potentially very hazardous.

Surfing In lake paddling, riding downwind on the crests of large waves. In white water, riding the upstream side of a wave, with the current seeking to drive the canoe up and over, gravity holding it from doing so. The canoe may perch in this position for some time.

Swamp When a canoe fills with water without capsizing.

Sweep canoe The last canoe in a brigade, usually paddled by experts ready to assist those in front.

Sweep stroke A wide, shallow stroke, the blade barely submerged, used to pivot the canoe.

Tandem   A two-seated canoe; two persons paddling.

Technical   Describes a set of rapids where intricate and precise maneuvering is required.

T-grip   A paddle handle in the form of a T.

Thigh straps   Straps attached to gunwale and to the center of the bilge. When in use, these bind across a kneeling paddler's thighs, affording him better control.

Throat   The flare of a paddle shaft where it blends into the blade.

Throw line   Length of rope used in rescue efforts.

Thwart   Cross braces running from gunwale to gunwale.

Tip   Bottom end of a paddle blade.

Tippy   Refers to an unstable canoe.

Tongue   A smooth V of swift water at the head of a pitch or between two obstacles, usually indicating deep water.

Track   Paddling in a straight line.

Tracking   Towing a canoe upstream with a tow line.

Trim   The manner in which a canoe rides on the water: its level fore and aft, as well as port to starboard.

Trip leader   Person in charge of a group who oversees safety aspects.

Trough   The hollow or depression between two waves.

Tumblehome   The inward curving of the sides of a canoe from a point at or slightly above the waterline to the gunwales.

Waterline   The level of the water on a canoe's sides when afloat.

Waterline length   Length of a canoe measured at the waterline, as opposed to the overall length.

Way   Forward or rear motion; momentum; as in "under way."

Wet pack   A waterproof bag used for carrying extra clothing, sleeping bags, etc.

Wet suit   A close-fitting garment of foam sandwiched in nylon that provides insulation against cold water.

White eddy   Pool at the foot of a drop-off, creating a marked backflow on the surface; usually highly aerated.

White water   A set of rapids.

Windward   Direction from which the wind is blowing.

Wrapped   When a canoe is pinned and bent around a rock.

Yoke   Device attached permanently or temporarily amidship, usually padded to protect the shoulders, for portaging a canoe.

Index

~·~·~·~·~